REAL ESTATE MARKETING

Developing a Professional Career

Norbert J. Stefaniak, Ph.D., C.P.A.

Professor Emeritus
School of Business Administration
University of Wisconsin-Milwaukee

REALTOR®, CRE® Emeritus
Equitable/Stefaniak Realty

WALKER – PEARSE, LTD., Publishers, Wisconsin, U.S.A.

REAL ESTATE MARKETING

Developing a Professional Career

By Norbert J. Stefaniak

Published by:

WALKER – PEARSE, LTD., Publishers
Post Office Box 14753
West Allis, WI 53214 U.S.A.

Printed in the United States of America

Publisher's Cataloging-in-Publication
 (Prepared by Quality Books, Inc.)

Stefaniak, Norbert J.
        Real estate marketing: developing a professional career /
    Norbert J. Stefaniak. — 1st ed.
        p. cm.
        Includes bibliographical references and index.

    Library of Congress Catalog Card Number: 98-60298

    ISBN 0-9662954-4-7

        1. Real estate business 2. House selling. 3. Real
    property — Marketing. 4. Real estate agents — Vocational
    guidance. I. Title.

HD1375.S84 1998   333.33'0688
                                   QBI98-107

To my loving, understanding and patient wife, Betty

and all of the "Mother's Day Silver Cup Ten"

also

To my special brother and lifelong

business partner, Gene

Acknowledgements

The author is grateful to the thousands of practitioners, scholars, students and friends that have shared ideas or raised meaningful questions that stimulated further inquiry into different areas of this field. Over the past 50 years the following quotation that has been adapted from a great American philosopher has served as a guide in the search of knowledge.

"Every person that I meet is my superior in some way, from that person I can learn something."

This little bit of advice can be especially helpful to the new entrant into this field. It may prove to be more rewarding to spend more time listening than talking. By asking simple, basic questions, one can open gates to the flow of knowledge.

The generous contribution of MGI Communications, Inc. of Wauwatosa, Wisconsin, in producing most of the graphic illustrations used in this text is sincerely appreciated.

It is recognized that there are few books in the education field that are much more than restatements of past scholarly endeavors. It is with an uncomfortable feeling to think that this author may have drawn from this historical reservoir of knowledge without giving due credit in some cases. May those who may have been offended be kind and understanding of this author's inadvertent shortcomings.

Special thanks are extended to Dennis Sobanski and Robert Bartelt, my loyal teaching and research assistants. The painstaking editing work of Kevin Malloy and Anne Spaltholz enabled this project to be completed.

Foreword
by
Tom Dooley

The more things change, the more things stay the same!!

In his nearly half century of practicing, teaching and raconteuring in the real estate field, Norb Stefaniak, Professor Emeritus in the School of Business Administration at the University of Wisconsin-Milwaukee, and a principal in one of Wisconsin's leading residential brokerage firms, has weathered the winds of change and watched with keen interest as "wild schemes and ideas" became mainstream operational standards for the realty profession. Through it all he has taught and guided thousands of students and agents to a clear understanding of what real estate is all about.

All the while, he has witnessed the stability of four main essentials for success for real estate practitioners: their market, their clients, their office and their career.

In this book, Dr. Stefaniak addresses each element in such a manner that when novice licensees read it, they will realize they have found the passport to occupational greatness while veteran agents will treasure the work as the definite source for continuing mastery of their profession.

As witness to his knowledge and absorption of change, the author devotes one entire chapter to how a real estate market currently operates and another to how it is likely to change.

In addition to explaining the principles involved in every facet of the real estate business, Dr. Stefaniak demonstrates the meaning of his instructional words with practical applications and procedures.

Persons who have advanced to the level of company ownership will find the chapters on "Company Operations", "Staff and Procedures", and "Management and Budgets" to be replete with proven ideas leading to a profitable and professional enterprise.

Every reader, even those just considering an entrance into the real estate field, will be able to better chart his or her career path after perusing the chapters entitled "Professional Status" and "The Future of the Professional".

Plato once said that the essence of a great education was a log with Socrates seated on one end and an eager student on the other. Pull up a log (or a comfy chair) and grab Dr. Stefaniak's book. You'll soon be the recipient of a great education in real estate!!

—CONTENTS—

Chapter 1 **INTRODUCTION** **11**
Brokerage Pyramid; Real Estate Field – Various
Functions; Role of the Real Estate Broker;
Basic Body of Knowledge and Objectives; Real
Estate Courses; Theory (the "Why"); Experi-
ence and Knowledge; Theory vs. Practice;
Rules of Thumb; ARELLO Statistics; Ease of
Entry

Chapter 2 **YOUR MARKET: HOW IT OPERATES** **32**
What is a Market?; Real Estate Markets; Real
Estate Market is Unique; Residential Market
Model; Housing Turnover; Standing Stock;
Supply; Demand; Supply vs. Demand; Sellers'
Market; Buyers' Market; Household Cycle;
Housing Decisions

Chapter 3 **YOUR MARKET: HOW IT CHANGES** **56**
Market Change and the Broker; Patterns of
Change – Seasonal, Cyclical, Long-Term
(trend) and Irregular; Real Estate Cycles;
Interpreting Market Change; Market Indicators
(volume and pace) – New Building Starts;
Ownership Turnover; Mortgage Recordings;
Vacancies; Foreclosures; Number of Days on
the Market; Stimulators (or dampeners) –
Financing Terms, Population Change, Level of
Employment, Marriages, Rate of Housing
Inflation

Chapter 4 **YOUR MARKET: PREDICTING VOLUME
AND SELLING PRICES** **85**
Importance of Forecasts; Primary Indicators of
Market Activity; Comparison of Market Stimu-
lators to the Ideal; Basis for Judgment;
Affordability ("ACE"); Pricing vs. Appraising;

The Appraisal Process; Seller's Pricing Rationale; Pricing Estimate (short-cut); Overpricing

Chapter 5 YOUR CLIENTS: THE SELLERS   111
Who are the Sellers?; Reasons for Selling; Selling Process; Broker's Responsibility to the Seller; Importance of Listings; Probability of Getting a Listing; "Pockets of Activity"; Obtaining Listings; Expenses of Sale; Type of Listing Contracts; Increasing Salability; Timing of Sale; Servicing the Seller; Comparative Market Analysis; Competitive Problems; For Sale by Owner; Older Homeowners

Chapter 6 YOUR CLIENTS: THE HOME BUYERS 140
The Changing Market; The Younger Market; Home Ownership; Owning vs. Renting; Price Range; Monthly Payment; Pre-Qualifying Buyers; Resistance to Increasing Interest Rates; The Broker's Role; Sources of Buyers; Buyers Psychology – Consumer Behavior; Creating Buyer Interest; Offer to Purchase

Chapter 7 YOUR CLIENTS: THE INVESTORS   170
Benefits to the Investor; Kinds of Investors; Income Statement; Depreciation; Components of Value; Cone of Value; Rates of Return; Simple Investment Models; Pyramiding; Investment Leverage; Income Tax Aspects; Starker Type Exchange; Net Cash Flow; Internal Rate of Return

Chapter 8 YOUR OFFICE: THE COMPANY AND OPERATIONS   197
Operating Functions; Forms of Business Organization; Capital Requirements; Managerial Talent; Degree of Control; Extent of Liability; Tax Position; Independent Contractors; Limited Liability Company; Company Name; Office

Location; Management Principles; Company
Policy Manual

Chapter 9   **YOUR OFFICE: STAFF AND**
            PROCEDURES   **219**
            What is Success?; Why Do Salespeople
            Leave?; Size of Sales Staff; The Cycle of
            Effort: Recruiting and Training Sales Person-
            nel; Motivation; Pareto's Law; Enthusiasm;
            Sales Manager's Role; Selecting a Sales Man-
            ager; Economies of Scale; Public Relations;
            Anti-Trust Laws

Chapter 10   **YOUR OFFICE: MANAGEMENT**
            AND BUDGETS   **239**
            Business Plan; Expenses Per Desk; Break-even
            Analysis; Listing and Sales Quotas; Market
            Share; Revenue Pace; Revenue and Expense
            Budgets; Mission Statement; Short-Range
            Goals; Long-Range Plans; What is Your
            Business Worth?; Impact of Inflation;
            Management Control

Chapter 11   **YOUR CAREER: PROFESSIONAL STATUS** **262**
            High Pay, Hard Work; Definition of a Profes-
            sion; Personal Goals; Goal Setting; Commit-
            ment to Success; Professional Designations;
            Code of Ethics; Education; Organize Your
            Professional Career

Chapter 12   **YOUR CAREER: THE FUTURE OF**
            THE PROFESSIONAL   **291**
            Changes in the Last Fifty Years; The 80s and
            the 90s; Concerns of the Real Estate Practitio-
            ners in the 90s; The Closing Years of the
            Twentieth century; The "UP-Desk"; Looking
            Ahead Into the Twenty-First Century; Nine
            Statements that Focus on the Future; Threat or
            Opportunity?; Some Challenging Questions

CHAPTER 1 – INTRODUCTION

"Experience may be the best teacher . . .
but the 'tuition' is high." *Richard Andrews*

The material in this book is directed toward the aspiring real estate practitioner and the dedicated real estate student who have their eyes set on higher heights in this field. It is assumed that they are, or will be, licensed in the near future. Those already licensed should understand the basic elements of the average residential real estate transaction. This would include workable knowledge of the listing contract, the offer to purchase, fundamental concepts of financing and closing the transaction. These are the bare essentials necessary for one to collect a real estate commission. Most state licensing authorities regard the real estate license as a *privilege* to legally operate in the field. It is a regulatory requirement for entry into the business. But the likelihood of success will increase and accrue to those who develop a level of expertise beyond these minimum standards.

Immediately, this raises a question about the parameters of this extra fund of information and insight. Specifically, what body of knowledge should the broker or the salesperson thoroughly understand if they desire to move toward true professional status in the real estate field? This book endeavors to answer the question by identifying and amplifying the pertinent areas of concern. Accordingly, the material is divided into four major sections: Your Market; Your Clients; Your Office; and Your Career. These four major sections can be viewed as integral parts of a total structure as illustrated in the following manner.

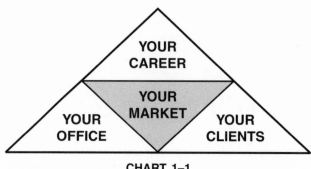

CHART 1–1
THE REAL ESTATE BROKERAGE PYRAMID

The cornerstones of the system are your office and your clients. The interaction between the two takes place in the focal area of negotiation, your market. The effective combination of these base components is capped with your career, serving as the apex of the system. Each of these four major divisions is further organized into several chapters dealing with subject matter consisting of principles, procedures and applications related to the real estate brokerage business.

Students of real estate and those entering the field with limited experience will be able to build a sound foundation for making their future experience all the more meaningful. It should be pointed out that others working in real estate related fields, although not actively in the brokerage phase, also may discover new, exciting and valuable dimensions to their work.

For the newcomer it is hoped to create a degree of awareness that it takes more than obtaining a real estate license to effectively participate in the real estate market.

The Real Estate Field

The term "real estate" is used in two common ways. The first way describes the commodity, that is the property, the land, the building and all of the rights attached thereto. The second identifies the broad spectrum of activities that it encompasses. In spite of popular usage in some circles, the general term, real estate, should not be limited to the brokerage field alone.

The real estate industry is much broader, more complex and much deeper rooted than is commonly realized. Let us consider some of the elements of this far-reaching field of real estate:

1. Real Estate Brokerage ⟨ the listing and selling of real estate wherein the broker acts for the owner (or buyer).

2. Property Management ⟨ the handling of rentals as well as looking after the property in the best interests of the owner.

3. Industrial Brokerage ⟨ the sale and leasing of industrial property.

4. Real Estate Appraisals ⟨ professional determination of real estate values.

5. Land Subdividing ⟨ the "manufacture" of urban land into buildable sites.

6. Real Estate Research ⟨ scientific investigation into fields such as marketing, finance and management.

7. Real Estate Counseling ⟨ the rendering of expert advice on the professional level to real estate clients.

8. Real Estate Finance ⟨ arranging for mortgage funds to facilitate real estate transactions.

9. Property Development ⟨ the complete process from sub-dividing through construction.

10. Real Estate Investments ⟨ operation of real estate corporations, syndicates and trusts for the benefit of participating investors.

11. Construction ⟨ building new houses, apartments, offices, stores, etc.

12. Trading & Exchanging 〈 facilitating the transfer of
equities for real estate
investors with particular
emphasis on mutual tax
and investment advantages.

Command of the mechanics and the technical aspects of practice puts one into the vocational category. Understanding the body of knowledge on which these procedures are based is one of the prime requirements toward professional standing.

The Role of the Real Estate Broker

By "marketing real estate" we are specifically referring to the real estate brokerage function, which includes a complete range of business services that effect the transfer of title in real property from seller to buyer, whether it be for owner-occupancy or investment purposes.

It is the declared objective of this book to focus on the role of the real estate broker and members of the broker's staff. Brokers and salespeople serve as intermediaries in the real estate market. They facilitate transactions by serving as a vehicle between prospective sellers and prospective buyers. The successful culmination of their efforts result in market transfers of title. The range of this market would include all transactions that have taken place or are in some stage of negotiation. But not all real estate transfers are considered to be market transactions. There are special cases wherein title is transferred in what are deemed to be non-market transactions. Examples of this would be the passing of deed on an intra-family basis without any realistic bargaining taking place; the inter-corporate transfer of real estate title among controlled corporations; deeds issued to correct errors in title; and the sale of small portions of land to adjoining owners, representing an extremely restricted kind of demand. It is also recognized that there is a category of transactions generated between buyer and seller without the aid of a real estate broker. Therefore, one can readily identify three major categories of title transfers that make up the total of deeds recorded in any one period of time: 1) Those transactions handled by real estate brokers; 2) those transactions handled directly between seller and buyer; and 3) what we have called non-market transactions. These three comprise the sum total. If the real estate broker is going to play this vital role, facilitating transactions, what kind of educational background, what body of knowledge, what level of experience must one possess in order to do this job effectively? It does suggest a combination of formal training, plus appropriate experience. The formal training should be broad in nature in order to provide a sound base on which to build a career. At the academic level this most likely would involve economics, sociology, political science, psychology, law, business ethics and specialized course work in the real estate field.

Basic Body of Knowledge and Objectives

In a practical sense, the real estate broker's work deals with clients, location factors, market forces and operation, general business conditions, political influences and change, the legal framework, social customs and practices and regulatory programs, both public and private. This broad range of exposures suggests that the broker's activities are not of an isolated, unilateral nature. In fact, they are just the opposite. The following chart attempts to describe the general nature of these relationships.

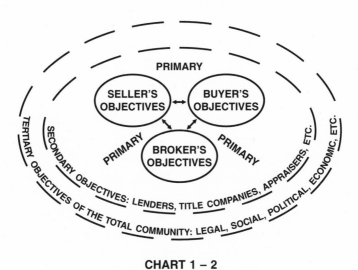

CHART 1 – 2
INTER-RELATED OBJECTIVES

Objectives are important because they provide guides for the decision-making process. The seller of real estate has as a prime objective the liquidation of one's equity in the marketplace. The form in which one retrieves this equity might be in cash, taking back a purchase money mortgage, or even selling on a low down payment installment sales contract to provide a desired form of tax shelter. The client's personal financial planning certainly enters the picture. The seller also may prefer some kind of time schedule that comprises a part of an objective, the time within which one expects the property to be sold and liquidated. Not all sellers prefer cash. Some prefer to trade their existing equity for that in another piece of real estate in order to defer the income tax impact. Some sellers test the market and, in essence, are almost unwilling sellers by virtue of their stated position, "I'll sell if I can get my price." The matter of seller's motivations is treated in much greater detail in the fifth chapter.

The objectives of the buyer relate to owner occupancy or investment purposes. The buyer's objectives are contained within the realm of one's financial capabilities. The kind of real estate that one may be looking for is related to shelter, investment goals, or occupancy for business purposes.

The broker's objectives include (a) the completion of a transaction in order to earn a commission; and (b) the creation of a favorable impression in hopes of developing other business relationships in the future. Like most other business people, the broker is not solely trying to maximize income. Other high ranking goals include staying ahead of the competition, independence, prestige and estate planning.

These three sets of objectives, the seller's, the buyer's, and the broker's comprise the primary set in the real estate market. The higher the degree of compatibility of these objectives, the greater the efficiency of interaction in the form of completed transactions and satisfaction. Obviously, the greater the divergence, the lesser the chance of success, and the greater the economic waste of resources involved. Actually, the broker, in performing the market function, is matching the seller's objectives and buyer's objectives, and in the process, completes a transaction. Real estate brokers ren-

16

der a marketing service for which professionally treated clients are willing to pay a commission.

Another set of objectives could be labeled secondary in nature as they are supportive of the primary real estate transaction. These secondary groups provide the financing, title evidence and other services that facilitate the eventual transfer of title. While secondary objectives are ancillary in nature, they can negate the transaction if its terms are not consistent with the operating policy of these secondary groups.

The third set is the tertiary objectives, which make up the institutional framework within which the market negotiation takes place. Tertiary objectives are those of the total community and refer to the legal, social, political and economic forces. These tertiary objectives of society tend to set kinds of limits within which real estate activities are conducted. It has been said that, except for narcotics, no product or commodity is more rigidly regulated and controlled than real estate.

It is apparent then that there are three major sets of objectives operating in the real estate market: primary, secondary and tertiary. While all have varying degrees of impact on the real estate market, we are particularly concerned with the primary set of objectives since it is within this category that the real estate broker conducts the major part of one's business activities. It is obvious that without satisfying primary objectives there would be no transactions, hence there would be little need for the related service activities of lenders, title companies, surveyors, etc. And, of course, there would be a lesser degree of concern on the part of the total community with regard to tertiary objectives.

The broad set of inter-related objectives just presented calls for an equally broad involvement on the part of real estate broker operating in a particular market. Such extensive involvement necessitates a wide base of knowledge and experience. This base covers many individual subject areas. A good deal of the literature available to the real estate industry today follows the traditional approach in which knowledge is compartmentalized into the conventional format:

Fundamentals of Real Estate
Real Estate Law
Real Estate Finance
Real Estate Appraisals
Real Estate Management
Real Estate Investments

The noticeable feature of such an approach is the lack of integration of subject matter. It seems as if the information is presented along independent channels of thought and it is left up to the reader or the teacher to do the integrating by identifying any appropriate inter-relationships that exist. While this book covers the very same areas of real estate information, it attempts to integrate by emphasizing the role of the real estate broker rather than the entire industry. Therefore, these subject areas such as location, the real estate market, value, financing, investment analysis, etc. all are treated within the context of the real estate brokerage business. In another way, the style of this book seems to follow the philosophy of the professional football coach who advocates "a return to fundamentals;" that is, the perfection of blocking and tackling before going on to the double and triple reverses. In the real estate field we might view it as a fresh look at the basic principles, a new foundation on which to build a career.

The body of knowledge that an aspiring professional should master is comprised of principles and applications. Principles are but generalizations from experience that have established validity and therefore are widely accepted but have not been elevated to the order of laws. It might be put this way: The *why* of doing things is explained through principles, whereas the *how* follows proven experience. While the "how" may prove to be more financially beneficial in the short run in that it provides immediate benefits, the "why" provides the basis for the development of a sound, long-term career. We know that there are some practicing real estate brokers that understand the mechanics thoroughly but aren't quite sure why things work as they do. Their situation might be compared to individuals who knows how to turn on the water faucet but don't care to concern themselves with why the water gets there. The eventual result may be that when economic downturns affect the "supply of water," those persons may be eliminated from the business because of their inability to cope with challenging conditions. It seems the real estate business has been affected to a degree throughout the years by a philosophy emanating from self-styled success. A certain number of brokers achieving success in the real estate business seem to be compelled to teach others on the ground that "not all people have been successful . . . but I have been successful . . . therefore I am morally bound to teach others what I know." While such a dedicated attitude may be admirable, it does not necessarily mean that what that person has to teach is the most appropriate kind of knowledge available.

Experience and Knowledge

You may have had the occasion to observe the real estate "old timer" who walks through a residential building without taking a single written note, carefully observing, and at the end of the tour blurts out "seventy-nine five." Yes, the building is worth $79,500. But why? L.W. Ellwood addresses this issue at the front of his book, "Ellwood Tables – for Real Estate Appraising and Financing."[1]

EXPERIENCE and JUDGMENT

I believe experience can teach lessons which may lead to sound judgment. I believe sound judgement is vital in selecting the critical factors for appraisal. But, I also believe the bright 17 year old high school student in elementary astronomy can do a better job estimating the distance to the moon than the old man of the mountains who has looked at the moon for 80 years. So, I find it difficult to accept the notion that dependable valuation of real estate is nothing more than experience and judgment.

I would not give a red cent for an appraisal by the "expert" who beats his breast and shouts; "I don't have to give reasons. I've had 40 years experience in this business. And, this property is worth so much because I say so".

After all, value is expressed as a number. And, no man lives who, through experience, has all numbers so filed in

---

[1]Publishing rights are now owned by the Appraisal Institute, Chicago, Illinois 60611

the convolutions of his brain that he can be relied upon to choose the right one without explicable analysis and calculation.

Knowledge is a wonderful gift but it is a most unusual one. We can pass on our wealth and other material riches to our successors through a well-established legal process that is initiated by merely signing a will. But to attempt to pass on our personal expertise and knowledge is a far more challenging process. In some cases the transfer may be less than complete and as a result a portion of this peculiar kind of wealth is lost and buried.

Experience may be a good teacher in the sense that it provides one with practical knowledge. It is especially useful in a local market wherein conditions continue to remain substantially the same. However, a change in circumstances beyond the realm of experience may cause the real estate broker to be hard pressed for a confident decision. Then there also is the matter of performing in a different market area. Would the previous experience apply? Further, what is the quality and the quantity of the experience? Is the experience varied and of a new nature every year, or is it the same kind of experience year after year. Really, it could well be one year's experience repeated many times! Yes, experience is important, but it would be all the more meaningful and valuable if it were accumulated against an organized framework of knowledge.

Unfortunately, haphazard accumulation of experience lacks the systematic framework for organizing this useful information within our minds. Properly related experience can teach lessons that may provide the basis for sound judgment. In turn, sound judgment is essential in selecting and weighing material factors in making real estate decisions. This is where education comes into the picture.

Proper education provides a broader base on which to build a bigger and better understanding of real estate activities. The expert practice of real estate is based on a body of knowledge that draws from many educational disciplines . . . economics, law, political science, accounting, sociology, psychology, management (decision making) science, etc. Real estate as an industry is more than just listing and selling. It encompasses a wide range of functions: subdividing, development, construction, appraising, finance, management and brokerage.

This book will demonstrate that most of the popular rules of thumb that are so widely accepted by the practitioners are definitely related to a formalized body of knowledge. The underlying structure is composed of theory, principles and procedures that comprise the framework within which real estate activity is conducted.

The present day real estate industry still bears some of the stigmas attributed to the fast dealing and free wheeling land developers operating at the turn of the preceding century, as well as the effects of the wholesale foreclosures of the 1930s. However, in some ways the real estate business has come of age only since the "Great Depression" of the '30s.

⟨ It was then that the monthly amortized mortgages began to become a matter of policy with most loaning institutions.
⟨ It has been since then that all states have adopted real estate license laws.
⟨ It has been since then that insured and guaranteed mortgage loans have been introduced.
⟨ It has been since then that the trade associations have been more effectively active in real estate affairs.
⟨ It has been since then that improvements in appraisal techniques have been developed.

In recent years the "education explosion" is bringing about an improving image of the real estate broker. However, memories of the past still linger on in the minds of the public.

Inability to cope with criticism related to the "old days" may cause the real estate broker to go on the defensive to explain the justification for services and the amount of commission. This is a sign that the public has not been adequately updated as to the current status of the real estate industry. The functional role of real estate is vital to the growth and prosperity of every community. City growth is the sum of individual real estate investment decisions, both private and public. In varying degrees, all real estate practitioners are "city builders" operating within a rather complex framework that they very often fail to recognize. Too often practitioners reject the theoretical aspects of the business on the grounds they prefer to be called practical people. It seems as if they don't want to accept the notion that many of their actions are applications of theory. They use procedures that are, in fact, well founded on strong theoretical principles, but still prefer the so-called "bread and butter" approach to the business.

The public must be informed to understand that there is a higher degree of sophistication to modern day real estate operations. The aspiring professional real estate broker must be able to explain *why* in an intelligent manner. If that broker is unable to do so, he or she is not sufficiently prepared to do a professional job.

Theory vs. Practice

For the most part, practice in the field preceded accepted theory. The theorist analyzed and described in a logical manner what the better practitioners already were doing. Over the years, scholars have searched and fitted existing concepts from other fields to various segments of real estate market practices. So, as we look over the body of knowledge on which this industry is based, we soon discover that present and future value concepts come from the field of finance; amortization tables are another form of annuity tables; pioneering location theory was based on applications of geometry; the depreciation concept came from the field of accounting; market cycles came from the field of economics; some of the valuation procedures came from the field of mathematical statistics; and so on.

To paraphrase a respected popular scholar/professor, "Practice is brick; theory is mortar. Both are basic requirements and both must be of good and tested quality if we want to construct a sturdy building." To utilize practical experience to build a bridge over a creek is one thing, but to translate that experience into building a bridge over a river may be an entirely different matter.

The body of knowledge on which real estate practices are based is very broad in nature. However, identifiable roots can be found in research and publications coming forth from the land grant universities established after the Civil War. The initial focus was on agricultural land, but by the end of the 19th century, attention was turning to the urban area as well. Noticeable in this area was the pioneering work of Richard T. Ely at the University of Wisconsin. His research and activity in the field of economics and other related fields, though under scrutiny at the time, were staunchly defended by the University of Wisconsin Board of Regents in 1894 by the board's statement:

"In all lines of academic investigation it is of the utmost importance that the investigator should be absolutely free to follow the indications of truth wherever they may lead.

Whatever may be the limitations which trammel inquiry elsewhere, we believe that the great state University of Wisconsin should ever encourage that continual and fearless sifting and winnowing by which alone the truth can be found."

The Class of 1910 memorialized this second paragraph on a bronze plaque at the entrance of Bascom Hall on top of the University of Wisconsin's famous Bascom Hill.

In 1940, Ely, along with George S. Wehrwein, published the classic book, "Land Economics". During this period other researchers followed Ely's lead but sharpened their focus on real estate as a subject. This group included Dorau and Hinman at Northwestern and Fisher at Michigan, who later headed up the research efforts at the Department of Housing and Development (HUD) in Washington, D.C. in the 1930s and 1940s. Fisher served as a mentor to Richard U. Ratcliff who went on to the Wisconsin campus. Shortly after World War II, it was at Wisconsin that Ratcliff wrote the "bible" of the real estate field. His "Urban Land Economics" became the basic textbook for real estate instruction at colleges throughout the country. During this same time period, Arthur M. Weimer of Indiana University and Homer Hoyt of urban consulting fame published a series of editions of well-known

"Principles of Real Estate." It is worthy to note that nearly all of these authors as well as their contemporaries had some degree of interchange with the developing library of the National Association of Real Estate Boards.

Trade Associations

Just after the start of the 20th century, trade association activity began to blossom at an impressive level. Organized activity on the part of real estate brokers and salespeople began around 1908. The national headquarters of the National Association of Real Estate Boards (now the NAR, National Association of Realtors®) was established in Chicago. It is now headquartered in Washington, D.C. Among services to members was the development of an extensive real estate library that dates back to the 1920s. Today it is the finest and most complete real estate library in the country. Presently, membership in the NAR is over 700,000 and includes activity in all 50 states, the District of Columbia, Puerto Rico, Guam and the U.S. Virgin Islands. Members subscribe to a Code of Ethics and abide by established Standards of Practice. Besides extensive member services, the NAR is very active in legislative matters at the local, state and national levels.

The importance of real estate in our nation's economy was re-emphasized by President Bill Clinton in a 1993 address to the Board of Directors of the National Association of Realtors® in Washington, D.C.:

> "The main engine of economic growth is people like you. I respect the work you do. There's no greater goal for America's families than to be able to live in their own homes." The President went on to say, "I respect you because I know that you live by your wits. You live by your efforts. You don't have a guaranteed income. How well you do depends on how hard and how smart you work, but it also depends on decisions made by people in this town that set the parameters in which you operate."

The pursuit of home ownership as a goal by American families is evidenced by the gradual increase in ownership from about 40 percent in the 1920s to 65 percent in the United States today. These are 1995 figures based on owner occupied housing units.

Rules of Thumb: An Example

There is ample evidence that a good number of the participants in the real estate market tend to make decisions based on so-called "rules of thumb" and clichés that have been inherited from past practitioners, acquaintances and hear-say. In most cases a "rule of thumb" turns out to be an estimate or average statement of a particular real estate procedure or practice. A very common one is used in connection with approximating the market value of a two-flat in many cities. This rule of thumb simply states that "100 times the monthly rent equals the value of the property."

CHART 1 – 3 Two-Flat RULE OF THUMB			
"100 times monthly rent = value of the property."			
Gross Monthly Rent	–	$400.00	– lower unit
Gross Monthly Rent	–	395.00	– upper rent
Total Gross Monthly Rent	–	$795.00	– both units
Apply two 0's . . . $795 plus 00	=	$79,500	estimated value

The above example assumes that the gross monthly rental of the lower unit in a two-flat is $400.00 and the corresponding figure for the upper unit is $395.00 a month. By adding the two you arrive at a monthly total of $795.00. The final step is to attach two zeroes to the $795.00 total and arrive at a value figure of $79,500.00.

However crude, this short-cut version seems to be a take-off from the stock market notion of price/earnings ratio, although the latter is based on net earnings rather than gross revenue. What's more, this over-simplified technique is further ingrained in the market operation by buyers and new owners using the procedure in reverse. The owner of a newly acquired two-flat reasons, "Since I paid $79,500 for this property, if I drop the last two zeros, that means I should collect total monthly rents of $795 for the two units."

This over-simplified technique of valuation came into prominence in the 1920s and has been in wide use ever since. Apparently its ease of application accounts for its continuing use and popularity. Because of the seemingly superficial method of application, one can't help but wonder how many of the users really understand the underlying significance of these estimates. The fact of the matter is that they actually are applying a short-cut version of a formal capitalization process. It is based on the basic financial formula of:

$$\frac{I}{R} = V \quad \text{or} \quad \frac{\text{Gross Annual Income}}{\text{Annual Rate of Return}} = \text{Estimated Value}$$

Using the figures employed in the above illustration, we discover that in the process of adding two zeroes to the monthly rents, the broker actually is capitalizing the gross rental income on the basis of an annual rate of 12 percent. This is born out by substituting the information in the capitalization formula as follows:

$$\frac{I}{R} = V \quad \text{or} \quad \frac{\$795.00 \times 12 \text{ Months}}{\text{Annual Rate of Return}} = \text{Estimated Value}$$

The first step in the solution is to cross-multiply, which converts the equation to:

$$\$79,500 \quad R = \$9,540.00$$

Therefore

$$R = \frac{\$9,540.00}{\$79,500.00} \quad \text{or} \ \underline{12\%}$$

Thus we can see that the rule of thumb is equivalent to capitalizing gross rental income at an annual rate of 12 percent. The annual rate can be checked by applying it to the estimated value. Twelve percent of $79,500.00 is $9,540.00. Annual rent of $9,540.00 divided by 12 months gives a monthly rental figure of $795.00, which agrees with assumed conditions of the rule of thumb example.

Gross capitalization rates can be stated in forms other than percentages. For instance, the 12 percent rate of gross return is equivalent to an annual gross rent multiplier of 8 1/3 times. This is arrived at by dividing 100 percent by 12 percent giving a ratio of 8.333. To convert this to a monthly gross rent multiplier we would multiply 8 1/3 by 12, producing a monthly multiplier of 100. This constitutes a brief explanation of the basis for adding the two zeroes to the monthly rental total. Experience in the real estate market will provide you with the knowledge that the size of the gross rent multiplier will vary with different kinds of property since newer residential properties may command a multiplier of eight or nine times while older properties may warrant a multiplier of only five or six. Rooming houses, because of the uncertainty of rental collections from transient clientele and the condition of the property, may command an annual gross rent multiplier of only two or three.

It should be pointed out that the arrived at rate of 12 percent is based on the straight-line capitalization technique that assumes the income flows in perpetuity. As previously stated, since the emphasis is on *gross* rent with no recognition given to vacancies nor operating expenses, another assumption is that vacancy rates and the ratio of operating expenses to revenue are fairly constant from property to property. This suggests that there are some severe limitations associated with the use of this method. Further, this particular rule of thumb may most likely be an "average" in your market area and is subject to adjustments based on the quality of the neighborhood, condition of the property, investor demand, redevelopment prospects, degree of risk, etc.

The subject of capitalization will be discussed in greater detail in Chapter 7 dealing with analyzing real estate investments. The accepted procedure for estimating a listing price is presented in Chapter 5: "Your Clients – the Sellers".

Ease of Entry

Who are the participants in the process of marketing real estate? Primary participants are brokers, salespeople, sellers, buyers and lenders. A report issued in 1965 disclosed that there were nearly 800,000 licensed real estate brokers and salespeople in the United States. By 1995, that number more than doubled to more than 1,800,000 according to an annual report issued by the Association of Real Estate License Law Officials (ARELLO). In the period from 1965 to 1995, total U.S. population increased from about 200,000,000 to about 260,000,000, or a total increase of approximately 30 percent. On the other hand, active real estate licenses (brokers and salespeople) increased from about 800,000 to over 1,800,000, or a total increase of about 125 percent! Comparing active licenses to the 1995 total population indicates that in 1995 there was one real estate licensee for about every 142 people on a nationwide basis. Using an average family size of 2.6 persons per housing unit would convert the 142 measure to the equivalent of about 55 families. Five states have about one-half of the total number of active licensed real estate brokers but only about one-third of the total national population. These five states are California, Florida, Massachusetts, New York and Texas. All of these states have large, well-populated urban areas. A more detailed examination of the report discloses that the relationship of population to licensees varies considerably from state to state. The ratios range from 50 to 500+ people for each real estate licensee. The following chart groups these ratios for the 50 states and the District of Columbia.

CHART 1 – 4		
POPULATION PER REAL ESTATE LICENSEE		
Range of Population to Each Licensee	**States or District**	
50 – 149	Arizona California Colorado Connecticut District of Columbia Florida Hawaii Indiana	Maryland Massachusetts Missouri New Hampshire New Jersey North Carolina Rhode Island Virginia
150 – 249	Delaware Georgia Idaho Illinois Kansas Michigan Minnesota Montana Nevada New Mexico New York	Ohio Oregon Pennsylvania South Carolina Texas Utah Vermont Washington Wisconsin Wyoming
250 – 349	Alabama Arkansas Iowa Maine	Nebraska South Dakota Tennessee
350 – 449	Alaska Kentucky Louisiana	North Dakota Oklahoma West Virginia
450 – 549	Mississippi	

The above tabulations were based on comparisons of adjusted census figures (1995 estimates based on 1990 census figures and current growth rates) and the 1995 report of real estate licensing activities. It should also be pointed out that there are a good number of licensees that cannot be considered full-time real estate practitioners. Some only renew their licenses each year for purposes of convenience. This category includes employees of lending institutions, governmental agencies, insurance companies and the like. While they are not actively seeking real estate commissions, they find it useful to be licensed since they are fully employed in a real estate related field. Another large group is made up of part-time salespeople gainfully employed elsewhere who sell real estate to supplement their incomes. Some members of this group have the objective of becoming full-time as soon as they acquire sufficient experience or accumulate sufficient financial reserves to provide the confidence to work on a straight commission basis. A detailed analysis of the licensees in the Milwaukee metropolitan area indicated that only 40 percent of licensed real estate brokers had a business listing in the telephone book. This figure suggests that a good number of licensees making up the unlisted group obtain their livelihood from sources other than the real estate brokerage business. A similar check of other counties in Wisconsin where the population was less dense than Milwaukee disclosed the percentage of active brokers to be considerably higher.

In round numbers, the 1,820,000 active licensees in the United States in 1995 consisted of approximately 640,000 real estate brokers and 1,180,000 salespeople. This represented a ratio of 1.8 salespeople per broker. On a state-by-state basis, similar ratios ranged from a high of 7.4 in Louisiana to a low of 0.5 in Wisconsin. This rather restricted range suggests that, by and large, most real estate brokerage firms are limited in size. This is understandable since the real estate brokerage business is based on a high degree of personalized service. This particular characteristic of the real estate business provides part of the foundation upon which professional service can be cultured and rendered. In the post World War II years, the ranks of real estate licensees swelled by increasing numbers of new entrants into the field. In recent years these new entrants comprise 10-15 percent of total licensees. However, this 10-15 percent increase of newcomers is partially offset by those retiring, those leaving and those failing to renew their licenses. The net gain of total licenses issued each year is about 3 percent compounded annually, the equivalent of a complete turnover in slightly more than one generation. The significant dimension of this 3 percent per year net increase in licenses issued is that it is much higher than the one percent per year average annual increase in the population of this country. A long-term projection of this trend seems to suggest overcrowding in the field. But it should not be overlooked that the sales of existing single family homes from 1968 to 1994 have increased at an annual rate of 3 percent compounded at the national level.

Another phase of the Milwaukee study revealed that over a 30 year period – 1960-90 – of the real estate brokers active at the outset of this period only 40 percent still were active ten years later. Over a 20 year segment only two out of ten were still on the scene. This survey, limited to the Milwaukee area, indicates that after a single generation of 20 years, eight out of ten brokers decided not to continue in business for a wide variety of reasons that might include everything from success and retirement, down to complete failure. The rate of new entries into the field may provide a strong basis for the "ease of entry" label attached to the real estate industry, but the turnover ratios represent the other side of the coin and indicate that there is an "ease of exit" as well.

While the statistics in this section may seem somewhat drawn out, it is important to recognize them for what they represent . . . your competition. It is strongly suggested that individual brokers, or groups of brokers within a local area, make similar determinations in order to better understand the number and nature of the participants in that particular local market area. "Market share" is an important management tool and will be discussed in Chapter 10 about office management and budgets. While this book will address the various phases of real estate marketing, primary emphasis will be on the residential phase.

CHAPTER 2 – YOUR MARKET: HOW IT OPERATES

*"Only one person in a thousand really understands
the real estate market . . . yet we seem to meet
that person everyday." Richard Ratcliff*

What Is A Market?

In economic terms, a market is defined as the area in which sellers (supply side) and buyers (demand side) are in communication with one another and within which negotiations (for goods and services) take place. Does this describe a real estate market? In the very broadest sense it does. But in applying this general definition to the real estate market more specifically, certain limitations can be recognized. Such limitations are related to the nature of the commodity as well as the participants in this particular market. First of all, the commodity, that is the land and its improvements, is firmly placed at a fixed site. The fact that real estate is relatively immobile means that it cannot be shipped from market to market. However, this immobility gives it locational value. Secondly, the participants in a real estate market, the buyers and sellers, appear to have less face-to-face contact with each other than in many other markets. This is due to the fact that in most instances the seller is represented by a real estate broker. Using the property as the focal point of negotiation, the broker provides the channel of communication between the seller and the buyer. In the usual transaction the buyer comes in contact with the property through the efforts of the real estate broker. In some respects, the real estate broker serves as a kind of marketplace. Perhaps the buyer and seller may meet only at the final closing, if at all. A third noticeable difference is the time gap between the date of the contract to buy and the actual closing of the transaction and the transfer of title. This may involve a time delay of one to two months, or more.

Real Estate Markets

There are three major categories of real estate markets:

National • Regional • Local

Classifications of this type seem to place primary emphasis on the supply side of the market. Since each parcel of real estate is available only at a given location, it is chained to the particular market in which it is situated. Due to this fixity of location, many real estate economists describe a real estate market as being local in nature. In terms of supply, geographical areas are mere delineations for analytical purposes since local areas make up regions and regions in turn comprise the total national picture. In some cases, supply in other geographical areas has little impact on a specific local market. This is particularly true for residential real estate. However, the supply side of every real estate market is not confined to the local area. Manufacturing firms may shop in a regional market, composed of several different cities, simultaneously considering their various alternatives in choosing a new plant site. The managers of local office buildings may attempt to attract national tenants to their locations. These national firms, in turn, may be considering the advantages and disadvantages of office buildings in a number of different cities from coast to coast. The geographical differences in the source of units of supply and the source of units of demand are illustrated in the following diagram:

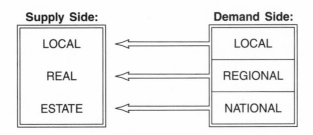

CHART 2 – 1
TYPICAL RESIDENTIAL REAL ESTATE MARKET

The demand side of the market has far broader dimensions and can be composed of units derived from the local, regional and national levels. For example, the typical local residential market is made up of demand that primarily is generated in the local area. However, additional demand comes from regional and national sources through normal moving, transferring of employees, retirement, etc. A more meaningful understanding of the real estate market can be obtained by classifying the supply side of the local market into sub-markets. Sub-markets might consist of geographical districts, neighborhoods, types of property, price ranges, land uses, etc.

In addition to identifying a real estate market in terms of the space in which it operates, it also is important to be aware of the functions that it performs. The market mechanism influences the highest and best land use through a competitive process wherein prospective buyers bid against each other for particular sites. The successful bidder develops the site within the scope of existing land use regulations. This in turn determines the amount of capital improvements (investment) that will be made and the actual timing of the development. The operation of this competitive process also provides the framework and mechanism for price determination. The intensity of demand also has an impact on the rate of new construction and the supply of space made available for urban development. These processes apply to the initial development of raw land and to the sale of existing real estate facilities. It should be recognized that there are certain market imperfections that hamper the efficiency of these market operations. These imperfections include non-availability of real property of the type that is in current demand, unrealistic prices asked by potential sellers, lack of financing to enable the completion of the intended transaction, insufficiency of market information, etc.

The Real Estate Market is Unique

The market in which the real estate industry operates is somewhat unique. In many merchandising activities, retailers regularly count on repeat business from a certain number of customers each week or month. Real estate brokers don't have this "order taking" kind of repeat business that manufacturer's agents or other kinds of retailers have. In the real estate business, tomorrow's customers are usually new ones. A repeat customer may reappear every six or seven years since this is the average life of a residential mortgage. For the most part, brokers must continually look for new clients in the marketplace.

One of the basic characteristics of marketing in the real estate brokerage field is the high dependence on turnover of tenancy, both rental and ownership. Therefore it is implicit that the broker identify who is likely to move, who is likely to sell, who is likely to buy and who is likely to rent. In order to understand these movements a little better, it is advisable to know how the components fit together.

Residential Market Model

The following illustration shows an overview of the residential housing market. (See Chart 2 – 2). The top tier indicates the ratio of home owners to renters. Recent national housing statistics reveal that about 64 percent of the housing units are owner-occupied and the balance, 36 percent, are tenant-occupied. The second phase of this chart deals with the often-quoted census statement that "one out of six families move each year." In a general sense, this may be interpreted that, on average, 17 percent of the housing units experience a turnover during the course of one year. However, it is well established that the rate of turnover is not the same in both the ownership and rental categories. As a matter of fact, the turnover in rental units is considerably greater. National surveys indicate that one out of three rental units change over each year. On the other hand, only one out of 13 owner-occupied units experience a change in occupancy on a yearly basis. These latter ratios indicate that of the 17 percent turnover in housing units each year, seven out of ten households move into rental units, whereas three out of ten will purchase new or existing housing facilities. Accordingly, the 17 percent changeover can be estimated as follows: 12 percent to rental units and 5 percent to purchased units. Of the 5 percent that bought homes, 1 percent decided on new homes while the other 4 percent purchased existing houses.

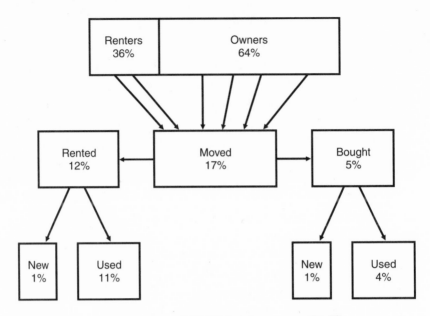

CHART 2 – 2
RESIDENTIAL REAL ESTATE MARKET
Annual Summary

A review of the arithmetic in Chart 2 – 2 may be helpful at this point. Starting at the bottom, it can be seen that the 1 percent in the "new" category plus the 4 percent in the "used" add up to the total of 5 percent buying housing units during the year. The 5 percent buyers combined with the 12 percent renters amount to the 17 percent that move each year. The 17 percent, of course, is part of the total of 100 percent which is comprised of 64 percent owners and 36 percent renters. The reader must bear in mind that these figures represent national averages and do not necessarily apply to one's particular local market. After reviewing this chart one may be amazed with the small number, one percent of new home buyers each year. This may appear to be particularly low in view of the vast amount of home building that has taken place since the end of World War II. However, a survey of the statistics on new-homes starts for the past 25 years demonstrates that the volume of new home construction regularly fell within a bracket of one to two percent. What this means is that the existing stock of housing was increased, on average, by one to two percent each year at the national level.

The glamour of new homes and the attendant promotion and publicity have consistently attracted much attention to the new construction industry. This magnetism of newness tends to keep the public's attention focused on its activities. However, the facts are that the sale of existing units is several times that of the construction of new housing units each year. This disproportionate situation is understandable because of the nature of these sub-markets, the new construction and existing homes markets. Extensive publicity and concentrated promotional efforts are well organized in the hands of a relatively limited number of builders in a local market. When contrasted to the organization of the existing home market, there are many more brokers and individual home owners participating as sellers than builders. Sheer numbers and attendant lack of organization result in much less-concentrated sales and promotional activity in the existing home market than is found in the new market. Further, brokers are dealing with "one of a kind's," whereas the builders are mass merchandising by reproducing the display model home many times, thus affording them economies of scale.

It should be pointed out that this overview of the residential real estate market is very general in nature, based on some facts, averages and estimates. It represents a summary of what happens in the course of a given calendar year in the residential housing market. The market model is static in nature. Closer study of this over-simplified model reveals that the total market stays in balance in spite of a whole year's activity, the ratio of ownership and rentals remains the same. While the chart shows that there was a 17 percent turnover, 12 percent made rental choices and 5 percent made buying choices, thus restoring the tenure balance back to the 64 percent and 36 percent levels. It is quite apparent that further refinements would have to be taken into account in order to develop a more sophisticated model. Such refinements would include taking into account the vacancy factors in both the rental and ownership categories; demolitions and conversions that would affect the size of the existing stock; changes in population and in the number of households; and similar market-related measurements. In line with the objectives of this book, the broker's chief concern should be the matter relating this market model to the operation of one's real estate brokerage business. The broker is reminded that there are several important dimensions to housing turnover. Housing turnover may involve these combinations affecting tenure dynamics:

a. Renter to renter
b. Renter to owner
c. Owner to owner
d. Owner to renter
e. Tenure losses (due to out-migration, death, etc.)
f. Tenure replacements (in-migration, marriages, etc.)

Some of these changes relate to listing, some to selling and some to both listing and selling. Since these tenure changes are more closely associated with the demand side of the market, they will be discussed in more detail later in this chapter as part of the demand story.

The Standing Stock

At any given point in time the standing stock of housing is the sum total of all owner-occupied units, plus all renter-occupied units, plus the vacancies in both the ownership and rental categories. Another way of quantifying the standing stock is illustrated as follows:

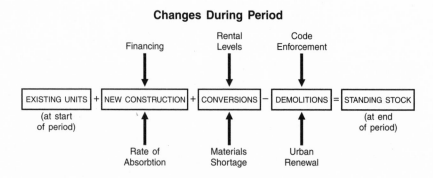

Changes During Period

EXISTING UNITS (at start of period) + NEW CONSTRUCTION + CONVERSIONS − DEMOLITIONS = STANDING STOCK (at end of period)

Financing → NEW CONSTRUCTION
Rental Levels → CONVERSIONS
Code Enforcement → DEMOLITIONS

NEW CONSTRUCTION ← Rate of Absorbtion
CONVERSIONS ← Materials Shortage
DEMOLITIONS ← Urban Renewal

CHART 2 – 3
THE STANDING STOCK

The quantity of existing units, the standing stock, is altered by the number of new housing units constructed as well as the number of units created through conversion of existing facilities. In turn, new additions to the standing stock are influenced by the optimistic outlook of builders who carefully watch the rate at which the market is absorbing the new units that they and their competitors are building. The accumulation of "overhang," an inventory of unsold units, will cause the builders to change their pace of activity. This pace also is affected by the availability of mortgage financing. It should be noted that financing can serve as a stimulator as well as a deterrent to a real estate market. The effects of financing are more fully described in the section dealing with the interaction of supply and demand.

The term "conversion" describes a process whereby existing facilities are physically changed, usually to provide more housing units. This may be accomplished by converting a large two-flat into four housing units of smaller size than the original ones. It also might involve the changing of a retail store structure into residential facilities. There are, of course, many other possibilities in the area of conversions. The volume of building permits indicates that conversions tend to occur in greater volume when there is a critical shortage of building materials for new structures and at times when vacancies are at their lowest level with rents near peak levels. In the aggregate, demolitions are stimulated by urban renewal programs, expressway construction and code enforcement related to building standards, health and safety. It is obvious that the standing stock is an ever-changing quantity as it is affected by new construction, conversions and demolitions.

Supply

Theoretically, all units in the standing stock are part of the supply side of the market. This is based on the notion that all properties can be sold or rented if "the price is right". However, experience tells us that this is not quite the case. Some owners may refuse to sell regardless of the price. This also is true of most of the owners and tenants who have moved recently. They are reluctant to change so soon and therefore the units that they now occupy are no longer in the market for the time being.

The main characteristics of the supply of housing can be brought into sharper focus by recognizing these major features:

1. The supply of housing is relatively slow to change.
2. This inherent stability tends to make supply a more important factor in long run analyses.
3. In most communities the existing supply of housing displays greater influence on the local real estate market than the current additions to supply.
4. Increases in supply are created by:
    a. The decision of owners to place their existing property on the market.
    b. Construction of new housing facilities.
    c. Conversion of existing facilities into a greater number of housing units.
    d. Doubling up, thereby making more units available.
5. Decreases in supply are the result of:
    a. Demolitions due to urban renewal, expressway construction, health department orders, etc.
    b. Withdrawal of a property from the market by the owner.
    c. Destruction caused by flood, fire, storms, etc.

    d. Functional and economic obsolescence of properties.

The current supply of housing is made up of all units offered for sale or for rent. The supply of housing is much more stable than demand. Supply, in most cases, is slow to change. This is quite evident in the following table dealing with national and regional housing statistics adapted from the United States Census:

TABLE 2 – 1 TOTAL HOUSING UNIT CHANGE IN U.S., 1970 -1990 (rounded to nearest thousand)					
	(Occupied Housing Units)			Absolute Increase	Percent Increase	Average Compounded Yearly % Increase
Regions:	1970	1980	1990	1970-1990	1970-1990	(to nearest 1/2%)
Northeast	15,483	17,471	18,873	3,390	21.9%	1%
North Central	17,537	20,859	22,317	4,780	27.3%	1%
South	19,258	26,486	31,822	12,564	65.2%	2½%
West	11,172	15,574	18,935	7,763	69.5%	2½%
United States	63,450	80,390	91,947	28,497	44.9%	2%

While the average compounded yearly increase for the United States was about 2 percent, the increases varied by region. The Northeast and North Central regions increased at a rate of 1 percent per year whereas the South experienced a 2½ percent per year gain. The West region showed a similar gain with a rate of 2½ percent. Wider variations occurred on a local basis, ranging from a 5 percent average annual increase in the Phoenix, Arizona metropolitan area to a modest average annual increase of 1 percent in the Boston, Massachusetts metropolitan area. Some of the other metropolitan areas showing housing increases above the national average were Atlanta, Dallas/Fort Worth, San Diego, Las Vegas, Washington, D.C., Denver/Boulder, Memphis, Orlando and Oklahoma City. Among those metropolitan areas with increases lower than the national rate were Kansas City, Milwaukee/Racine, New Orleans, Toledo, Baltimore, St. Louis, Detroit/Ann Arbor, Spokane and Wichita. In order to gain a better understanding of a particular local market, the broker should consult the Census of Housing reports applicable to one's area. This information is readily available in most public libraries.

The fact that real estate has a relatively long life suggests that gradual change is taking place through the process of aging. As individual properties become older, they tend to become less desirable and therefore pass down the ladder of housing preferences. The process whereby formerly higher-priced properties pass down to other users at lower prices is called "filtering". This redistribution of housing space is the chief means by which lower income groups are provided housing. It has its inadequacies due to the declining quality and condition of properties reaching the lowest rung on the ladder. An example of filtering would be the movement of turn-of-the-century mansions to multiple family status by conversion, and then their eventual downward slide into rooming house use. However, change in the type of use is not a prerequisite for filtering to take place. Single family homes tend to pass to families of successively lower incomes from generation to generation.

Demand

Compared to supply, demand is a much more dynamic factor in real estate market analysis, exerting its influence particularly in the short run. The major components of demand are quantity and quality. The quantitative aspects of demand relate to population change, rate of household formation, net migration and family composition with special emphasis on the age groupings of its members. The qualitative aspects of demand are closely associated with the level of family income and the availability of mortgage financing. In an attempt to define the quality of demand, the economist is careful to point out the difference between the "need" for housing versus the "effective" demand for housing. The real estate broker does about the same thing when attempting to qualify a prospect. Much like the economist, the salesperson makes a determination as to whether or not the prospect can effectively buy or rent the property. In short, does the prospect have the financial ability to complete the transaction? Effective demand has an immediate impact on the market in that it can be expressed at the present time. Buyers having need for another housing facility but lacking the necessary financial qualifications are considered to be a part of potential or future demand as their personal positions improve.

Major factors affecting the demand for housing are:
1. A change in the number of households.
   a. Marriages; other household formations

      b. In-migration
      c. Population increase (natural)
  2. Intra-area mobility of households
      a. Change in housing needs
      b. Change in income level
      c. Involuntary moves due to urban renewal, etc.
      d. Desire for improved housing standards
      e. Other motivations: status, prestige, etc.

An increase in population does not necessarily create an increase in demand for housing. If population increases naturally, that is the excess of births over deaths, a portion of this increase may be accommodated in existing units. For example, a new baby may share a bedroom with a brother or sister. Other kinds of adjustment can be made by converting existing space to more usable room or adding rooms to the house. Actually this represents a delayed type of demand to be expressed 18-20 years later when the child has developed to the point of emancipation from his or her household unit. On the other hand, population increases due to in-migration most likely will cause an immediate demand for housing as the family or adults arrive on the local scene. Marriages usually result in increased demand for housing except in cases where doubling-up occurs. Under certain circumstances the newly married may find it advisable to live with relatives for a given period of time because of financial reasons, family situations or military obligations.

With respect to individual household groups, demand for housing facilities is an ever-changing matter. This notion is reaffirmed by the estimate that one out of six families moves each year. Individual circumstances are changing constantly. Younger families soon outgrow their housing facilities as the size of their family expands. In the case of mature families, housing space eventually may become excessive. Also, families may move up and down the income ladder, thus altering their ability to afford housing costs. Other events such as divorce, untimely death, disabling injury, loss of employment and prolonged illness enter into the picture as well.

All of these factors influence the rate of turnover, which is the sum total expression of market demand.

Supply vs. Demand

Consideration has been given to the major factors that cause the supply of real estate to expand or contract. It also was pointed out that the demand aspect of the real estate market increased or decreased in intensity, but that demand was much more volatile than supply. Viewing these factors separately for the moment, one can visualize different combinations of change with the help of Chart 2 – 4. On a quantitative basis, either supply or demand can be expanded or contracted as illustrated in Step A. However, their separate direction of change may be the same or the opposite. Such change in quantity and direction will be discussed later in this chapter.

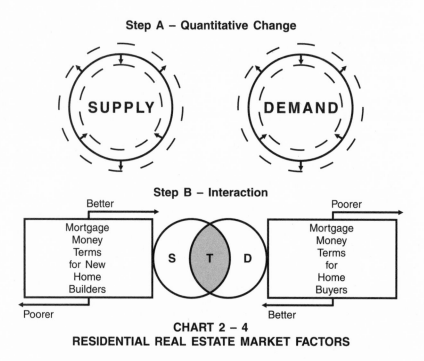

CHART 2 – 4
RESIDENTIAL REAL ESTATE MARKET FACTORS

Sufficiently large expansion of either or both of these market factors will produce an overlap of these two quantities as shown in Step B of Chart 2 – 4. This simplified schematic concept of the real estate market is based in part on the notion that the size of the supply area or the size of the demand area can change due to the peculiar factors that affect each of them as discussed in previous sections. However, the role of improving mortgage financing conditions is depicted as a special force that may drive these areas closer together or allow them to become less engaged as mortgage money becomes less available or less attractive due to changes in borrowing terms. It is this kind of overlap of supply and demand, as shown by the shaded area in Chart 2 – 4, Step B, that represents the active part of the real estate market. It represents the vital area in which supply units (S) and demand units (D) are compatible and result in market transactions (T). Real estate market activity is created on the common ground where the forces of supply and demand interact.

The mobility of the occupants of households within an urban area may be viewed as a grand game of "musical chairs" played in the marketplace to the tune of "change." The likeness of this children's parlor game to the real estate market seems quite appropriate in the case of renters as they move from rental unit to rental unit. There is also a good deal of applicability in the "for sale" market since nearly one-half of all household groups leave an existing unit in search of another one. Real estate statistics indicate that five out of every ten home buyers have an existing home to sell. Their decision to buy another home is tied to an almost simultaneous decision to sell. In market parlance, many buyers are also sellers in the very same market.

The real estate market is known for its fluctuations. These recurring fluctuations create challenges for the real estate broker. But problems thus generated are not to be feared because, in effect, the real estate broker is a problem solver. There may be an oversupply of housing, an undersupply, intensive demand, light demand, or lack of financing. These are some of the problems with which the real estate broker must cope. From a practical point of view, brokers equate the level of supply with the availability of listings and the intensity of demand with the number of qualified buyers currently looking for homes. The interaction of these two market forces takes place within the area of the availability and terms of mortgage financing. Experienced brokers will be ready to admit that more often than not, one or more of these three market factors (supply, demand, financing) is out of proportion with respect to the others, thus creating a problem. The mere fact that buyers and sellers have problems means that they are more likely to turn to the real estate broker for solutions. One might even extend this type of logic to the point that if there were no market problems, perhaps there would be little or no need for real estate brokers' services. There was some evidence of this in recent years when a noticeable number of sellers decided to by-pass the real estate broker and attempt to sell their homes on their own. In spite of their knowledge and experience deficiencies, many of these so-called "do-it-yourselfers" were able to consummate transactions.

When reported, most real estate market information tends to be organized on a city, county, metropolitan, regional or national basis. Such information may be useful in identifying broad trends but provides limited insight as to the functioning of specific sub-markets within the urban area. Within the wide range of urban housing available today, it is not at all unusual to find markedly different levels of activity from one neighborhood to another. There may be an actual shortage of willing sellers in a desirable neighborhood while at the very same time there may be an over-supply of units offered for sale in the least desirable neighborhoods. However, the sum total of all real estate activity in the local area merely indicates an average of what is taking place. In short the levels of supply and demand may be strikingly different as one moves from one section of the community to another. It would be extremely helpful to real estate brokers to keep abreast of the status of the sub-markets within which they do business. A simple but useful classification groups local sub-markets into three kinds:

1. Seller's Market
2. Buyer's Market
3. Stable Market

Admittedly, these divisions are broad in character, but they do serve to describe an outstanding feature of the sub-markets. A brief graphic description of a "seller's market" is depicted in the following chart:

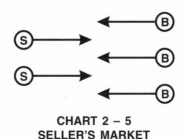

CHART 2 – 5
SELLER'S MARKET

The letter "S" stands for seller and the letter "B" designates buyer. In this illustration there are three buyers interacting with two sellers. This indicates that the three buyers must compete with one another since there are only two sellers. This places competitive strain on the buyers. The sellers are in a strategic position, hence the description, "seller's market." Real estate prices tend to be bid up under these circumstances.

The opposite is true in the next chart:

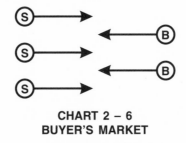

CHART 2 – 6
BUYER'S MARKET

In Chart 2 – 6 there are three sellers as opposed to two buyers. Now the intensive competition shifts to the seller's side of the market. In this case the limited number of buyers are in the superior bargaining position. This is called a buyer's market. If conditions such as this persist for any length of time, chances are that real estate market prices will begin to soften.

There is a third situation representing middle ground between these two types of markets, namely, a stable market. These are the so-called normal market conditions wherein the market is moving at a fairly constant pace. Factors of supply and demand are in reasonably good balance. This assumes that mortgage financing is readily available. It should be pointed out that the degree of attractiveness of financing affects both the demand side as well as the supply side of the real estate market. More attractive financing terms not only make a greater number of buyers qualified to buy but also buoy up their confidence to make the home-buying decision. Parallel effects can stimulate the supply side of the market as well. Traditionally undercapitalized builders and leverage-minded investors react to easy money in much the same fashion, thus providing new units of housing for both the sale and rental markets. A contraction of the supply and favorable terms of mortgage money will have the opposite effect. Qualified buyers at the margin are relegated to the role of sub-marginal buyers, thereby being eliminated from the status of effective demand. Builders and developers find it difficult to finance their projects and therefore slow down the supply of new units to the market. A classic situation was observed during the Great Depression of the 1930s when the supply was adequate, financing was available, but the need could not be translated into qualified demand due to the wholesale unemployment that prevailed.

Household Cycle

The interaction of supply and demand frequently is presented in the form of a theoretical model. While this may be useful in the arena of abstract thinking, from a practical point-of-view the broker will find it much more useful to consider supply and demand as it expresses itself within the framework of the household cycle.

For real estate brokers to gain additional insight about how the market operates, they should be aware of the reasons why people desire to rent or own. To understand the reasoning behind this basic housing decision, brokers should look at occupancy in terms of the human relationships involved. In other words, brokers must understand the household and how it affects occupancy. First of all, one must cast aside any preconceived idea of the typical household. All too often in real estate as well as other fields, the word "household" is immediately thought to mean a related group of people consisting of a husband and wife and one or two children. While this is not entirely wrong, it presents an incomplete picture. It represents only part of one stage of a cycle through which most households pass. In this cycle there are stages of development and decline. Also, the makeup of household members in each stage varies considerably, which results in changing housing needs as the household progresses from one stage to the next along the cycle. For the purposes of the broker, the household cycle is composed of four stages as shown in the following table:

TABLE 2 – 2 THE HOUSEHOLD CYCLE			
Stage	Name of Stage	Description	Probable Tenure
1	The Formation Stage	Newly Marrieds; Housing Partners	Rental: Limited Size Apartment
2	The Growing Stage	Children of Pre-School Age	Rental: Larger Size Flat
3	The Maturing Stage	Children of Primary and High School Age	Ownership: Single Family Home
4	The Contracting Stage	Children Leaving for for College or own apartment	Ownership: Smaller Home, Condo *or* Rental: Smaller Apartment

Although they overlap, each stage creates different housing needs that will greatly affect the decision to buy or rent, and thus, the demand for owner or rental occupancy.

Seventy percent of all housing units are occupied by family households. About four-fifths of these family households are headed by married couples and the balance are single-parent family households. The remaining 30 percent of all housing units are occupied by non-family households consisting of one-person households and what might be referred to as "Housing Partners." "Housing Partners" are two or more individuals, usually not related, sharing a housing facility and often sharing the expenses. This type of occupancy is much more volatile than family household occupancy. It also tends to be of much shorter duration. With the absence of children, Stages 2 and 3 are not too meaningful for this type of occupancy. However, that part of Stage 3 related to ownership acquisition may have some application. Nevertheless, this type of occupancy is more significant in the rental market than in the "for sale" market.

Not to be overlooked are one-person households that comprise nearly 85 percent of non-family households, or about 25 percent of all households in general. Bear in mind that this number includes single occupants in all age categories and in all types of housing units. Like the housing partners category, this type of occupancy is more significant in the rental market rather than in the "for sale" market. One-person households occupy single family homes, multiple-family flats, condos and apartments. People in one-person households range in age from young adults to senior citizens.

The Formation Stage represents the period of the new or beginning family when a couple get married and leave their previous housing facilities to form a household of their own. The largest group in this stage is the young family in which the woman is under 35 years old and as yet has no children. During this period the couple's financial situation usually is marginal and undeveloped. The husband may have just begun his career and, therefore, his earning power is still limited. As a result, the couple has accumulated little or no savings, and more likely than not, the wife is working to earn extra money. For this stage in household development, the housing needs are generally at a minimum. The couple requires little housing space since there are only two people and they are gone most of the time, working during the day and actively enjoying quality time in the evening. With little savings, the couple may not have the money for a down payment on a home. Most households in the Formation Stage have neither the need for nor the ability to buy a home. As a result the majority of them meet their housing needs by renting a small apartment.

As these couples become more firmly established, their attention may turn to having children and raising a family. At this time the family begins its evolution from the Formation to the Growing Stage. During this period the family makeup will change gradually according to the number of new offspring that are added to the household. The family is considered to be in this stage as long as all of the children are of pre-school age. The addition of children to a family, whether one or more, has a strong effect on the change in family housing needs. When the first child is born, the married couple almost immediately needs an extra bedroom. Thus the one-bedroom apartment, which previously filled the couple's housing needs, is made inadequate merely by the arrival of their first born. The family now has the need for more space but still may not have enough savings to purchase a home — especially with the added expenses of their first child. As a result, the family may put off home ownership and move to a larger apartment. With the addition of more children to the family and the approach of the first child to school age, the housing needs of the family become more complex. More bedroom space is needed for the new child as well as yard space where the older child can play. Parents also begin to recognize the need for housing close to schools where their oldest child can start elementary school. It is perhaps at this point where the family feels its first strong desire to move to their own home. More than likely, however, they still lack the down payment and income. As a result the family continues to rent — this time probably a large flat or an older home with more room, privacy and play space and close to school facilities.

As the family's children get older, of primary and high school age, the family progresses to the Maturing Stage in its life cycle. This stage is very important because it usually represents the family's first experience in home ownership. This stage is rather flexible. In it, the family is considered to have children between eight and 18 years of age. At this stage, the need for bedroom space becomes acute. Usually some time after age eight, children demand their own bedroom facilities, especially if they are of opposite sex. They want more privacy and need more room for their increasing possessions. Thus, the small rented home or flat becomes too small to meet the increasing space needs of the growing and maturing family. With the passage of time, the family probably has stopped increasing in number, and the parents have managed to save up enough money for the down payment on a modest existing home that will provide more privacy and space. So the family moves again but this time to a home of its own. As the earning power of the family head approaches its peak and the children reach their teenage years, the family may desire a larger home to entertain and accommodate friends and guests. Additional space might be required for hobbies and other interests. Therefore, the family will desire more space and will buy a larger new or existing home or build one of their own.

The family enters the final stage in its life cycle when the children leave home either to go to college, get married, or join the labor force. This stage is known as the Contracting Stage. Usually there are no children under 18 years. In this stage, the family is reduced to the same two members it had when the cycle started. Because of the reduction in the family's size, the housing needs are reduced greatly from what was previously required. For a while, there is need for extra space to accommodate frequent visits by the children. However, the unneeded space soon becomes a burden on the aging couple physically, and perhaps financially, and they move to a smaller home, condo, or in some instances a small apartment just as when they first started their household cycle. It should, however, be recognized that elderly households do not revert to rental tenancy on as grand a scale as is generally believed. This fact is clearly shown by Table 2 – 3. As can be seen, households in the Contracting Stage have a ratio of ownership to rental of approximately three to one. In other words, it can be said that on average, nearly eight out of ten households in the contracting stage own their homes while only two out of ten rent.

A knowledge of the household cycle as previously described will aid the broker in understanding the market. Through it, the broker can partially determine who moves, who moves most often, why people move, and why people decide to rent or own when they do move. If the broker considers who is creating the demand in the residential market, he or she actually is asking who is moving in the broker's market. Taking into consideration the household cycle, one can partially answer this by saying young households that are growing are a major factor in the rental market, and more mature expanding and elderly households are more important in the home ownership market. In addition, the broker must consider the employment and other economic conditions of the area, the rate of immigration, urban renewal, etc. The broker can explain in part why they are moving or creating this demand by considering the changing housing needs as households develop and change. Why people rent or buy also can be explained in part by considering the household stage that the majority of the broker's market is in and their typical financial conditions of the time. The availability of high percentage mortgage loans (low down payment) such as VA and FHA financing may enable a household to purchase a house sooner than normally expected. Conventionally financed purchases require larger down payments, hence a longer saving period for the down payment may be needed. Other factors entering into this basic housing decision of buying versus renting will be discussed in Chapter 6: Your Clients – the Buyers.

The following table shows the tenure or housing status and the stage of the household cycle for urban households according to age of the head of household, adapted from HUD's
U.S. Housing and Market Conditions, August, 1995.

TABLE 2 – 3 THE HOUSEHOLD CYCLE AND HOUSING DECISIONS			
Household Stage	**Age of Head**	**% Own Homes**	**% Rent Homes**
Formation Stage	18 – 24	15%	85%
Growing Stage	25 – 34	43%	57%
Maturing Stage	35 – 44	64%	36%
Contracting Stage	45 – 54	75%	25%
	55 – 64	79%	21%
	65 & Over	77%	23%

Through this table the broker can clearly see that the demand for rental occupancy is most prevalent in the early stages of the household cycle while demand for owner occupancy greatly increases in the mid and later stages. But the broker might ask, "How can I meaningfully use this information?" As demonstrated, it can be seen that the household cycle provides some explanation of the nature of the demand for housing, both rental and ownership. However, not to be overlooked is that supply is "the other side of the coin" in the housing turnover process. In many cases the expression of effective demand (buying or renting) results in vacating existing housing facilities, thereby adding units of supply to that side of the market. To the real estate broker this gives information as to who is likely to buy and provides a source of buying prospects. For example, the households in the Formation Stage currently renting flats and apartments are ripening into the Buying Stage. The Growing Stage households are sources of both listings and sales as they buy larger houses. Contracting households in the advanced stages are likely sellers. It should be pointed out that household cycle analysis, while highly informative, is not the entire framework of the real estate market. Other factors having an impact on the market are inter-area movements, formation and dissolution of non-related households, or untimely deaths or other removals from the demand side of the market.

By way of continued explanation, the broker should realize that the so called "active areas" of real estate activity are further evidences of the household cycle in action. This may be especially applicable to a homogeneous residential subdivision that is just completing the time span of one generation. Observers, seeing the rash of "for sale" signs may begin to wonder what is happening to the neighborhood when nothing unusual may be happening at all. It may very well be that most of the occupants in the area are about in the same phase of the household cycle and are faced with a common problem. Individual households may have been thinking about moving but hesitated making the final decision. However, one or two households make the decision to move and this serves as a catalyst for further selling action. The initial sellers set off a chain reaction in that they triggered other moves. In short, the first sellers lead the way and give others courage to make similar decisions. Similar selling impetus can be found in newer residential subdivisions about five to ten years old. Here one may find evidence of change developing in the second phase of the household cycle, the Growing Stage. These owners may have purchased new two- or three-bedroom homes and now that their households are expanding, they are outgrowing the present home and are forced to move. In the cases cited, one can expect an abnormal amount of turnover if a majority of the owners entered the neighborhood at approximately the same time. This is particularly true of the development of new subdivisions because they are likely to attract people with similar tastes and in similar age brackets. Areas having a majority of households somewhere in the Formation and Growing Stages will have more demand activity than areas of equal size but with a majority of households in the Contracting Stage. This is evident because younger, developing households are more mobile than older, more stable households. According to the U.S. Bureau of Census figures, "the chances of a household's moving is four times greater in the early stages of the life cycle than in the middle and later years".

The rate of household formation is one of the main elements in understanding the future of a local real estate market.

Underlying household formation is the willingness and the ability to spend money for the starting of a household.

One's expectations of the future of the economy effects one's confidence and hence impacts on the rate of household formation.

The last part of the "baby boom" will be reaching age 35 by the year 2000. Households headed by persons 35 years of age or younger will then start to decline. This should cause a shift away from the demand for entry-level housing toward an increasing demand for bigger and better homes as well as increasing interest in second homes for leisure and recreation purposes.

It is obvious that changes in the size and composition of the residential population have a direct effect on the number and types of households in this country. Social and cultural factors come into play as well. But the basic fact remains that each household occupies a housing unit, therefore household formations create the need for additional housing.

CHAPTER 3 – YOUR MARKET: HOW IT CHANGES

We can be sure of three things . . . death, . . . taxes . . . and change." *Ben Franklin (adapted)*

Market Change and the Broker

The prominent categories of change in the real estate market are changes in volume of activity (the number of transactions) and change in the level of market prices of real property. Observers of past real estate markets have noted patterns of movements in volume, ups and downs that in some cases resemble the fluctuations in general business activity of the overall economy. There are periods when the market is on the move, when construction of new housing units is increasing, when vacancies are low, and when sales of new and existing homes are brisk. The pace of this activity builds to a climax and then there is a slow-down followed by a marked decline during which attitudes move toward the pessimistic side and watchful, anxious waiting replaces enthusiasm. Eventually a bottom or trough is reached, followed in turn by another period of rising activity. In reacting to these market changes, real estate brokers seem no different than other business owners. Outwardly, brokers assess present market conditions by comparing the volume to the past year. But inwardly they have a tendency to compare the current level of business with former peaks. The prosperous years of the past seem to be the easiest ones to remember. The poor ones are easier to forget. This is only a human trait. Logically, if one were to reflect on this subject, a real estate broker should compare the current market to the average of the past, thinking in terms of whether things are above average or below average, rather than comparing present performance to former peak levels.

Fortunately, the typical real estate broker is an optimist, with enthusiasm to offset a good part of the gloom that may be prevalent in the market at a given time. This is understandable since nearly all real estate brokers work on a straight commission basis. Obviously, they are willing to accept the risk embodied in this "no sale, no pay" sector of the business world. The very structure of a real estate brokerage business is such that success, if measured by the number of completed transactions, doesn't occur in a steady stream. It is marked with characteristic ups and downs. However, some of this irregularity is offset by the relatively large dollar amount of reward on each transaction, since the average real estate commission may be thousands of dollars. In short, as far as remuneration is concerned, the lack of frequency is overshadowed by the larger individual amounts, thus accumulating to an attractive annual incentive. The individual broker, or the salesperson, who sells several properties a month, most likely is earning an above-average living. Assume this person lists and sells three or four properties in a given month. Also assume that each of these transactions occurs on a different day. This means that they have experienced success on six or eight days out of the month. On the flip side, if there have been six or eight days of success a month, there also have been 22 to 24 days of defeat or no success that very same month. Under normal circumstances, this could be a depressing situation. It is apparent that the broker's business life is permeated with a bust and boom philosophy. But from a selfish point-of-view, the aggressive real estate broker may be more concerned about individual performance rather than what the total market is doing. Relating personal sales achievements to the total market is one way to measure success. If a broker is trying to maximize personal income, getting a rightful share of the market is a primary concern. When the market is good, better chances of developing more business exist. When the market is tight, the broker has to be more competitive to attain individual goals. The level of activity in the real estate market is an indicator of potential to the real estate broker. It is evident then that ups and downs of transaction volume take place within the broker's office, within the broker's local market and in other areas as well. The brokers can determine the amount of change taking place in their business. However, it becomes more meaningful when the broker can relate and compare his or her level of activity with the local market. But if the broker does seek to make some sort of comparison, he or she soon finds that the real estate market does not produce a steady, level volume of activity. Instead, it is subject to constant change.

Patterns of Change

In observing the local real estate market, there are four different types of change that occur:

1. Seasonal variation
2. Cyclical fluctuation
3. Secular or long-term trends
4. Irregular deviations

Most local residential markets follow a seasonal pattern. This pattern has a 12 month duration and repeats itself each calendar year. Sales typically reach a peak in spring and again in late summer, with lower levels of activity during the winter months. Seasonal variation has a decided impact on a real estate broker's business, since it causes the month-to-month volume of listings and sales to fluctuate to a noticeable degree. This is evidenced by the following table showing deeds recorded in Milwaukee County for an 11-year period from 1984 to 1994. The figures employed represent deeds recorded, indicating that the transfer of title has taken place. Usually the decision to buy occurred some weeks or months prior to the actual closing of the transaction and the subsequent recording of the deed. Hence, there is some time lag built into the original deed recording figures. Sales involving conventional financing may be able to close in a few weeks time, whereas FHA and VA financed transactions may require several additional weeks. For purposes of this analysis, it was decided to apply a one month lag time between the sale and the date of recording the deed. This means that December sales are reflected in

January deed recording totals, January sales are recorded in February deed totals, etc. The figures were adjusted for the assumed one-month time lag, and then combined into quarterly periods.

TABLE 3 – 1 QUARTERLY DEED RECORDINGS IN MILWAUKEE COUNTY, WISCONSIN (Deeds with Transfer Fee)					
Year	1st Quarter	2nd Quarter	3rd Quarter	4th Quarter	TOTAL
1984	3,273-	4,435*	3,354	3,508	14,570
1985	2,761-	4,151	4,395*	3,334	14,641
1986	2,823-	4,707	5,227*	4,274	17,031
1987	3,134-	4,871*	4,297	3,362	15,664
1988	2,787-	4,579*	4,376	3,669	15,411
1989	3,000-	4,169	4,350*	3,604	15,123
1990	3,093	4,305	4,438*	3,076-	14,912
1991	2,643-	4,479*	4,119	3,067	14,308
1992	3,020-	4,943*	4,260	4,154	16,377
1993	3,140-	4,168	4,753*	4,327	16,388
1994	3,396-	5,274*	4,670	3,695	17,035
11 Year Average	3,006	4,553	4,385	3,643	15,587

* Highest quarter of the year
- Lowest quarter of the year

A careful inspection of the previous table reveals that over the 11-year time span, the second quarter produced the highest total each year on six occasions. The other five high quarterly totals within a given year occurred in the third quarter. The lowest quarterly totals occurred most frequently, 10 times out of 11, in the first quarter. So, based on the above deed recordings, the second and third quarter activity was consistently higher than the first and fourth quarters.

While the quarterly seasonal pattern is not exactly the same each year, there are good reasons for this format. Levels of activity in specific periods could be affected by extended unfavorable weather conditions, local economic conditions such as abnormal unemployment, lengthy labor strikes, non-availability of mortgage money and short-term lulls in new construction. The quarterly periods employed in Table 3 – 1 consist of three calendar months each (January-February- March, April-May-June, etc.) rather than four 13 week periods due to the form of the data. Therefore the very make-up of the calendar itself has an effect on these figures. Certain widely observed holidays such as Holy Week and Easter do not occur on the same date each year. In non-leap years, February has about 10 percent fewer days than six other months of the year. Even the changing physical make-up of the individual months, due to normal calendar sequence, causes some months to have four weekends, while others may have five. The number of weekends is significant in the sale of residential real estate because buyers typically house hunt on the weekends.

The pattern of seasonal variation inherent in these deed statistics can be revealed more clearly by restating the quarterly data to a base of 100, the average for a particular time period. Further understanding of seasonal variation is afforded by comparing the deed based observations to other statistical series as illustrated in Table 3 – 2 which follows:

TABLE 3 – 2 INDEX NUMBERS OF SEASONAL VARIATION: THE VOLUME OF REAL ESTATE ACTIVITY (For the Calendar Year)		
TIME PERIOD	MILWAUKEE COUNTY DEEDS RECORDED, ADJUSTED	UNITED STATES (1992-1995) EXISTING SINGLE FAMILY SALES
First Quarter	77	81
Second Quarter	117	115
Third Quarter	113	108
Fourth Quarter	93	96

The figures used in Table 3 – 2 were converted to index numbers for ease of comparison with 100 being the base or average. Thus, numbers under 100 are below average for that series. In viewing the above table of index numbers, one can detect a similar pattern of seasonal variation from quarter to quarter during the course of the calendar year. This holds true for both the statistical series involving deeds in Milwaukee County and the total volume of existing single-family sales activity in the United States.

TABLE 3 – 2A INDEX NUMBERS OF SEASONAL VARIATION: VOLUME OF EXISTING SINGLE FAMILY SALES U.S., 1992-1995 (For Calendar Year)					
Time Period	**Northeast**	**Midwest**	**South**	**West**	**U.S.**
First Quarter	74	85	82	79	81
Second Quarter	110	121	113	114	115
Third Quarter	123	105	105	107	108
Fourth Quarter	93	89	100	100	96

Further examination of seasonal variation by major geographical regions within the United States is shown in Table 3 – 2A. Adapted from U.S. Census figures, these index numbers reveal the presence of seasonal variation in all parts of the country, based on existing single-family sales from 1992 through 1995.

What are some of the underlying reasons for this kind of change in volume of activity during the course of the year? Perhaps the most significant factor is parents' reluctance to move their families during the normal school year. This, of course, applies to families with school-age children. Changes during the school year may place an undue burden on the child to adjust to a new environment involving home, school, church, friends and places of recreation. A second factor is the inconvenience associated with unfavorable weather conditions during certain seasons of the year, especially rain, snow and cold.

A third reason is the simultaneous variation in the level of new construction activity. This is particularly true in the real estate markets in the northern part of the country where the building season is limited because of extreme weather conditions. Remember that new home construction is the catalyst that starts a chain of real estate transactions as families move up the housing ladder. The availability of the new house permits the buyers to vacate an existing house. The vacant existing house enables the occupants of a smaller home to move into it. Their former existing home becomes available for still another purchaser. Thus, one move breeds another move in the real estate market. Even in warmer climates, we find that seasonal variation exists. However, this situation is not as pronounced as in colder climates.

A fourth reason for seasonal variation might be attributable to the clustering of year-end holidays that extend from Thanksgiving Day to New Year's Day. In typical American style, these celebrations involve the family unit, and therefore, interfere with the process of selling and buying of homes. This is not an ideal time for change since it might disrupt holiday activities. In addition, the strong time demands created by the holiday season definitely limits the amount of time left over for engaging in real estate transactions.

The deeds recorded are not an exact expression of the number of transactions that take place in a given real estate market. A certain number of deeds do not reflect the normal arm's length transaction, such as intra-family sales of property that never reach the market, inter-corporate transfers by corporations controlled by the same individuals, transfers of a minor portion of a lot to the neighbor or public authority, deeds issued in correction of other deeds originally drafted in error and deeds issued in fulfillment of land contracts that were initiated years ago. These are some of the non-market transactions that may enter into deed totals. A Milwaukee study revealed that 41 percent of the warranty deeds recorded in a given year did not represent bona fide market transactions. Similar studies in other cities produced percentages ranging from 25 percent to 50 percent of deeds not representing real estate market transactions. For these reasons, month by month comparison of deed totals should not be relied on as a precise measure of change in the volume of real estate activity. Deeds tabulated in Table 3 – 1 were limited to deeds with transfer fees only. At best, deed totals compiled on a *quarterly basis* can be used as a fairly reliable indicator of the change in the level of market activity. However, the purpose of the previous tabulation was to identify a kind of pattern, an average pattern of seasonal variation that occurs in a selected local real estate market. From it we have observed that the changes in levels of activity during the course of a calendar year indicate that the probability of sale is much higher during the spring and summer months than in the fall and winter months. Another dimension of seasonal variation is the shifting from a sellers' market to a buyers' market, particularly during the peak months when buyers are competing with one another for available properties. The opposite is true in the winter months when there are more sellers than available buyers. This seasonal variation also is reflected in the length of selling time for individual properties. Properties listed during the spring and summer months tend to sell faster than properties listed at other times of the year.

Seasonal and Cyclical Change

The seasonal variations discussed in the previous section are of short duration, namely 12 months, and are repeated every calendar year. If we assume that market volume does not change from year to year, then a graphic depiction of such a market for a nine-year period may look like this:

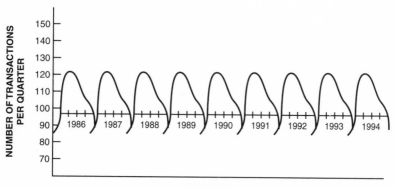

CHART 3 – 1
TYPICAL SEASONAL VARIATION
(Level annual volume)

The shape of the seasonal curve is based on Midwest index numbers found in Table 3 – 2A. Therefore the first quarter level is 85; the second quarter, 121; the third quarter, 105; and the fourth quarter is 89. The same pattern repeats itself for nine years, since we assumed no change in annual volume of real estate activity.

Now observe what happens when we change our assumptions to the extent that the market volume increases each year during the first six years and then tapers off into a decline for the last three years.

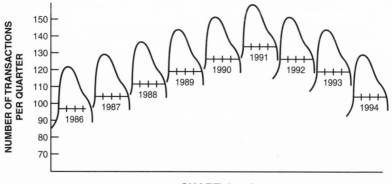

CHART 3 – 2
TYPICAL SEASONAL VARIATION
(Changing annual volume)

While the seasonal variation is still present, each year appears to constitute a separate system in that each seasonal curve is geared to a different base. However, the annual bases are not as independent as they appear to be in Chart 3 – 2. The fact is that they are interrelated in that sales volume is a kind of continuous series day after day, month after month. So in reality, next year's sales volume is a mere continuation of this year's . . . one picks up where the other one leaves off. Changes in volume are not as abrupt as they appear in the chart. Actually the change is a gradual one and therefore it would be more realistic to "tilt" the volume level for each year in the direction of the change that is taking place. This is done in Chart 3 – 3 which follows:

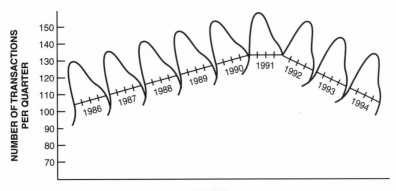

CHART 3 – 3
TYPICAL SEASONAL VARIATION
(Changing annual volume)
— sloped in direction of change

The volume levels for the first six years tilt in an upward direction, indicating a gradual increase in market activity. The volume levels for the last three years tilt in the opposite direction, indicating a decline in the level of market volume. The 12-month seasonal variations are an integral part of a larger structure, namely, the real estate cycle. The cyclical change encompasses the upswings and downswings in market volume over much longer periods of time. Certain real estate economists have attempted to identify regular real estate cycles having time lengths of approximately 18 years. Others deny the existence of such regular real estate cycles. The fact remains that historically, the volume of activity in the real estate market has gone up and down. Refer to Chart 3 – 4 that shows changing volume of sales from 1979 through 1995.

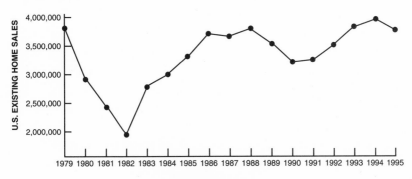

CHART 3 – 4
REAL ESTATE CYCLES
(Existing Home Sales) — Single Family

So, based on past experience, whether we describe changes in volume as cycles or fluctuations, we do know that there is some change that does occur over periods greater than one year. We will take the license to continue to refer to these long-term fluctuations as real estate cycles, but not commit ourselves to any specific duration. With these thoughts in mind, we will proceed to point out that just as the calendar year has its four seasons, so the business cycle has its four phases: expansion, peak, decline and trough. While real estate cycles may be of different duration and not necessarily coincide with business cycles, they seem to pass through the same kinds of phases as shown in the following chart:

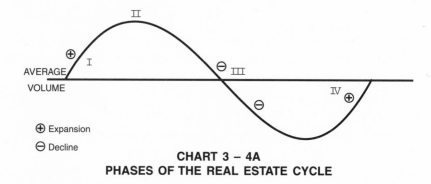

CHART 3 – 4A
PHASES OF THE REAL ESTATE CYCLE

In explaining the nature of the various phases illustrated in the above chart, our starting point, or point-of-reference, will be at the extreme left side of the chart.

Phase 1 – This condition could be described as a normal market wherein supply and demand are in reasonably close balance. As we move upward along the cyclical curve, the level of market activity begins to accelerate because of an increasing surge of demand. Land subdividing is on the rise. New construction is becoming more active. Mortgage money is available. Listings are more difficult to obtain but they are selling faster than before. More investors and speculators are entering the market. More people are going into the building and real estate brokerage business. Vacancies are on the decline and rents are inching upward. To the extent that new construction falls behind current demand, there will be a corresponding price impact on both new and existing housing. Each successive year seems to produce more optimism than the preceding one as most of the market indicators are setting new highs. Buyers, influenced by rising prices, display an urgency to buy as soon as possible since waiting may cost them additional money.

Phase II – The market now is reaching its crest and, while continued optimism prevails, it is now being tempered with certain signs of caution. The demand, while still high, is not as carefree as before. The buyers are showing more resistance and want to be sold rather than serviced by order-takers. Builders are beginning to feel the effects of over-building and start to hold back on new land acquisitions. Builders show signs of price consciousness and competition and begin to put more quality and extras into their houses. Brokers begin to realize that it's now easier to get listings, but that the demand pressure is beginning to dissipate. Mortgage terms begin to become less attractive as lenders become more selective, bypassing marginal buyers. Rents resist further escalation and begin to stabilize even though vacancies show signs of increasing. Real estate prices also resist further rises. The forces of expansion have run their course, the market has experienced its peak level of activity, and now we have reached the upper turning point. The remaining expansion fuel is inadequate to drive the market any higher or even to maintain the peak level of activity.

Phase III – This is the beginning of an extended downward movement of the real estate market. Indicators of market volume such as deeds, building permits and mortgages have passed their peaks and slide downward to the starting point in Phase I, but continue on past it to new lower levels. Buyers' attitudes have switched from active to passive. Now waiting seems to have its advantages as prices begin to drop. The longer the wait, perhaps the greater the savings. The urgency to buy virtually has disappeared. Land sales for development purposes are grinding to a halt. Of all real estate commodities, vacant land now seems to be the most unsalable of all. Listings are comparatively easy to obtain, but it takes much longer to sell them. Lenders are expressing signs of caution. Although they have mortgage funds available, they have the time and actually are screening loan applicants more carefully with a watchful eye on the declining quality of the collateral. Vacancies are on the rise and landlords are offering such inducements as a month or two of free rent and similar concessions in order to get tenants to sign a lease. What was described as "ease of entry" into the real estate field for new brokers and new builders in Phase II now could be relabeled "ease of exit" as the market drops.

Phase IV – This is the trough or lower turning point in the real estate cycle. This is about as bad as things are going to get. All market indicators are reaching the point where they are bottoming out. However, vacancies and foreclosures are at record highs. A noticeable number of the brokers and builders have left the real estate field and are now in some other kind of business pursuit. Only the more qualified, both knowledge-wise and capital-wise still are around. They have met the test and challenge of a declining market. From here on things will start to improve. As confidence gradually is restored things begin to improve and eventually the average or normal volume of real estate market activity is reached, completing the entire real estate cycle, with a new one in the offing.

Real estate analysts have stated that real estate cycles, however irregular they may be, have longer durations than normal business cycles. Real estate cycles generally are described as covering 15 to 18 years or so, while general business cycles are considered to run for periods of seven to eight years. In other words, real estate cycles tend to be about twice the length of major business cycles.

Is there any relationship between business cycles and real estate cycles? Upswings and downswings in regular business cycles are reflected in employment figures, reflected in the amount of overtime worked, reflected in the amount of savings that individuals are able to accumulate. It also colors their expectations of the future. Confidence in the level of business activity in the future may affect the timing of decisions to marry, to move and to go into debt. There is no question that the factors just mentioned have an impact on the demand of real estate. On the other hand, it would seem that if the population always were increasing, there would be a steady demand for housing commensurate with the population increases, since housing is a basic necessity of life. But need for housing and effective demand for housing may be two different things. Doubling up and overcrowding siphons off some of the demand. Then too, not all of the demand is for the purchase of housing facilities. There may be a financial necessity or a positive preference for renting rather than owning. A comparison of the increase in population to the changes in the annual volume of single family residential construction appears in the following chart:

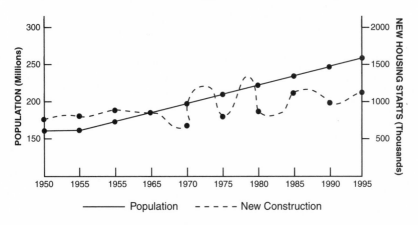

CHART 3 – 5
UNITED STATES POPULATION AND NEW CONSTRUCTION
(Single Family Starts)

While the population totals of the past four decades show a constant increase, the volume of new residential construction has been quite erratic. Construction activity emerged from the doldrums of the 1930s to reach highs in 1950 and again in 1956. Another wave of recovery appeared to be developing in the early 1960s only to be arrested by another downturn in 1965-1966. Other peaks were reached in 1972, 1978 and 1986. These were interspersed by low years of activity in 1975, 1982 and 1991. Although the peaks of activity do not have the same amplitude, there is definite evidence of marked changes in these particular time segments of real estate activity. Total deed recordings followed a similar pattern. Even in a mature urban area such as Milwaukee, where the population has been increasing at approximately the national rate, cyclical variation in the level of real estate activity was also in evidence.

The existence of a partially managed economy, such as we have in this country today, might lead one to conclude that cycles are becoming a thing of the past. While it is true that we now use more built-in defenses against business fluctuations, and the severity of the downturns are becoming less harsh, it would seem foolhardy to believe that variations in volume of business activity, particularly in real estate, are not likely to occur again.

Secular or Long-term Trends

Secular trends represent the average level of activity over long time periods and usually are represented by straight lines as opposed to the curvilinear swings of a cycle. A trend line depicting U.S. population as seen in Chart 3 – 5 naturally will have an upward slope due to the gradually increasing population. Extension

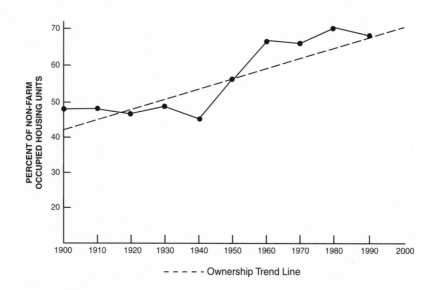

– – – – – Ownership Trend Line

CHART 3 – 6
HOME OWNERSHIP IN THE UNITED STATES
(Based on Owner Occupied Housing Units)

70

of such a trend line into the future must be based on the assumption that birth rates, mortality rates and immigration rates will remain the same. This is quite a bold assumption in view of the rapid drop-off in birth rates experienced in recent years. The "urge to own", so typical of American families, presents another kind of trend line in chart 3 – 6 shown on the previous page.

The trend of home ownership in the United States has followed an upward trend over the past 60 years. As a matter of fact, home ownership has increased about 50 percent in the past six decades, from a low point of 41 percent to 64 percent in 1993. These figures relate to national totals and vary considerably from city to city. In general, the larger the city, the lower the ratio of home ownership. Cities like New York and Chicago have about 50 percent owner-occupied units, while surrounding suburbs may have ratios in the 90 percent plus categories. Rural areas have higher ownership ratios than urban areas. These marked differences can be explained in terms of the past development of rental facilities and consumer attitude toward the expansion of this type of housing unit.

Irregular Forms of Change

The first three patterns of change that were discussed, seasonal, cyclical and secular, related to recurring types of changes; while their particular forms were not extremely precise, they were somewhat identifiable. This is in contrast to the fourth type, irregular factors, that may appear at sporadic times in history and some that may never reappear again. Examples of such irregular factors would be:

- Wars and other international armed conflicts
- Serious illness or untimely death of a U.S. President
- International threats and crises
- Acts of nature such as hurricanes, major floods, widespread tornadoes

These irregular factors tend to create economic and political uncertainty and embody these important aspects:

1. They can't be effectively forecast since they occur quite unexpectedly
2. It is rather difficult to predict the duration of these events
3. They exercise a peculiar impact on the market

In most cases these irregular factors will cause an almost immediate and abrupt change in the volume of real estate market activity. It should be noted that there are a few kinds of irregular factors that are capable of driving the market upward as well as downward. Buying scares and speculation could drive the market into a frenzy in contrast to many other irregular factors that for the most part will bring the real estate market to a screeching halt. So, in most instances, these irregular occurrences will cause a sudden drop in real estate volume. This means that far fewer transactions will take place. However, if we are talking about residential housing, it must be emphasized that the lack of present transactions does not mean the complete dissipation of demand. The need for housing has not suddenly disappeared and the buying qualifications still may be there, but the confidence to express this demand is lacking at the present time. This pent-up accumulation of housing demand might be compared to water stored behind a dam with little or none passing through. For the most part, it is being held behind the wall. When buyer confidence is restored, buyer resistance disappears and we witness a release of this pent up demand. Such sudden changes in the market might be referred to as "boomlets". These little boomlets merely reflect a short adjustment period where latent demand surges forth causing a sudden increase in volume. Once the boomlet has run its course, the market is restored to its normal pace. The broker should be cautioned about expressing over-optimism as to the real status of the market during the course of one of these boomlets. Such possible misinterpretation might lead the broker to jump to the erroneous conclusion that the market is moving into an upward swing of a long real estate cycle.

Other kinds of irregular factors include civil rights disturbances, specific government actions such as urban renewal projects and monetary policy expressed at the national or regional levels. This was particularly true in 1966 when for a six or eight month period the market decelerated to the slowest pace in 20 years as a result of the syphoning off of mortgage money from savings and loan institutions to other kinds of lending.

Interpreting Market Change

We have seen that seasonal variation is an annual system of change within the framework of a multiple-year real estate cycle. Further, a series of curvilinear cycles can be mathematically averaged out to form a trend line. Irregular factors, by their very nature, follow no special form. The all important question at this point is how do these four forms of change blend together into some meaningful configuration? With four patterns of change involved, many combinations are possible. For example, a cyclical upswing could offset the traditional fourth-quarter seasonal downturn. Or, a cyclical downswing might further accentuate the fourth-quarter seasonal downturn. Is it necessary that each kind of change be isolated and identified in order to understand and predict market change? What is considered a general but satisfactory approach to recognizing the effects of these various kinds of market changes? Real estate brokers are forever faced with the uncertainty connected with next month's market . . . next quarter's market . . . and next year's market. What does it hold in store for them? How will future market conditions affect their brokerage business? They have every reason to be concerned since the status of the market will influence the level of their sales volume and as a result, their profits. It would be a boon to the real estate industry if good market information were readily available in usable form, but that isn't the case. While much information is available, it is not usually reported in the most desirable form, and what is more important, it is not effectively analyzed for the real estate broker's specific purpose.

The process of predicting the nature of future market activity is not pure guesswork or hunch. There are some market indicators that provide adequate evidence for making reasonable estimates of future activity. But there is one thing that the real estate broker can be sure of: the market will change in some manner or other. It may express itself in the form of a change in market volume, market prices, consumer preferences, mortgage terms, housing styles or many others. The common denominator that underlies every kind of market in this country is *change*. Once convinced of this fact — that one's market will not stand still, that it will change, the intelligent broker, out of necessity, will assess the amount of change and what direction it will take in the time periods ahead.

Market Indicators

While there are numerous factors involved in real estate market analysis, they can be organized into two basic categories: (a) measurers of market volume and pace and (b) stimulators (or dampeners) of market volume and pace. This classification provides the basis for a simple, yet practical approach to market analysis. For this reason, only the more important factors, as categorized below, will be discussed at this time:

A. Measures of Market Volume and Pace
   1. Building Starts
   2. Ownership turnover
   3. Mortgage Recordings
   4. Vacancies
   5. Foreclosures
   6. Average Number of Days Per Sale
B. Market Stimulators (or Dampeners)
   1. Financing Terms
   2. Population Change
   3. Level of Employment (or Unemployment Rate)
   4. Marriages (Household Formations)
   5. Rate of Housing Inflation

The broad category, Measures of Market Volume and Pace, represents measures of the past and present activity in the broker's market. By checking these measures, the broker can determine the direction of recent activity: whether it is rising, stable or declining.

Building Starts – Records of building permits are public information easily obtained from the building inspector's office or other public offices in charge of issuing such permits. In many cities monthly and annual totals are published in the local newspapers, thereby making this information readily available to the real estate broker. To a large extent, speculative building starts represent the degree of optimism of local builders in future market activity and are influenced by builders' subjective estimates. This applies to contractors building on speculation, but in the case of custom builders having acquired orders from model homes, building permits represent current market experience. This information is useful since it provides the broker with an indication of the attitudes toward market expectations and experience of others in the field. Another dimension of building starts is the time lag that appears between the date of issuance of the permit, the start of actual construction, and the date of completion of the structure for occupancy. Adjustments for these time lags can add much insight into the tone of the real estate market in the months ahead. The trend of new starts of owner-occupied residential units usually is the bellwether of the degree of activity in the existing homes market. The trend of new construction should be qualified by the rate of absorption; that is, the pace at which the market is utilizing the new units added. An increasing inventory of unsold houses, new construction overhang, is a danger sign that calls for further analysis.

Ownership Turnover – This second measure of market activity attempts to relate the annual number of real estate transactions to the ownership portion of the standing stock of housing. Real estate transactions are reflected in the total number of deeds recorded. Owner occupied units are arrived at by applying the current home ownership ratio to the number of housing units in the market area. For intercensus years, housing totals of the most recent census report may be adjusted year by year by adding new starts and subtracting demolitions. The ratio of deeds recorded to owner-occupied housing units provides one kind of estimate for the turnover of housing in the "for sale" market. Such ratios are, of course, estimates due to the nature of deed recordings and owner occupancy measurements, but year-to-year comparisons provide some generalization of the direction of housing sales. The broker is cautioned that this ratio would include the sale of both new and existing units. Therefore, if further refinement is required, the two segments can be separated, since new starts already have been identified.

Mortgage Recordings – Since about nine out of ten home purchases are financed by a real estate mortgage, the total number of mortgages recorded tends to follow deed totals. Periodically mortgage totals may reflect some refinancing to a certain extent, especially during times of declining mortgage interest rates. It also should be recognized that mortgage totals would include financing for all forms of real estate — residential, commercial and industrial. The presence of commercial and industrial activity is quite evident when the number of mortgages recorded is compared to the dollar volume of these mortgages. Mortgage recordings serve as additional information in the interpretation of deed recordings and market direction.

Vacancies – For most residential markets the level of vacancies seem to fall within a range of 3 percent to 6 percent under normal conditions. Increasing rates of vacancy generally are indicators of declining market activity and decreasing vacancies usually accompany rising market volume. However, one should not overlook other possibilities. Market demand and activity could remain relatively stable, but an accompanying abnormal supply of new units out of proportion to demand most likely will result in an increase in vacancies. This is another reason to look at the different measures of market activity in relation to one another, as well as in terms of good judgment. Vacancy figures can be obtained from local utility companies whose records will reveal the number of requests for installations and disconnections for water, gas, electric and telephone service. On occasion, the post office has conducted local vacancy surveys in cooperation with real estate and building trade associations.

Foreclosures – The rate of foreclosures serves as a quality rating of the mortgages outstanding, that is of past real estate transactions involving mortgage financing. However, they also indicate a measure of lenders' and buyers' future level of confidence in the real estate market. Foreclosures represent the impact of the forces of economic change on home ownership ability. Lack of employment, rising costs of living or stringent financing terms are a few of the factors influencing the number of foreclosures. Like vacancies, foreclosures move in a direction opposite to that of market activity. Therefore, an increase in foreclosures depicts a decrease in market activity and vice-versa. In some respects a part of the accuracy of foreclosures as an indicator of current and future market levels has been nudged out of focus by changing policies of lending institutions. A noticeable number of lenders may, in an effort to maintain goodwill and to develop a more favorable public image, take assignment of delinquent mortgages in liquidation of the mortgage debt instead of foreclosing. This serves several purposes in that it eliminates costly foreclosure expenses and saves the delinquent mortgagor from having a foreclosure blot on one's credit record. It is the lender's way of attempting to minimize losses. This procedure suggests that the number of payment delinquencies, rather than foreclosures, would be a more sensitive measure of real estate market conditions. An astute observer, in commenting on the validity of foreclosures as market indicators, likened the situation to an iceberg. The small portion of iceberg visible above water was compared to foreclosures, while the submerged portion, many times the mass of that above water, was termed mortgage payment delinquencies. The point being that foreclosures alone do not reveal the whole story of the nature of problems connected with mortgages outstanding.

Number of Days Per Sale – Brokers can determine this measurement from their own records. It represents the average number of days between the date of the listing and date of sale. In order to eliminate the effect of some extraneous factors, it is advisable to calculate the median rather than the arithmetic mean or average. This is done by arranging the individual results on each sale in an array from low to high, and then selecting that measure that is at the mid-point of the array based on the number of transactions, rather than the value of each item. If the median number of days between listing and sale shows decline in relation to past periods, it indicates that the market is reflecting an increasing level of activity and sales volume. In short, the tempo or pace of the market is on the rise. When the number of days so calculated increases, the opposite is true. Here again the broker is cautioned to exercise good judgment for it is possible that a change in the number days between listing and sale might be the result of over or under-pricing of listings, which may very well affect their salability. Changes also might be attributable to such internal variations as change in intensity of advertising and sales promotion, size of sales staff, or differences in sales personnel.

Because the measure of market volume and pace are an expression or product of market activity, they can indicate *where* activity has and is taking place and to what extent. But, these indicators are less reliable for predicting *when* changes will take place. As a result, the broker should be aware of other factors operating in the background of real estate activity that cause the great volatility in the market, thus influencing activity and changing the market indicators. Without these stimulators and depressants, the market would be quite passive and would continue indefinitely at the same pace. But because they are ever present, these dynamic factors must be thoroughly understood and watched. When this is done, the broker will develop greater confidence and remove some of the doubt about future movements within the local real estate market.

Financing Terms – Buyers may be encouraged or discouraged to participate in the real estate market by the nature of the terms of mortgage financing. Favorable conditions from the buyer's point-of-view would be lower down-payment requirements, lower interest rates, longer amortization period and lower closing costs. The movement of mortgage terms in these directions make more buyers eligible for borrowing and increases their confidence in the market. When mortgage terms move in the opposite direction (larger down payments, higher interest rates, shorter terms and higher closing costs) buyers not only become less enthusiastic about purchasing real estate, they may become involuntarily eliminated from the market due to higher qualifying requirements for mortgage loans. The direction and severity of change in mortgage financing terms portends, in part, the trend and the pace of the market in the periods ahead. For government-regulated mortgage loans, FHA and VA, changes of this kind also are reflected in the number of discount points required by lending institutions. Although the burden of the payment of the discount points may not be the responsibility of the buyer in some cases, it does have an impact on the attitude of the seller, the broker and the lender.

Population – As explained in Chapter 2, changes in population can be categorized as natural (births compared to deaths) and migratory (in versus out-migration). These two kinds of population change vary considerably in different sections of the country. Estimates of change over the past decade, based on census figures, are illustrated in the following table:

TABLE 3 – 3 PERCENT CHANGE IN POPULATION IN FOUR REGIONS OF THE UNITED STATES 1980 – 1990		
REGION	TOTAL CHANGE	INCREASE OR DECREASE DUE TO MIGRATION
North East	3 % +	—
North Central	1% +	—
South	13% +	7% +
West	24% +	11% +

Since these are regional estimates, they represent averages within certain regions and do not necessarily apply to every city and town in that region. Estimates must be made for specific urban areas to be valid in real estate market analysis. Natural change in population is easily calculated from the vital statistics published or made available by county governmental units. Estimates of net migration can be obtained by subtracting the natural increase in population from the total change in population for a given year. The result is the approximate portion of the population increase or decrease that is due to net in and out migration.

Population changes involve numbers of people as well as make-up or characteristics. While there are many useful population characteristics, perhaps the most meaningful to the broker's understanding of how population changes stimulate the market is to find out who is the most likely to move. The number of people of rental or ownership age in a given market represents the total potential demand that may exist at that time.

	TABLE 3 – 4 WHO MOVES MOBILITY STATUS OF THE POPULATION – 1992		
Region	Non-Movers (same home in 1991)	Movers – (to same county)	Movers – (to different county)
Northeast	88%	7%	5%
Midwest	84%	10%	6%
South	81%	11%	8%
West	79%	14%	7%
United States	83%	11%	6%
Age Category			
Under 20	82%	10%	8%
20 – 24	63%	23%	14%
25 – 29	67%	21%	12%
30 – 44	82%	11%	7%
45 – 54	89%	6%	5%
55 – 64	93%	4%	3%
65 & Over	95%	3%	2%

You will recall from Chapter 2 that about 17 percent of the population moves each year. From Table 3 – 4 it can be seen that the mobility status of the population, on average, is higher in the

South and West Regions as compared to the Northeast and Midwest Regions, according to the U.S. Bureau of Census.

The lower half of Table 3 – 4 shows the mobility status of the population by age brackets as tabulated in 1992.

Each category represents the percentage of each age group to total population. From this, the broker can draw valuable conclusions about the possible stimulation of market activity, present and future, by the local population. This chart, in no way, indicates the present level of activity in the broker's market. It simply indicates the potential for activity that will be conditioned by other market forces. In effect, potential demand must be screened or filtered through several qualifying steps before it expresses itself in the form of transactions in the real estate market.

The household cycle provides the format for estimating future potential. The distribution of the population in the "Under 20" age category represents ripening rental and ownership demand, a minor portion of which will begin to express itself almost immediately and continue to increase for decades into the future. As applied to Table 3 – 4 and most areas of the country, this large pre-rental and home ownership segment of the population will show its effects first in great increases in rental demand and then will mature into increased demand for owner-occupied units.

Employment – The effects and implications of employment with respect to the real estate market are far reaching, some of which are beyond the scope of this book. Basically, employment for market analysis purposes has two aspects: degree and quality. The degree of employment is reflected in the unemployment rates prevailing in the local area. The quality of employment is reflected in the incomes and the types of jobs provided, which, in turn, characterizes the local economy. Incomes are commensurate with the expertise required for jobs — skilled, semi-skilled, or unskilled. The quality of employment reveals the type of demand for housing in that the majority of lower income families provide a strong market for rental units. As families move up the income scale, the incidence of home ownership increases. Accordingly, well-paid skilled and technical workers will most likely be home buyers, and they will demand better and higher priced homes than workers in lower income brackets. This segment of the market may be more stable than unskilled workers who are much more vulnerable to lay-offs and the effects of automation. A rise in unemployment rates usually foretells an impending slackening in the level of market activity. This bears out the prime importance of income on the demand for residential real estate.

Marriages (Household Formations) – While the number of people of rental or ownership age gives the broker an indication of the general trend that the population is taking, another population factor that would perhaps have more immediate effect as a stimulant of market activity is net household formations. Net household formations involve marriages as well as family dissolutions (divorces and unmarried children leaving home) and deaths. For the broker's purposes it may be more practical to concern one's self with the number of marriages in the market area since information on marriages is easily obtained. Care, nonetheless, must also be applied since each new marriage does not necessarily create an immediate demand for an additional unit of housing space. In times of economic stress, or other unusual circumstances, families tend to double-up until some future date. However, in general, the change in the number of marriages is reasonably acceptable as an indicator of change in the number of household units. When economic conditions are favorable, optimism toward the future runs high. This confidence sets the stage for an increase in the number of marriages. The opposite is true of a declining economic situation. An ever-increasing dimension of the rental market is the growth in the number of non-related households. There is an upward trend for young people to pool their financial resources and rent the newer apartments in order to enjoy the amenities of living with the younger crowd.

Rate of Housing Inflation – Until the early 1970s, real estate economists did not seem to pay much attention to price inflation as it affected housing transactions. Following World War II, long-term mortgage interest rates remained relatively steady, inching upward in the range of about four to six percent. Single family home prices moved up gradually at an average rate of about two to three percent a year. But while an annual price increase of three percent a year may not cause too much alarm, a look at compound interest tables will tell you that an increase of three percent a year compounded for 23 years results in the doubling of prices over that time period. The 1970s saw the rapid escalation of real estate prices, spiraling wages and booming oil prices. Inflation in residential real estate for the country as a whole reached a peak in the middle to late 1970s when prices were escalating at the rate of more than 1 percent a month . . . over 13-14 percent a year! Following this residential real estate price surge, long-term mortgage interest rates quickly followed and reached a high of 18-19 percent in the 1981-82 period. While mortgage interest rates may vary a percentage point or two from coast to coast, inflation rates do not occur as uniformly. Some areas experienced inflation rates above the national level while rates in other areas were lower. Variations in inflation rates proved to be different in neighborhoods within the same urban areas, usually dependent upon the strength of demand for location, housing style or price range. The following Table 3 – 5 shows the approximate annual change in median price changes over the period 1968 to 1994, according to the National Association of Realtors®, Washington, D.C. *Real Estate Outlook: Market Trends and Insights* (copyright).

Period	Median Price U.S.	Percent Increase
TABLE 3 – 5		
EXISTING SINGLE FAMILY HOMES PRICES		
1968 – 1994		
1968	$20,100	
1969	21,800	8%
1970	23,000	6%
1971	24,800	8%
1972	26,700	8%
1973	28,900	8%
1974	32,000	11%
1975	35,300	10%
1976	38,100	8%
1977	42,900	13%
1978	48,700	14%
1979	55,700	14%
1980	62,200	12%
1981	66,400	7%
1982	67,800	2%
1983	70,300	4%
1984	72,400	3%
1985	75,500	4%
1986	80,300	6%
1987	85,600	7%
1988	89,300	4%
1989	93,100	4%
1990	95,500	3%
1991	100,300	5%
1992	103,700	3%
1993	106,800	3%
1994	109,800	3%

There is a noticeable amount of interplay among the various market stimulants, especially in the area of home buying. The amount that buyers are willing to pay for a property largely depends on how much they can borrow. The amount that they can borrow is directly related to the prospective buyers' present and future income.

The manner in which these measures of market activity and related stimulants can be combined into some meaningful analysis is presented in the next chapter.

CHAPTER FOUR — YOUR MARKET: PREDICTING VOLUME AND SELLING PRICES

"To be forewarned is to be forearmed . . ." *Major John Lindemann*

It has been said that a real estate brokerage business, in spite of the relatively low number of transactions, is an ***overtime*** business rather than a part-time one. The myriad of activities (listing, selling, financing, closing transactions and managing a staff plus an office) place a strong time demand on the real estate broker's work day. As a result, those functions that are most directly related to earning commissions tend to receive the highest priority time-wise. The high degree of involvement in current transactions minimizes the time that the broker has available for planning and market forecasting. One can understand why a good number of brokers appear to subscribe to an almost fatalistic philosophy of accepting the market as it unfolds day by day on the notion that whatever will be, will be. Some take a passive attitude on the grounds that they feel there is little or nothing that they can do to change or even influence the market's course. They accept the challenge of market conditions, relying on their competitive ability to get their desired share of it.

The situation may be likened to that of sailing a boat. Ignorance of possible changes in weather conditions is not necessarily harmful. Unsettled weather may change for the better, in which case the journey continues on without hindrance. On the other hand, weather conditions could turn in the other direction. There are obvious signs that give warning of impending trouble. Dark clouds, increasing wind velocity, decreasing barometric pressure, dropping temperatures, increase in humidity, etc. are all signals that there may be more severe weather ahead. The smart sailor will

85

heed the warnings and take the necessary precautions. No sailor has to, but experience tells him or her that it is prudent to do so. It is possible to survive by ignoring these signals, but chances of survival over the long run are much less for those who ignore the warnings and rely on pure luck. There is no statute forcing one to adhere to market warnings, save the economic law, but successful operators are those who have some kind of defense to go along with their offense. In spite of this, some less efficient operators have attained financial success as the effects of an upswing in real estate market cycles were sufficiently strong to overshadow their particular shortcomings. Once established, they were better equipped to survive the storms of subsequent downswings of the market. Had they started their businesses at another phase of the real estate cycle, it might have been a different story!

What alternatives are available to progressive brokers who desire to increase their level of efficiency by utilizing the company's resources in line with the market potential for the time periods ahead? After considering the amount of time they can afford for this function, their analytical talents and their financial resources, the broker is in a better position to choose a course of action among these several possibilities:

1. The broker, with the help of staff members, can prepare one's own real estate market forecast.
2. A real estate consultant can be hired to perform this task.
3. The broker can attempt to imitate the actions of the leaders in the field, trusting that their judgment is the best.
4. The broker can sidestep the entire issue and leave the results to pure chance.

The judicious use of a forecast made at the beginning of a year, or other time period, will enable the broker to adjust the various facets of his or her organization to effectively cope with the manner in which one expects the market to react. If the unfolding year proves the estimates to be fairly accurate, the broker will find that such forecasting and planning has improved the operating efficiency of the company and most likely resulted in increased profits. The task of accumulating and analyzing the many relevant market factors may seem to be an insurmountable task to the average broker. The broker may envision market forecasts as precise reports that contain computer-like accuracy. Some of this fear and doubt may be dispelled when the broker realizes that forecasts are but estimates. While striving for a high degree of accuracy or perfection is admirable, it is not absolutely necessary or even practical when dealing with an ever-changing mechanism such as the real estate market. With the kind of market information described in Chapter 3, the broker is in a good position to develop an acceptable forecast of the market for the months and year ahead. While real estate consultants may approach this challenge by first identifying the dependent and independent variables involved, one can simply proceed by considering measures of market activity along with market stimulators and dampeners. Market indicators and probable sources of such information are set forth in the following table:

TABLE 4 – 1 PRIMARY INDICATORS OF REAL ESTATE MARKET ACTIVITY	
Indicator	**Information Source**
Building Starts	Building Inspector's Office; Newspaper or Trade Association Releases
Ownership Turnover: Deed Recordings Housing Units	County Recorder's Office Census of Housing
Mortgages	County Recorder's Office Local Title Companies
Vacancies	Utility Company Reports on Discontinuance of Service; Post Office Surveys
Foreclosures	Local Lending Institutions; County Recorder's Office
Average Number of Days on Market	Broker's Records; Multiple Listing Service
Financing Terms	Local Lending Institutions; Broker's Market Experience
Population Change	Bureau of Census; Health Department (Vital Statistics); Association of Commerce
Unemployment Level	U.S. & State Employment Services; Association of Commerce
Marriages (Household Formation)	County Recorder's Office Local License Bureau
Rate of Housing Inflation	Based on Median Price of Home Sales

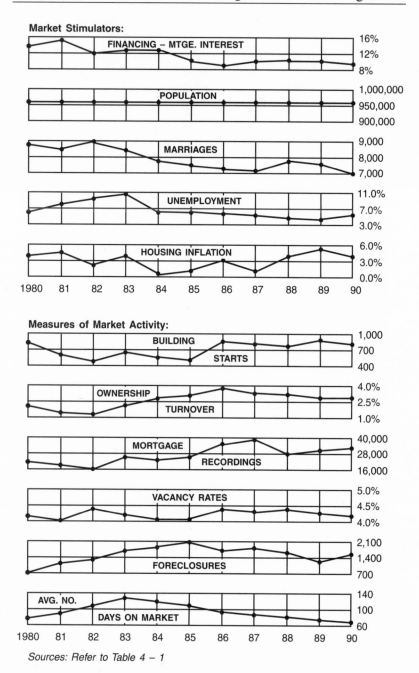

CHART 4 – 1
REAL ESTATE MARKET INDICATORS
(Milwaukee County, WI 1980 – 1990)

The list is limited to eleven indicators, five market stimulators and six measures of market activity. Ideally, more information would be desirable, but the five market stimulators are perhaps the most convenient to work with in terms of availability, cost to obtain and ease of interpretation.

In the event the broker finds that obtaining the above information is too time consuming or costly, it is suggested that the broker pool efforts with other interested brokers and share the responsibility involved in a joint venture. Among other possibilities would be the formation of a market information committee within the local real estate board to assemble and distribute this kind of information.

When assembled, the information is then organized within the framework of an analysis form as shown below:

TABLE 4 – 2 REAL ESTATE MARKET ANALYSIS AND FORECAST			
INDICATORS	**"IDEAL" DIRECTION**	**ACTUAL LOCAL TREND**	**FUTURE MARKET IMPACT**
Market Stimulators:			
Financing Terms	↘	↗	—
Population	↗	↗	+
Marriages (Household Formation)	↗	↗	+
Rate of Unemployment	↘	↗	—
Rate of Housing Inflation	↘	↗	—
Measures of Market Activity:			
Building Starts	↗	↗	+
Ownership Turnover	↗	↗	+
Mortgage Recordings	↗	↗	+
Vacancies	↘	→	0
Foreclosures	↘	↗	—
Average Number of Days on Market	↘	→	0

The chart contains three vertical columns. The first column indicates the "ideal" direction in which each stimulator and measure should be going in order to have a perfectly positive market, one in which all factors indicate improving conditions. A perfectly negative market would be just the opposite – one in which all factors would indicate deteriorating market conditions. The second column should be filled in by the broker, recording the results of the information that has been collected about one's own local market, similar to the trends illustrated in Chart 4 – 1. The arrows in the second column indicate the current trend or the actual direction in which each stimulator and measure is now going in the broker's market. After recording local trends in column two, the broker is now in a position to compare current trends with the ideal direction listed in column one.

From the use of the actual tabulated trends in the second column combined with other useful information tempered by good judgment, the broker can determine the appropriate entries in the third column which will in effect result in a short-term forecast of the local real estate market. In line with the instructions at the top of column three, the broker enters one of three possible expectations for the months ahead: a plus (+) for expected movement in the general direction of the ideal; a minus (-) for expected movement counter to the ideal; and a zero (0) for lateral movement, neither in the direction of nor away from the ideal. These expectations are initially applied to the current trends of the five market stimulators. The directions of these five stimulators are then used as conditioners in order to estimate the probable direction of future market activity.

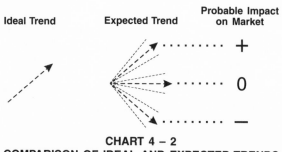

Ideal Trend   **Expected Trend**   **Probable Impact on Market**

CHART 4 – 2
COMPARISON OF IDEAL AND EXPECTED TRENDS
(In Cases Where the Ideal Trend is Typically Upward)

For example, assume the "ideal" in the above illustration represents the trend of the number of marriages in the local area. In nearly all circumstances, an increase in the number of marriages represents an increase in the demand for housing units. However, in many markets the major portion of this demand will go to the rental market rather than the single family home buying market. Local experience related to these new entrants will prevail in determining the impact on the "for sale" market. If the trend of number of marriages is expected to decline, the impact on the market may be negative, hence a minus (-) in the third column.

If the volume is expected to remain about the same, then this predicted lateral movement should not alter the present level of market activity, therefore a zero (0) is listed in the column three. Should the trend be in a an upward direction, or if there is a noticeable preference shift toward home ownership on the part of those new households, then a plus (+) would be in order.

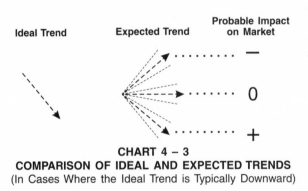

Ideal Trend   **Expected Trend**   **Probable Impact on Market**

CHART 4 – 3
COMPARISON OF IDEAL AND EXPECTED TRENDS
(In Cases Where the Ideal Trend is Typically Downward)

Before any entries are made in column 3, the broker should consider his or her personal estimates related to the five stimulators: financing terms, population change, marriages (household formations), the level of unemployment and the rate of housing inflation. If for any reason the broker feels that one or more of these stimulators may change direction in the near future, *regardless of past trends*, he or she must indicate this by placing the proper sign (+, -, or 0) in the third column. Having determined that each stimulator will promote either a positive, negative, or stable market, the broker then relates these expectations to the other six factors — the measures of market activity. By analyzing these six measures in terms of the impact of the expected future direction of the stimulators in one's market, then you can determine whether it appears as though any change in their direction will take place in the near future. If it appears that change will occur, these six measures must be altered accordingly with the proper sign as was done for the stimulators. For example, if one of the stimulators, say financing terms, is expected to change direction, how will it most likely affect the measures of market activity? Further downward movement of the ideal trend could mean lower interest rates. This condition would have a stimulating effect on building starts, ownership turnover, number of mortgages and the average number of days on the market. The extent of these positive forces would be proportional to the impact of the change in financing conditions. It will be recalled that as a market-influencing factor, significant changes in financing terms can cause abrupt changes in market pace. Easier financing terms in a rising market can be likened to adding fuel to a fire. On the other hand, tighter money conditions can put the brakes on an improving market. In a declining market, less favorable mortgage terms will accelerate the rate of decline. Improved mortgage terms will arrest the rate of descent of a declining market. Not to be overlooked is the special case where the market appears to be at a low ebb and on dead center. In this case improved financing conditions are not very effective in stimulating the buyers to act in the marketplace.

Another example of the impact of a change in one of the stimulators on the other measures of market activity would be a sudden improvement in the level of unemployment. This could be caused by the establishment of a new industry or government activity in the local area. As soon as local unemployment is soaked up, outsiders will be attracted to the newly created job opportunities. This will put immediate pressure on available rental facilities and cause vacancies to disappear rapidly. The average number of days to make a sale will drop appreciably. Building starts will be slow to respond because of the very nature of the construction industry. However, once building activity starts, it will set off a chain reaction in the existing homes sector of the community as people strive to upgrade their housing standards based on the new, higher level of economic activity.

Basis for Judgement – Once this procedure has been completed for all of the five market stimulators and the six measures of market activity, the broker is in a position to examine an overview of the probable path of future market activity in the local area. By considering the number of each of the three signs (+, –, or 0) in column 3, the broker should be able to forecast the general direction of his or her market activity (whether up, down, or little change) and its strength. In cases where the plus signs actually outnumber the minus and zero signs, the broker has reasonable assurance that for the coming year the market should be moving on an upward trend and activity should be above average.

As a result of knowing the direction and strength (or weaknesses) of the probable level of market activity, the broker is in a better position to operate his or her business more efficiently. More appropriate listing and sales strategies can be planned. The broker also is in a better position to place his or her resources and emphasis in the areas where they are most likely to produce the greatest returns. In addition, forecasting will allow the broker to time expenditures more effectively. Thus, forecasting helps the broker create a realm of efficiency where wasted time and wasted efforts are minimized and profits are increased in the process.

It should be recognized that this type of analysis relates to the total market. Individual sub-markets may vary. Some areas may experience increasing volume of sales while others may experience declining volumes. This calls for a more careful look at individual neighborhoods' "average number of days on the market" to help identify selective listing and selling opportunities.

Finally, with the exception of the so-called "irregular factors," changes in residential sales volume are usually not too great from year to year. An examination of the historical performance of residential real estate markets indicates that year to year changes, for the most part, fall within the range of approximately +10% and -10%. In a 26 year period, 1968-1994, the annual rate of change in the volume of transactions involving the sale of single family homes in the United States fell within a range of +12% to

-12%, except for seven of those years. Four of those seven years were in to the early 1980's when the market hit record lows. On the positive side, about three out of four years in those 26 years experienced a market volume change in the range of +12% to -12% per year. Such ranges are typical of established urban areas and, of course, cannot be applied to burgeoning towns that are affected by such explosive growth factors as the establishment of a new industry or government facility, the implementation of a new town's program, or major tract building projects. The latter cases represent deviations from the ordinary and are subject to special interpretation.

Present statistical procedures are available to combine all eleven of these variables into a complex mathematical model for forecasting purposes. However, it seems that most real estate brokers would find it difficult to justify the time and cost involved in collecting and processing such data. Fortunately, it would appear that by the year 2000, or shortly thereafter, this type of information will be available and affordable through the rapidly expanding information network. Along with this, no doubt, will be the development of relatively low cost computer software programs that will enable the broker to process this type of information within the broker's desired time frame and financial budget. It should be emphasized that the "abbreviated" procedures presented focus on this specific short-run objective: to *estimate* the direction and probable strength of the real estate market in the months and year ahead . . . . a *general* guide for marketing and management planning.

The previously presented procedures are not intended to produce precise measurements. The rationale was based on simple ordinal ranking of measurements . . . that is, "greater than", "less than", etc.

By utilizing the same market stimulators in a more precise manner, they become part of another set of procedures labeled with the acronym, "ACE", an overview of the typical buyer's behavioral pattern. These three letters represent the overall attitude

94

and outlook of the typical single family home buyer in the marketplace:

TABLE 4 – 3 ACE		
A	=	affordability
C	=	confidence
E	=	expectation

Affordability – In layman's language, this means, "Will I be able to handle the monthly mortgage payment without putting undue strain on the household budget?"

Confidence – This is an inwardly focused issue. This refers to the buyer's assurance that his or her future income will be dependable. What about expected pay raises? What about possible promotions? What if I get laid off? What if my employer sells or merges or moves out of state? Will the "down-sizing" trend affect my employer? There is a genuine concern for job security.

Expectation – This issue is more external in nature. What does the general economic future hold in store? How will inflation or an economic recession affect my equity? How would changes in the Internal Revenue Code affect my ownership position?

Affordability

The Economics and Research Staff of the National Association of Realtors has developed a Housing Affordability Index. The basic index takes into account the median family income, the current 30 year fixed rate mortgage terms, and the median price of a single family home. In short, it is the percentage of a median priced home that a median income family can afford, assuming the family makes a 20% down payment and spends 25% of its gross income on principal and interest payments. The calculations are shown in the following Table 4 – 4.

TABLE 4 – 4
HOUSING AFFORDABILITY INDEX

Assumptions: Median Price   = $100,000
             Loan Amount   =   80,000   (20% down payment)
             Loan Terms   = 7% fixed rate, 30 year term
             Mo. Mtge. Payment   = $532   (principal and interest)
             Median Family Income = $36,000   (pre-tax)

Calculations: $532   (Monthly Mortgage Payment)
                                      x4   (Qualifying Ratio, 25%)
                                   $2,128   (Monthly Qualifying Income)
                                     x12   (Months per Year)
                                  $25,536   (Annual Qualifying Income)

$$\text{HAI} = \frac{\text{Median Family Income}}{\text{Annual Qualifying Income}} \times 100$$

$$= \frac{\$36,000}{\$25,536} \times 100$$

$$= 140.98 \quad \text{rounded to } \underline{141}$$

To explain the index, a value of 100 means that a median income family has exactly enough annual income to qualify for an 80% mortgage, 7% fixed rate interest, 30 year term, on a median-priced home with 25% loan qualifying ratio. An index number higher than 100 indicates the buyer has more than enough income to qualify for the loan on a median priced home assuming the same financing terms and conditions. While the index describes average prices and average income along with current mortgage financing conditions, the period to period comparisons of indices provide insight into the trend of general market conditions.

Confidence

There are a number of indices of consumer confidence published on a monthly basis. Most notable are the University of Michigan Consumer Confidence Index and that of the Conference Board, based in New York City. Both are quoted regularly in business journals and business sections of local newspapers. Other related information at the local level could be found in retail sales levels and the number of marriages, both reflecting levels of consumer confidence.

Expectation

The consumer's outlook and attitude toward the future is highly influenced by what that consumer sees on television, hears on the radio and reads in newspapers and magazines. Two topics that seem to be especially influential are unemployment and inflation. Rates in these two areas are frequently quoted in all forms of public communication. It has been suggested that one of the ways to sense consumers' expectations of the future is to combine these two rates in the form of a simple index. In short, add the unemployment rate to the inflation rate to get an overview of consumers' expectations. Both measures are readily available in the marketplace. However, in place of the popular Consumers Price Index put out by the U.S. Department of Labor, it is suggested that the broker use another measure more closely related to real estate. A Rate of Housing Inflation can be calculated by comparing the percentage change of single family home median prices from period to period. Some urban economists combine the unemployment rate with the general inflation rate (CPI) and refer to it as the "Misery Index". This seems to accentuate the negative aspects without giving due attention to the positive side in the use of such a title. Research indicates that a Rate of Housing Inflation tends to be more sensitive and hence more focused and more meaningful for purposes of local real estate analysis.

The "ACE" approach, although not very complicated, still recognizes most of the basic information contained in the five market stimulators. It tends to reveal the tone of the local real estate market by answering the questions:

"Are single family homes affordable for typical local households?"

"Are consumers sufficiently confident to make housing decisions?"

"How does the economic climate affect consumers' attitudes toward the future?"

Rather than relying on precise measurements, this approach reveals the tone of the real estate market in the trend of the three related indices . . . upward, downward, or sidewise. By studying the trend of the *local* Housing Affordability Index, the Consumers Confidence Index and the Rate of Housing Inflation, one can judge and estimate the future direction of that particular real estate market's movement.

Once again, this procedure provides a way to determine a local market's *direction* in the months and year ahead. The *intensity* of that movement should be adjusted within the normally expected +10% or -10% range of volume. Of course, if unusual local conditions exist, adjustments may have to be made beyond the normal range of annual change.

Continuing study and work with market measurements develops a kind of "sixth sense" that complements the standard approaches to real estate market forecasting.

Pricing vs Appraising

In the field of real estate brokerage, particularly in the area of marketing residential real estate, the term "appraising" has been subjected to a degree of misuse. There appears to be some tendency on the part of brokers and salespeople to use this term rather casually. To the well informed person in the real estate field, appraising involves a formal process that includes an estimate and opinion of value, usually in the form of a written statement prepared for a fee. Many states require a separate license to perform such service. The report includes an adequate property description and a definition of the value being appraised as of a given date. The value conclusion is based on a thorough analysis of pertinent facts combined with professional judgment. The concept of valuation in the mind of the professional appraiser is illustrated in the Chart 4 – 4:

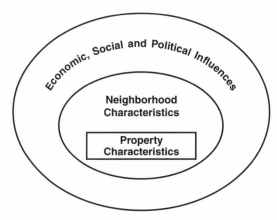

CHART 4 – 4
MAJOR INFLUENCES ON REAL ESTATE VALUE

There are two major sets of characteristics and forces involved. The first set is internal in character and deals with such physical attributes of the property as frontage, land area, the extent and condition of improvements and the relationship of improvements to the quality of the land. The second set is external to the property and deals with the neighborhood and other outside influences such as economic, social and political forces that affect real estate value. The neighborhood category includes surrounding land uses in the immediate areas that affect accessibility, convenience, favorable and unfavorable exposures. It also deals with demographic factors such as population trends, age mix, household composition and turnover factors. The economic influences involve employment opportunities in the community, family incomes, consumer spending patterns and the economic health of the area. Social forces deal with the institutions of property ownership, family life, citizens' rights and responsibilities. Cultural patterns and mores also enter into the picture. The political area encompasses man-made laws for regulation of society, the forces that maintain or change such regulation and the policies of government at all levels. The interpretation of these internal and external factors is known as the appraisal process. A general description of this process follows in Chart 4 – 5:

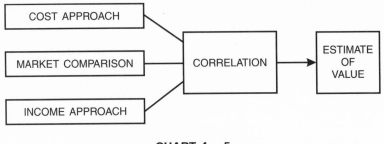

CHART 4 – 5
THE APPRAISAL PROCESS

This diagram identifies the traditional approaches to value; namely, cost, market and income capitalization. The correlation of these three avenues enables the appraiser to make a final estimate of value. In the residential field, an estimate of market value is the goal commonly pursued. Market value for this purpose appears to be highly influenced by court decisions. As a result, market value so defined is considered to be the highest price at which a well-informed seller would sell and at which a well-informed buyer would buy, assuming neither party is under any unusual pressure to act. It also assumes that the property has been exposed to the market for a reasonable length of time, that full title is being passed by seller to the buyer and that there are no unusual financing conditions. One observer pointed out that this definition of market value can be described as how much a hypothetical buyer is willing to pay to a hypothetical seller. Although this definition may appear to be somewhat idealistic when compared to actual market circumstances, it has been highly influential on valuation procedures and in legal proceedings.

The *cost approach* to value calculates a building's value based on replacement cost less depreciation to date. The calculations are usually made on a square foot or cubic foot basis for residential properties. The land value determined by market comparison is added to this net figure. Adding the depreciated value of the building to the current land value gives the indicated value via the cost approach. The replacement cost-new is calculated in terms of equal size and utility and by present day construction practices rather than the cost of an exact replica. Depreciation represents a loss in market value from all causes rather than a number from an accounting cost allocation schedule of depreciation.

The *market data approach* to value consists of selecting several recently sold properties of comparable size, style and construction. The more recent the transaction and the more similar the location, the greater the degree of validity for comparative purposes. Since there are usually some differences between the comparable properties and the property being appraised, adjustment for these differences must be made. Differences may be in lot size, location, time of sale, building size, building features, age, condition and the like. After adjusting for differences, these comparable properties are used as a basis for arriving at the indicated value of the subject property.

The *income approach* to value may not be applicable for residential valuation purposes, especially in the case of owner occupancy where it may be difficult to measure the equivalent market rents. Where used, the income approach may simply consist of the use of a gross rent multiplier to convert estimated gross income to a capital value. Based on current market experience, the estimated monthly rental of comparable facilities is multiplied by an appropriate gross monthly multiplier that reflects the relationship of gross rents to property value at the time of the appraisal. It is obvious that the quality of value indicated by this technique is a function of the quality of the rental equivalent and the judgment exercised in selecting the proper multiplier. The value so derived becomes the indicated value via the income approach.

While the design of these procedures suggests that these approaches are independent avenues of value analysis, it should be noted that most of the significant data assembled is market-related.

Finally, the indicated value from each of the three approaches can be correlated into one single estimate of value. The correlation process should not be interpreted as simple averaging, but rather as a thorough reexamination of the quality of the data, a rechecking of the calculations, and as a reassessment of the degree of validity of each approach. This weighing and sifting process enables the appraiser to exercise judgment in the direction of the approach, or approaches, that are most reliable in terms of reflecting market value. The appraisal report is concluded with a certified statement on the part of the appraiser, stating the estimate of market value as of a particular date.

The degree of sophistication embodied in the appraisal report depends on the nature of the specific appraisal assignment and the amount of professional appraisal time for which the client is contracting.

It is quite apparent that professional appraising is based on formal training and extensive experience in the valuation field. Asking your broker for an appraisal is somewhat like asking your pharmacist to recommend a prescription for an ailment, by-passing the medical doctor. While pharmacists may provide useful recommendations, the fact remains that in nearly all cases they are not professionally qualified to conduct a thorough diagnosis and interpret the results properly. This is also true of the real estate broker trying to play the role of a professional appraiser. In most cases the broker is not qualified to conduct a complete analysis and present recommendations in proper form. The exception, of course, is where the broker is legitimately performing a dual role in the real estate market. It is possible for a broker to rightfully hold both designations if he or she has been properly qualified. However, the broker usually expects to be compensated by way of a commission rather than by earning an appraisal fee. Furthermore, being both broker and appraiser for the same property and the same client raises serious ethical questions. Can an appraiser retain complete objectivity in the valuation process when he or she may be competing for the listing with other brokers? It does suggest that brokers should avoid making so-called "free appraisals" and confine their evaluating to the estimation of probable selling prices in line with their brokerage activities and responsibilities.

The preceding discussion provides the basis for identifying the proper role of a real estate broker. The broker's role should be to "price" properties rather than to "appraise" them. Pricing should not be confused with appraising. If an appraisal is called for, then it is recommended that an independent appraiser be called in for that purpose.

Pricing establishes a realistic asking price that will meet the objectives of the broker's principal, the seller. In most cases sellers are ignorant of the formal appraisal process. On the other hand, sellers are well aware of the cost inputs regarding their property. Initial purchase price, subsequent improvements, real property tax assessments, and preparation of annual income tax returns cause one to be a fairly good record keeper. If sellers are at all typical, their primary objective will be to obtain the highest possible selling price. This, of course, assumes the sellers have the time to allow the broker to give the property maximum market exposure. Asking prices must be realistic and within market range since pricing sets the stage for negotiation. Inordinately high asking prices cause properties to become stigmatized and thereby are effectively removed from the market since the asking price is out of market range. In such cases there is little opportunity to initiate the bargaining process between seller and buyer since the high asking price is out of communication range of the prospective buyer. Asking prices "open the bidding" while transaction prices tend toward the level of market value, except in extreme cases. Pricing is one of the market functions in which the broker participates and one in which the broker can be very influential. Depending on the motivation of the seller, imprudent pricing could prove to be a disservice to the seller in either direction. If the broker sets the asking price too low, the seller will be deprived of the just selling price. The subject of seller motivations will be treated in far greater detail in the next chapter. For the time being, it should be recognized that reasons for selling cover a wide range from inadequate shelter to economic and psychological factors. Real estate prices are somewhat volatile and change with the economic conditions in the marketplace. Prices are affected by seasonal volume and the swing of the real estate cycle. This is best reflected in the relationship of the supply of properties for sale to the level and intensity of demand expressed by prospective buyers. An overview of this interaction of supply and demand is expressed in Chart 4 – 6.

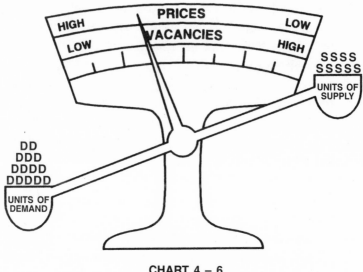

CHART 4 – 6
SUPPLY — DEMAND — PRICES — VACANCIES

As units of demand (D) outweigh the units of supply (S), the indicator moves to the left, resulting in higher prices and lower vacancies. High prices are usually accompanied by low level of vacancies and declining prices and are accompanied by increasing vacancies.

Seller's Pricing Rationale

In addition to motivating forces there are two distinct attributes of sellers in the residential market. First, they are reluctant to accept the idea of depreciation. Consumers readily accept the planned obsolescence of automobiles, appliances and clothing. After driving one's new car for one year, the consumer realizes that this used car has suffered a loss in market value and knows very well he or she must settle for a price lower than paid originally. However, it seems that most sellers are not willing to transfer this kind of consumer behavior to the real estate market.

Their limited experience and casual recollection provides them with convenient memories of friends and relatives who sold properties profitably for the last several decades. A good deal of such profit-taking was the result of the inflation which the economy of this country has experienced since the end of World War II. It is almost an axiom that no one ever sells a residential property at a loss. The federal income tax regulations have been structured so that gains on the sale of one's principal residence could be deferred if the seller reinvests in another principal residence of equal or greater value within two year's time. On the other hand, losses experienced in the process of sale were not deductible. There are other detailed aspects of these regulations, but the tone is such that it has a noticeable impact on the seller's subjective or personal asking price. See Chapter 5 — Your Clients – The Sellers for 1997 changes.

The second attribute relates to the peculiar dual-role of participants in a residential real estate market. Nearly one-half of all sellers in the market are also buyers in the very same market. In the process of selling their home they automatically become buyers, since most have to find another residence. As a result, they may be shopping both sides of the market at the same time. Confronted with asking prices of properties currently offered for sale, they subjectively inflate their own asking prices accordingly. It is commonplace to hear the expression, "Well, if this property is worth $XX,XXX, the mine is worth more than $XX,XXX since mine is obviously better!" Pricing may be looked at as the first step in bringing sellers and buyers together through the efforts of the real estate broker. If sufficient interest can be generated by the broker, the prospective buyer will express a degree of interest in the form of a written offer to purchase. A certain amount of bargaining may follow and produce counter-offers that may culminate in acceptance of the offer. The offer and subsequent negotiation ripen into a contract upon mutual agreement between buyer and seller with the aid of the broker. After the necessary financing arrangements are made and appropriate evidence and papers are prepared, the transaction is completed with the formal transfer of the deed at closing. Brokers participate in influencing asking prices but market prices are created by the negotiation between willing sellers and qualified buyers in the marketplace. It is an important part of the broker's job to explain the price justification if the seller is too adamant or the prospective buyer fails to recognize all of the price components.

In dealing with a prospective seller, the broker's immediate objective is to obtain a listing of the property for sale. In order to discuss listing price effectively, the broker must understand how the seller's subjective asking price may be formulated. In a good number of cases the seller's interpretation of a fair asking price is composed of these elements:

a. Initial acquisition costs
b. Cost of subsequent improvements
c. Estimated selling costs
d. Observed market increase since acquisition
e. Cushion for bargaining (informed sellers only)

The sellers' acquisition costs are well-documented in the copy of their closing statement at the time they purchased the property. It includes the contract price for the house plus financing fees, survey, appraisal, mortgage policy, recording fees and other expenses incidental to closing the transaction. Subsequent improvements may include such items as the construction of interior or exterior additions, remodeling and other extras that may have become part of the real property such as carpeting, cabinets, lighting fixtures and the like. In this regard, the "do-it-yourself" owners have a tendency to add in an estimate for their own time and materials, regardless of the quality of the workmanship. Selling costs are made up of the real estate broker's commission, the cost of title evidence, discount points for financing (where applicable) and any final costs directly related to marketing the property. The amount added for observed market increases may not be too well documented. A certain portion will be based on hearsay or imperfect market information. Nevertheless, the sellers believe they are entitled to price increases which they believe have occurred in the marketplace. In some instances the broker will discover, upon investigation, that these so-called market increases have been based more on rumor than fact. The fifth component of what sellers might term their fair asking price is an arbitrary cushion to enable them to have "a few yards of goods for bargaining purposes." This dimension applies more to sellers with above average market knowledge. Their exposure or experience tells them that asking prices tend to be on the high side of the market and that transaction prices tend to fall below that level. Inflated asking prices seem to be traditional in the real estate market. They set the stage for the often practiced pursuit of bargaining . . . a seemingly time honored American custom. These beliefs are reinforced by reports of sales in the local newspaper where the asking prices and selling prices are disclosed. Personal contacts and transactions of acquaintances may very well provide similar information. Further, periodic multiple listing reports reveal dollar gaps between sellers' asking prices and eventual selling prices.

Testing the Sellers' Asking Price

The sellers' "Fair asking price" is subjective in nature in that they reflect their personal desires and a certain amount of self-esteem. The broker's obligation is to test or validate this price. There are three convenient and practical ways of going about this task:

1. Real estate assessment verification
2. Residual cost test
3. Recent sales comparisons

Real estate assessment ratios may serve as a useful guide to identifying the general market range of values. Local tax assessors have the responsibility of assessing real property for "ad valorem" purposes at uniform ratios based on full market value. However, due to staffing problems and the size of the job, not all properties are reassessed each year. While this creates some inequities and subtracts from the degree of usefulness of this information, gross estimates are possible. The fact remains that the tax assessor did have an opinion of market value of the property at the time of the assessment. Current property taxes divided by the current tax rate will produce the assessed value. This information, assessed value, is also available through inspection of the local tax rolls that are in the province of public information. The local assessor can provide the broker with the prevailing assessment ratio; that is, the ratio of assessed value to full market value. The proper ratio enables the broker to convert assessed value to full market value in the opinion of the assessor.

If the required ratio is not available or seems inappropriate, brokers may want to establish it themselves. This can be accomplished by gathering information on recent sales in the area. The real estate taxes can be converted to assessed value as explained previously. Then the ratio for each property can be calculated by dividing selling price by the assessed value. These ratios can be arranged in an ascending array, from lowest value to highest. The median, or middle value, of the array would be selected as being representative of the group of selling prices. Such a procedure eliminates extreme values at either end of the scale. Having developed the representative ratio, the assessed value of the specific property is then multiplied by it. This value figure can be compared to the seller's asking price. Differences should be questioned. It may be that the property assessment has not been updated, in which case the new buyer may have to pay higher taxes in the future. This could have an affect on the buyer's offering price. At any rate, the procedure does provide some basis for testing the reasonableness of the seller's asking price. An illustration of this real estate assessment procedure is shown in Table 4 – 5.

TABLE 4 – 5 PRICES FOR 1228 WEST MAIN STREET					
R.E. Taxes Assessed Value				$ 2,970 $49,500	
1 Address	2 Selling Price	3 Real Estate Taxes	4 Total Assessed Value	5 Ratio of Selling Price to Assessed Value (col. 2 + col. 4)	Array of Ratios (from col. 5)
1143 W. North	$96,750	2,781	$46,350	2.09	1. 1.79
1326 N. 12th	100,350	2,943	49,050	2.05	2. 1.84
1812 W. Center	90,000	3,024	50,400	1.79	3. 1.85
908 North 10th	103,500	3,348	55,800	1.85	4. 1.90
1129 W. Main	98,550	3,213	53,550	1.84	5. 2.04
1004 N. 14th	99,000	2,916	48,600	2.04	6. 2.05
1448 W. National	102,600	3,240	54,000	1.90	7. 2.09

Median = 1.90

Estimated Price:		Estimated Price Range:	
Assessed Value	$49,500	Estimated Price –5%	$89,348
Median Ratio	x 1.90	Estimated Price +5%	$98,752
Estimated Price	$94,050		

The residual cost test is an adaptation of the appraiser's cost approach to value. The broker first makes a determination of the market value of the lot, exclusive of the building and garage. This land value estimate is then subtracted from the owner's asking price. The residual amount is then allocated to the building and garage. By applying square foot or cubic foot replacement costs to the building and garage areas, the broker is able to estimate the replacement cost-new. If the replacement costs are less than the residual amount, this indicates that the asking price may be somewhat overstated. This is significant, since buyers often have the alternative of buying an existing home or a new one. Aside from the time needed to construct a house and occupancy target dates, it would not seem likely that a buyer would pay more for a used house than for a new one. This procedure serves to establish an upper limit of a reasonable asking range.

The third test, recent sales comparisons, assumes comparable sales information is readily available. Such information may come from the broker's own files or the multiple listing service. Other sources, not as current, but providing some guidance, would be the face value indicated in the owner's title insurance policy, or the amount of the transfer fee noted on the recorded deed. These transfer fees are listed at time of recording at a rate fixed by each individual state. The time factor is extremely important in using a transfer fee for market information.

In discussing asking price, the broker should frankly discuss all evidence that bears on pricing in order to help the seller set the asking price within a realistic range of the market.

Overpricing

The penalty for overpricing is shouldered by both the broker and the seller in varying proportions. Overpricing lengthens the selling time and increases all promotional costs. Overpricing causes buyers to expect more at the higher asking price and thereby discourages prospective buyers. Overpricing also stigmatizes the property and creates an unfavorable image of the broker in the marketplace.

The ill effects generated have a short-run impact on the seller and persist as long as the property is on the market. After sale, the seller is removed from the market with respect to a particular property but brokers remain in the market and have to live with their mistakes.

Some estimates of the true costs of such imprudent practices are detailed in the following chapter along with a more professional listing price technique called "Comparative Market Analysis".

CHAPTER 5 —
YOUR CLIENTS – THE SELLERS

"Good listings are not found . . . they are cultivated!" *Nathan Shapiro*

Who are the Sellers?

The seller is the real estate broker's principal in a listing agreement. The real estate broker, acting as an independent contractor, is the agent of that principal. As a kind of short-term employer, the seller pays the commission in the real estate transaction. Without a principal to give an assignment, the real estate broker has no selling function to perform and can earn no commission nor income. Therefore, it is basic to the real estate brokerage business to find prospective sellers and obtain listing agreements with such sellers. Listings to the real estate broker are like merchandise on the shelf for the retailer. Limited selection or near-empty shelves seriously impair sales volume. In order to find potential sellers the real estate broker must know who they are. How can they be identified in the real estate market? In order to answer this question appropriate attention must be given to the underlying motivating forces that cause owners to sell. The common denominator of motivating forces is change. It may be expressed as a change in the state of the household cycle, change in employment status such as promotion, change in location of employment such as a job transfer, or it could be change in the standard of living as one moves upward or downward on the income ladder. It could also represent a change in physical housing needs expressed in the form of number of rooms, amount of recreational area, or similar space requirements. Studies of behavior within households observe that the arrival of additional children requires more people to live in the same limited space, thus posing a unique pressure to move. Parents seem to be much more attached to the family which they are raising than to the physical structure in which they live. There is an overriding concern for the welfare of the children. The house becomes a "thing" which must be replaced in the best interests of the family. Hence, the decision to move.

The ever present factor of change can render housing facilities inadequate or excessive when compared to ideal standards. While change may create needs, these needs must be qualified. In order to be effective in the marketplace, real needs must be accompanied by the economic capability of acting or curing. Property owners may be well motivated to act but may not be in a financial position to do so. For example, a factory worker with limited income may need more housing space. While need is obviously there, the situation cannot be corrected until that worker experiences an increase in pay. A young executive might have the opportunity to accept a better job in another city, but may stay right where he or she is because of family ties. Homeowners with housing problems consider selling as one of their alternatives. It should also be remembered that these problems concern people and structures and/ or how the people relate to these structures. Potential sellers are motivated people faced with a series of housing alternatives.

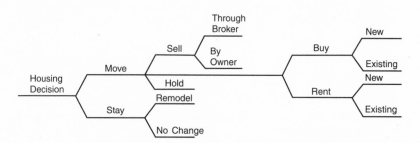

CHART 5 – 1
THE DECISION TREE OF THE HOMEOWNER
CONFRONTED WITH CHANGE IN HOUSING NEEDS

The decision tree in Chart 5 – 1 outlines the major steps related to housing alternatives. The upper series (move) involves more decisions than the lower series (stay). Homeowners deciding to move have to make a "sell or hold" decision on their present property as well as a "buy or rent" decision regarding their next housing accommodation.

Reasons for Selling

Instead of asking, "Why are they *selling*?," perhaps it would be more meaningful to ask "Why are they *moving*?" Selling is probably a decision in an attempt to adjust an identified need. Essentially, people are not deciding whether they are going to sell or not, but, rather, they are deciding whether they should move or not. Hence, the selling decision follows the decision to move. People may consider moving because of dissatisfaction with their present housing situation. When the dissatisfaction becomes unbearable, they feel compelled to act. Because of the financial and sentimental aspects of this decision, sellers tend to procrastinate. Some would rather put off the decision than make it immediately. In many cases the decision to move, followed by the decision to sell, is preceded by extensive discussion within the household and with other individuals as well. Quite often people are put into a position of uncertainty, "Should we or shouldn't we move?" Obviously, the stronger the pressures, the sooner the decision will be made. A person facing inter-area job transfer must act quickly. On the other hand, casual sellers lack strong motivation to move and take the attitude "We'll sell if we can get our price." Therefore, they can afford to play a waiting game.

The following table represents an overview of why households move each year, adapted from various census materials, social studies, budget counseling publications and market experience.

TABLE 5 – 1 WHY ONE OUT OF SIX HOUSEHOLDS MOVE EACH YEAR	
MAJOR REASON	**% of Total Households**
1. Inadequacy of present facilities	7%
2. Financial pressures	6%
3. Forced or involuntary (non-financial)	3%
4. New family or household formation	1%
TOTAL % OF ALL HOUSEHOLDS MOVING EACH YEAR	**17%**

Further detail related to Table 5 – 1:

1. Need for more suitable housing facilities due to changing needs and/or desired social status . . . over 70% of these buy houses.

2. The compelling force is strictly financial rather than degree of satisfaction with present facilities.

3. These moves are forced through sale, fire, flood, natural disasters, eviction, demolition, etc.

4. New partners and maturing children desiring emancipation from their families, preferring an independent household.

At times sellers are reluctant to disclose their true reason for moving. Persuading clients to provide the real reasons that are motivating them to sell isn't as difficult a process as might be expected. Probably the broker's best tool is empathy. Often, if the broker can show a sincere interest in the sellers and their problems and not just a dollar interest in the property, a strong feeling of confidence in the broker can be developed on the part of the clients. When the sellers' true motivation and background is known, the broker can show the proper concern and recommend the right kind of action that will be compatible with the true interests of the seller. It follows then that the real reason for selling is directly related to the quality of the listing. If the reason for selling is weak, this very weakness may be reflected in the listing, quite often in the form of over-pricing.

Selling Process

In the real estate business, brokers and their salespeople have one important thing to sell and that is service. Because the real estate broker's functions require representing the selling homeowner in dealing with potential buyers, this means that both the broker and seller are subject to all the legal implications involved in a principal-agent relationship. As a result, the broker must operate within a framework of certain responsibilities to the principal and to buyers if he or she is to earn a commission.

Broker's Responsibilities to the Seller

The obligations which define the broker's (agent) relationship to the homeseller (principal) are among the most important parts of the law of agency. These laws impose the following requirements on the agent:

- To employ adequate marketing efforts and act in good faith–
  As agent of the seller, the broker must make reasonable efforts to effectively market the property that the owner has listed with him or her.

- To attempt to acquire the best possible price and terms –
  The broker must give the property adequate market exposure while keeping informed of market prices and conditions. The broker must submit all offers (both oral and written) and can advise the seller about accepting such offers.

- To be truthful and accurate in one's statements –
  The broker is obligated to distinguish between opinion and fact. The law does not allow the broker to exceed the limit of authority that has been delegated by the principal. Therefore, the broker cannot bind the principal in any actions beyond the scope of authority so delegated.

- To provide full disclosure of material and information –
  The broker must convey to the principal all relevant information that the client might need in determining whether or not to accept an offer.

- To be capable of completing his or her work –
  The principal (seller) must allow the agent (broker) sufficient time to sell the listed property before one can pursue contract relief.

- To continue to perform as long as one is relied upon –
  After the broker initiates his or her services in connection with the attempted sale of the principal's property, the broker must continue such efforts as long as he or she is relied upon by the seller.

115

Broker's Responsibilities to the Buyers

Even in cases where brokers are hired as agents of the seller, the broker owes certain responsibilities to the buyers:

- Render full service –

    Upon entering into an agency relationship with a prospective buyer, the broker is required to make sincere efforts to serve the buyer in his or her full capacity.

- Provide full disclosure –

    Just as in his or her responsibility to the seller, the broker is required to provide the buyer all necessary information needed in order to arrive at a considered decision to purchase a property. In the event the broker is informed of material factors that would make the buyer refuse purchase, such information must not be withheld.

- Provide accurate and honest statements –

    As with the seller, the broker is required to provide the buyer with factual information, accurately and honestly. Should any of the broker's statements to the buyer constitute opinion, one must so qualify.

It is important that the broker maintain contact with the seller. The philosophy of the real estate market regarding the listing of a property for sale is that the sellers have selected a specific broker as their agent and, in so doing, expect a certain level of performance. This is in contrast to the buying side of the market where the focus is on the property. The buyer concentrates on the property first and the broker second. Accordingly, sellers expect constant effort and continuous communication with their real estate broker. They want to know the reactions of prospective buyers after a personal showing of the property. They would like to know what the reactions were of the people who attended an open house. They would also like to know how their property compares with competing properties offered for sale. This is an important point to remember. It should be recognized that the sellers are focusing their attention on one property (a single objective) while the broker has to divide his or her attention among many properties. However, this is no excuse for a lack of communication with individual sellers.

In the process of listing a property for sale, it would seem that the seller and the broker have overlapping objectives.

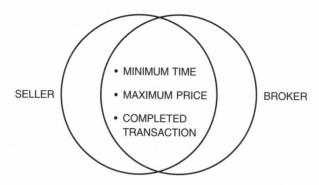

CHART 5 – 2
OVERLAPPING OBJECTIVES OF SELLER AND BROKER

The broker wants to successfully complete a sale and, likewise, the sellers want to achieve the same goal. The broker would like to accomplish this feat in as short a period of time in order to minimize his or her efforts and overhead and, hence, to create a wider margin of net profit. The sellers would like to sell the property in a minimum amount of time in order to minimize their inconvenience connected with the selling process. The broker would try to get the highest price available in the market because the broker's commission is tied to the selling price, but he or she also knows that the closer the buyer's offer to the listing price, the greater chance one has of getting the offer accepted and completing the transaction. The sellers, in nearly all cases, are trying to maximize the equity they can extract from the sale. Hence, they hope that the broker will conduct a complete search of the market and find a qualified buyer who will pay the top price.

There are two unusual attributes of sellers in the residential market. The first is that most of them are reluctant to accept the idea of loss in market value, depreciation. The second is that many sellers are also buyers in the same market, buying another home and selling their present one. As a result, they may be shopping both sides of the market at the same time. When they are confronted with higher asking prices, they subjectively inflate their own asking price accordingly.

In one sense, the broker really earns a commission by finding the premium buyer in the marketplace that perhaps sellers could not find on their own. Many brokers reveal that in the process of bringing in a low offer, the sellers are likely to come back with the familiar caustic statement, "We don't need to pay a real estate broker a commission to give our home away."

There are more important dimensions to an offer than price alone: certainty of closing the deal, occupancy dates, income tax advantages and the like.

From a legal point of view, the listing in writing is a contract between the seller and the broker. These are the principal parties to the contract and, as previously described, the contract centers around common goals. To many sellers, the commodity in the transaction of a real property sale is something special -- their home. They have a sentimental attachment to it; they have raised their family in it; they have molded the character of their children in it; they have entertained their close friends and relatives in it. Therefore, sellers have the tendency to treat it somewhat delicately. On the other hand, the broker has no such sentimental ties. The listing represents an economic opportunity. It is merchandise to be sold in the marketplace. In the process of rendering the brokerage service, one of the broker's important goals is to obtain a commission. For these reasons the psychological reaction to the property may be different on each side. In the context of the listing process, sellers think of marketing a *home* while brokers concentrate on selling a *house*.

Importance of Listings

The availability of listings fluctuates with the real estate cycle. There are times when listings are not only plentiful, but excessive. The latter situation would be in a typical buyer's market where the buyer is king and sellers compete with one another. At times of housing shortages, the number of properties offered for resale is comparatively low simply because ample opportunity for turnover is not available. Potential sellers have few alternatives. They don't have many choices of places in which to move. As a result, the number of transfers is held to a minimum. People are less willing to move; hence, there are fewer properties for sale.

New construction is an activating force that causes turnover in the market as people upgrade their housing standards. At times when new construction volume is low, the number of existing homes offered for sale is also low. There is a direct relationship. However, individual brokers should bear in mind that it is neither their function nor objective to sell every house in town. Brokers are basically looking for an adequate number of listings — a base on which to operate a successful business. When listings are difficult to obtain, the competition among brokers is more intense. When listings are easier to get, the competition is lighter. Looking at the real estate brokerage function in its simplest form, one can identify the critical path of action. The broker must obtain a listing in order to attract a buyer, to complete the sale and to collect a commission. Each one of these functions must be successfully completed. In some cases, certain steps need to be repeated as shown in the following chart. A rejected offer or a collapsed deal causes the process to start over at the showing stage.

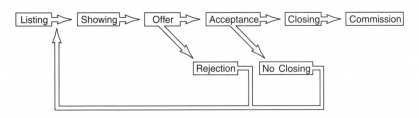

CHART 5 – 3
CRITICAL PATH TO EARNING A COMMISSION

As was explained in Chapter 3, there are annual recurring seasonal factors within the longer cyclical variations of the real estate market. Family groups are more reluctant to move during the course of the regular school year or during cold weather because of the attendant inconvenience. Families are more apt to move during the warmer months when school is out due to greater flexibility and so as not to impose any serious educational restrictions on their children. Therefore, in general, the opportunity for getting listings is much greater in the spring and summer than it is in the fall or winter. Of course, one must bear in mind that the level of competition from other brokers fluctuates in the same proportions, as evidenced by the size of the classified section in local newspapers during the month of May compared to the size of the classified section in the month of December.

Probability of Getting a Listing

The probability of getting a listing is directly tied to efficient use of resources. Even though one in six families moves each year, it should be remembered that this includes both owners and renters. In most markets the probability of a renter moving during the course of the year is about one in three, for a homeowner it is about one out of thirteen. So, if one were to contact households at random, via direct telephone calls, ringing doorbells or direct mail, the probability of finding a prospective seller is rather small. Chart 2 – 2 in Chapter 2 illustrates this point. If the broker talked to all households at random, including both tenants and owners, chances of contacting a household interested in selling an existing property would be four or five out of every hundred on an annual basis. If this annual measurement is distributed over a twelve month period, on average the probability drops to one chance in about 300. This emphasizes the nature of the listing hunt. Due to these odds, the so-called shotgun approach of ringing doorbells and direct telephone calling results in a rather low rate of productivity. This approach may not have a realistic payoff in terms of the time invested. In addition, the competition factor must be recognized. If only one out of 300 properties will be listed for sale this month, it is also reasonable to assume that other brokers will be competing for the listing. Thus, the broker will not be successful every time he or she identifies a potential seller. Since one will be successful only part of the time, a more realistic measurement might be closer to one in a thousand. "One in a thousand" means that once a potential seller is identified, one out of three times the broker will be able to get the listing, and two out of three times other brokers will get the listing. In other words, the broker must control 33 percent of the listing market in order to realize a one out of a thousand success rate. Rather than using a "shotgun" approach, it would appear that perhaps a "rifle" might be more effective by first identifying the target and then taking a direct approach.

"Pockets of Listings"

Experience proves that the "rifle" approach is less time consuming, less costly and more productive. One of the best indicators of where selling action is likely to take place as far as location of sellers is concerned, is embodied in the "pockets of activity" concept of residential sales. By plotting the exact location of each sale on the map, the broker will soon realize that sales tend to concentrate in clusters, taking on characteristics that might be comparable to patterns of children's communicable diseases. Measles and chicken pox tend to spread through neighborhoods, probably as a result of contact at the grade school level. A similar type of phenomenon takes place in the real estate market regarding the sale of residential property. Residential neighborhoods tend to be somewhat homogeneous in character. That is, people living in a neighborhood are very likely to have similar characteristics: there are noticeable degrees of similarity in age, family sizes and income brackets. These characteristics, however, are general in nature rather than specific. Because of this commonality, families in a given neighborhood tend to respond to similar stimuli. There is an identifiable behavioral pattern. It's a kind of "keeping up with the Joneses" philosophy. They observe with interest the decision on the part of the first homeowner in the neighborhood to sell. They begin to wonder why they are selling. It may be that the neighbor is buying another existing house, building a new home, or moving to another city.

Interest is aroused by the appearance of the "for sale" sign and is further intensified by the eventual "sold" sign. Real estate signs serve as a catalytic agent and induce thought provoking action. Other homeowners respond by reexamining their own positions.

"If the Smiths are building a new house, why shouldn't we?"

"We were toying with the idea of moving, but we never really faced the question squarely."

"We had never sold a house before and we were in doubt as to how complicated the process was. It all looks so simple now."

"The Smiths put their house up for sale, got close to the asking price and now, having retrieved their equity in their present house, are in a position to upgrade their housing standards."

"If the Smiths can do it, so can we."

As a result, we see a good deal of imitation of the Smith's action in the neighborhood and the more frequent this successful sale pattern is repeated, the greater the tendency of others in the neighborhood to do likewise. In many cases homeowners are not aware of the true market value of their property. However, when it is demonstrated by a nearby sale, they then come to realize that they may have more equity in their home than they had thought. When they find out that it is a rather simple process of retrieving that equity, they then have the courage to act that they lacked before. So, in short, the decision to sell is often an imitation of the successful actions of other people in the neighborhood.

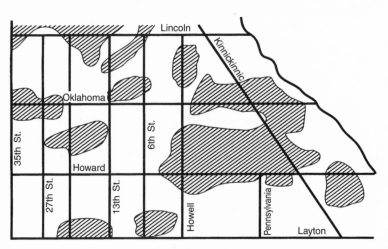

CHART 5 – 4
"POCKETS OF ACTIVITY"

The enterprising real estate broker will identify this behavioral pattern and upon a successful sale of a property, will immediately contact other homeowners in the area, inform them of the sale and offer his or her services to do the same for them. This is one of the more fruitful approaches to getting listings: getting into an area where potential sellers are more apt to consider listing or selling their property. The pattern which was described is typical of the average neighborhood. This type of behavioral pattern does not evidence itself as vividly in high priced neighborhoods and it expresses itself in a very unusual manner in declining neighborhoods. In changing lower priced neighborhoods there is a tendency for "panic selling." Realizing that the neighborhood is starting to break up, people want to sell. It may be for economic reasons; social reasons; or for environmental reasons. At any rate, when conditions such as these persist, it produces the classical economic situation of a glut in the market: a pronounced oversupply of a commodity being offered for sale where sellers are forced to accept a lower price. The positive side of this "pockets of activity" concept is particularly applicable in neighborhoods containing people in the aspiring brackets; the factory worker or foreign born person trying to upgrade his or her status; the young executive moving up the ladder and so forth.

Obtaining Listings

Two general approaches for obtaining listings have been identified: (1) the general approach, and (2) the specific approach. The general approach relates to general advertising in the newspaper, radio, television, using mass appeal and banking on a certain percentage of response. This approach, while it can be very effective, is a comparatively costly approach and calls for a large capital commitment in the form of an advertising and promotional budget. A smaller broker in a medium sized or large sized town may find this a very impractical and nonproductive approach. It is more appropriate for the higher volume broker. On the other hand, the specific approach for getting listings can be centered around such techniques as the pockets of activity concept and the so-called "sphere of influence" approach. Each individual engaged in the selling of real estate has one's own particular sphere of influence. This sphere is made up of people who are loyal to him or her and, when given the opportunity, will channel business in that broker's direction. This would include one's relatives, friends and the people with whom he or she does business, the people who render them professional service and the clients that they have served successfully. The combined efforts of all of these people within this sphere of influence produce what is know as "referral business." For the average size or smaller broker, this represents the greatest opportunity for getting listings.

A popular term used today is "networking". It is used to refer to the people within one's sphere of influence. It is the source of many of the broker's listing leads. The following Table 5 – 2 illustrates in a very simple manner how one might organize his or her own network. The theme was adapted from that of a very successful new car dealer, Ernie von Schledorn, who popularized the slogan, "Who do you know wants to buy a car?" The two lines at the top of the chart capsulize the highlights of a proposed telephone conversation to any person included in the five categories on the sphere of influence chart. Note the question asked and the promise to call back in about a week. Listing programs based on this idea have proved to be very productive where there was commitment and consistent follow through.

Table 5 – 2			
MY SPHERE OF INFLUENCE			
"I need your help . . . we've had record sales . . . we need homes to sell! Start thinking."			
"Who do you know wants to sell a house? I'll call you back in about a week."			
RELATIVES – NAME	**Phone No.**	**Dates Called**	**Comments**
1. 2. 3. 4. 5.			
FRIENDS – NAME	**Phone No.**	**Dates Called**	**Comments**
1. 2. 3. 4. 5.			

Table 5 – 2 cont'd on page 125

VENDORS – NAME	Phone No.	Dates Called	Comments
1. 2. 3. 4. 5.			
CHURCH, SOCIAL, ETC. – NAME	Phone No.	Dates Called	Comments
1. 2. 3. 4. 5.			
PAST CLIENTS – NAME	Phone No.	Dates Called	Comments
1. 2. 3. 4. 5.			

All brokers, regardless of size, have the opportunity to get listings by following for sale by owner ads in the newspaper. Another opportunity exists in servicing new property for sale by a builder, where the builder achieves a goal of selling new houses and the broker is able to sell the existing homes of the buyers of the new houses. These are but a few ways to get listings. There are many different ways available. The advice to the real estate broker is to select the technique which is most productive, to work on it, concentrate on it and perfect it. It cannot be a hit or miss application. One of the strongest requirements is persistence. The listing campaign must also be conducted twelve months a year rather than on an in and out basis. Good listings are not found, they are cultivated.

Expenses of Sale

A seller of real estate is obligated for certain expenses connected with the sale. For the most part, these expenses include the real estate broker's commission, bringing the title evidence up to date, the title transfer fee, the home warranty premium and recording costs related to the satisfaction of the sellers' mortgage. Nearly all other costs attendant to the sale are usually the responsibility of the buyer. In most residential markets, real estate commissions are a percent of the selling price. The full commission is charged regardless of the level of performance of the real estate broker because it represents fulfillment of the listing contract. The broker should bear in mind that the sellers have an opportunity to be selective. It costs no more commission-wise to sell with Broker A versus Broker B versus Broker C. Hence, they feel, or expect, that they will get more service from one broker than another and accordingly express a kind of preference for the broker that will give them the best performance for their commission dollar. The following are generally accepted requirements for earning a commission:

- The broker must prove that it was intended for him or her to receive a commission upon selling a property in question.
- The broker initiates a transaction in accordance with the seller's terms.
- The broker must establish that he or she provided the procuring efforts that brought the buyer and seller together.
- The broker must produce a purchaser willing and capable of meeting the seller's stated terms (or acceptable terms), and legally qualified to contract.
- The broker negotiates a completed transaction or what is construed as a completed transaction. If the broker completes a transaction, he or she is entitled to the stated commission. On the other hand, if a transaction has been advanced well to the point of completion but extraordinary circumstances prohibit full completion, it is possible for the broker to receive one's full commission. Examples would involve cases where the seller could not produce clear title, or the seller's spouse refuses to pass title to his or her interest.

Types of Listing Contracts

The types of listing contracts that are employed in the real estate market are related to the independence of the seller and the policies subscribed to by the broker operating in a particular market. In cases where listings are difficult to obtain and the sellers are aware of this condition, they may be willing to give an open listing at best.

The open listing merely guarantees a commission to the broker initiating a contract that the sellers accept. In short, in an open listing the broker is not only competing with all other brokers, but is competing with the sellers as well. This situation is less than ideal because the broker can perform, but never has full assurance that he or she will be compensated for their effort. As a result, there may be a tendency on the part of the brokers to put forth something less than full effort on open listings. Usually open listings aren't advertised as well, aren't shown as often and are given secondary attention with respect to other property listed for sale. On the other hand, the exclusive listing contract gives the broker the sole and exclusive right to sell the property and earn a commission if he or she performs by bringing in an offer acceptable to the seller. The fact that the contract is exclusive means that the sellers will pay a commission on any offer that is acceptable to them regardless of the source of that offer, be it a prospect generated by the broker, another broker, or by the sellers themselves. While this may seem harsh at times, it is an advisable arrangement to motivate the broker to work in the best interests of the seller.

The Multiple Listing Service is a cooperative arrangement where Realtor® members pool all of their listings. In most markets brokers belonging to the Multiple Listing Service are required to file new listings with the Multiple Listing Service within 48 hours after they are obtained. This cooperative arrangement then allows any member of the MLS to show and attempt to sell the property. This gives Realtor® members, particularly smaller companies, an excellent opportunity to become competitive in the total real estate market. If they were operating on their own, the extent of their sales might be limited to the company listings that they have under their control, in contrast to the MLS arrangement where they have a greater number of properties, a greater pool of properties from which to sell. Within the context of the listing process, the MLS service gives the smaller broker the opportunity to compete with the larger brokers. It enables all brokers to provide the selling power of the entire Multiple Listing Service in addition to one's own office. Thus, the listing broker is able to present a convincing story to the seller, explaining that he or she can, through the Multiple Listing Service efforts, give the seller's property maximum market exposure, which will give the broker the opportunity to find a premium buyer if one is present in the market. It should be observed that, in addition to maximum market exposure, the broker is also able to give maximum personal service since he or she is going to be in direct contact with the seller. In the operation of the Multiple Listing Service it is the participating brokers that pay the fees to the Multiple Listing Service, while the sellers pay the same commission that they would to a non-MLS broker. In short, the cost of the Multiple Listing Service is borne by the broker members rather than by the seller.

Increasing Salability

The sellers can enhance the salability of their property in these ways: 1) by participating in the financing; 2) by improving the physical appearance of the property; and 3) by cooperating and allowing the broker to perform his or her proper role.

The sellers can assist in the financing by assigning their existing mortgage, by taking back a second mortgage, or by selling on land contract (contract for deed). This is particularly true in periods when interest rates are high or mortgage money is difficult to obtain.

Using special financing techniques in other types of markets enables sellers to extract a price toward the high side of the market since buyers in this category are generally marginal buyers. Hence, with their small down payment, they lack the full ability to be completely effective in the bargaining process.

In order to attract a greater number of qualified buyers the broker should request cooperation on the part of the sellers by asking the sellers to present their property in its best light. This would include good housekeeping and minor chores to enhance the physical appearance of the property. A poorly kept house might cause buyers to have doubts about other aspects of the property. They may fear that the property has been abused. On balance, it is quite obvious that prospective buyers would react more favorably to a house that has good eye appeal as opposed to one that appears to be neglected. The old adage that "it's nothing that a scrubbing brush or a paint brush can't cure" might seem cute, but the condition still represents a barrier to the sale.

The broker serves as an intermediary in the marketing process. He or she facilitates the bargaining between sellers and buyers and, for this reason, the marketing process can proceed more smoothly if the two parties are kept apart. The broker serves as the channel of communication. The broker should be given every opportunity and cooperation to complete the sale.

Timing the Sale

The timing of the sale can have a material affect on the final selling price. If the seller has the ability to hold off for an extended period of time, then this factor is of little consequence. However, if the seller is under any particular pressure to act within a limited time period, that seller may be at the mercy of the market. If good fortune is with sellers they may be able to sell (offer their property for sale) during a seller's market and get premium price. On the other hand, if it's a buyer's market they are going to have to adjust their price downward in the process of competing with other sellers. By realizing the importance of timing, the broker can use this as an inducement to get a listing. For example, if the seller says, "Well, we're going to wait until school's out to put the property on the market," the broker can counter with, "Spring is the peak of the real estate market. Now is the time to offer your house up for sale because you have the greatest chance of getting the highest possible price. By waiting until the summer you will have passed the peak and you may have to settle for a lesser price. Even if the property is sold now we can arrange the occupancy date at some time in the future that will in no way disturb your children's school attendance." A similar kind of argument can be used in the fall, where the people are thinking about whether they want to list their property for sale. As we go into the fourth quarter of the year, the seasonal downturn sets in and, of course, the probability of selling drops. It might be smart to list the property as soon as possible in order to take advantage of a more promising market. Some observers have commented that real estate prices, even in a level market, can vary as much as 5 to 10 percent between a May sale and a December sale, all other factors remaining the same.

Real estate brokers should not look at a listing as a quasi-monopoly. This means that the broker should not have as his or her objective the tying up of the sellers by putting them under a listing contract. A broker has the moral and business responsibility to list only those properties that fall within one's sphere of operations. For example, if the broker has limited experience or lacks ability in the area of industrial real estate, that broker should not list an industrial property for sale. If one is incapable of professionally presenting an investment property, he or she should not list that investment property for sale. Instead, one should refer the property to a fellow broker who possesses that particular capability. Such working arrangements can easily be affected whereby Broker I, the investment broker, refers residential properties to Broker R. Broker R, in turn, refers investment properties to Broker I, the investment broker. So, in the long run, each broker maintains an image in the real estate market, serving his or her clients at a high level, and still benefits from this course of action.

By the same token, the broker should be realistic in taking on a given number of listings. The volume should be limited to the number that the broker can handle effectively. In most cases the real estate broker would solve this problem by adding staff members rather than turning down listings. This seems to be the positive approach. Remember that the overstocking of shelves with listings results in increased overhead, increased office work, increased advertising and increased servicing. For the office that lacks sufficient personnel, the servicing element may get so large that the staff will effectively lose a good part of its selling time. Hence, the company will not be as successful as it could be in selling and, at the same time, may create displeasure for some of the sellers.

Communication with and Service to the Seller

Most brokers are quite enthusiastic at the time they acquire the listing. They may make representations and promises to the prospective seller. If the broker could maintain this level of enthusiasm throughout the listing period, it would most likely result in a sale of the property and a satisfied seller. However, because of the demands within the real estate brokerage business, there is a tendency by brokers to neglect to communicate with their sellers. They fail to give the seller periodic reports as to the reactions of prospects who looked at the property. In the event that the broker is unsuccessful in selling the property during the initial listing period, he or she may have grave reservations about going back and attempting to relist the property because of the embarrassing situation that may have been created through the lack of communication. The broker, in effect, has educated the sellers by creating an awareness that there were no offers on the property and perhaps the sellers realize they should adjust their asking price. However, because of sellers' dissatisfaction with this particular broker, they most likely will switch brokers. Broker number 1, in effect, has set up the listing for broker number 2 at an adjusted asking price – not even receiving thanks for one's efforts.

Brand Name of Listing Broker

There is evidence of the brand-name concept in selling residential real estate. The reputation of real estate brokers, their performance in selling properties and their integrity, evidenced by the manner in which they treat clients, makes a company a desirable one with which to do business. People become aware of the company's name and reputation. When considering the sale of their home, in many cases, people respond to this kind of brand-name or high level image in the market. This is a definite asset in getting listings. Brokers developing this kind of reputation need spend little time convincing the seller that they are in the real estate brokerage business and that they render quality service. They don't have to make promises because the public is aware of their level of performance.

Determining a Price Range

Setting an asking price is part of the marketing function performed by the listing broker. The broker's job is to *price* . . . *not appraise* the residential property for the prospective seller. Based on available information on properties recently sold, properties currently offered for sale and present economic conditions in the home resale market, the broker uses his or her professional judgment to establish the price range in which the owner's property will probably sell. In many local markets the procedures used to determine the appropriate price range is referred to as a Comparative Market Analysis or a Competitive Market Analysis. This type of analysis will also provide the home owner with information on how long similar properties were on the market and the ratio between the listed price and selling price. The form of the analysis is illustrated in Table 5 – 3 on the next pages. It should be noted that the material used in Table 5 – 3 was first developed by ERA-Electronic Realty Associates, now ERA Franchise Systems, Inc.

A well researched market analysis should give the probable price range within which ready, willing and financially qualified buyers most likely will pay for a home generally similar to that of the owner's and located in a similar neighborhood. Sellers can ask whatever price they want for their homes. However, serious sellers want to set a price that will not only reflect the fair value of their investment in the home but a price that will also attract buyers. That is why a well prepared market analysis is very important to sellers as well as the real estate broker. It brings current market conditions that are relevant to the attention of the sellers in a manner that is very meaningful. The importance of the suggested price range in the work sheet of the CMA in Table 5 – 3 is discussed in Chapter 12 in connection with "Market Value Pricing".

TABLE 5 – 3
MARKET PRICE

Based on available information on properties currently for sale, properties recently sold and present economic conditions in home resales, our real estate professionals judge the market price of your property located at:

_____

To be in the price range from $ _____ to $ _____

• **Your Competitive Advantage**

Common Problems Arising from Improper Pricing:

- Lack of Showings
- Appraisal Problems
- House gets "Shop Worn"
- House does not sell

- Buyers are reluctant to make offers
- House competes with higher value homes
- Minimal MLS participation
- Competing houses become more attractive

Agreed Asking Price For Your Home Is: $ _____

_____   _____
Sales Associate   Date

TABLE 5 – 3 (Continued)

Questions about CMA's

What is CMA?

A CMA is a Competitive Market Analysis. Data is collected on homes similar to yours that have been on the real estate market recently. Style of home, number of rooms, bedrooms, bathrooms, amenities, etc. are used to determine a competitive market price for your home. However, every home is unique and there will be differences between each of them and yours. Also, the relative desires of the sellers and the buyers may have been different as well as the circumstances of sale.

Why is a CMA important?

A CMA will not only help determine a competitive market price for your home but also provide you with information on how long similar properties were on the market and the ratio between the asking price and the selling price. If you need to sell your home quickly, this information is key. A well-researched CMA is an excellent indication of what ready, willing and able buyers will pay for a home similar in size, style and location.

What is Market Price?

In simple terms, Market Price is the price a home will sell for within a reasonable period of time (usually 90-120 days) considering current market trends. As a seller, you can ask whatever you want for your home. The serious seller, however, wants to be informed about the trends in the market and wants to set a price that will not only reflect his/her investment in the property but will also attract buyers. That's why an *Equitable/Stefaniak* real estate agent is so important!

TABLE 5 – 3 (Continued)								

COMPETITIVE MARKET ANALYSIS

ADDRESSES:

Date _____   Subject _____

Prepared by _____   Sale #1 _____

Suggested Price Range   Sale #2 _____

$ _____ to $ _____   Sale #3 _____

	Features	Subject Property	Sale #1	Adj.	Sale #2	Adj.	Sale #3	Adj.
1.	Actual Sales Price Less Lot Value							
2.	Sq. Ft. Cost/Sq. Ft.							
3.	Bedrooms							
4.	Baths							
5.	Family Room							
6.	Construction							
7.	Garage							
8.	Age							
9.	Condition							
10.	Heating							
11.	Air Conditioning							
12.	Kitchen Equip.							
13.	Basement							
14.	Extra Features	BPP						
	A.							
	B.							
	C.							
15.	Terms							
16.	Adjusted Price							
17.	Date of Sale							
18.	Time Adj. Price							

Competitive Problems – Overpricing

One of the serious marketing problems that results in competing for listings is the matter of overpricing. This is particularly true in cases of properties offered for sale by owners. The fact that the property is offered for sale becomes public knowledge through the owner's sign or through an ad in the newspaper. As a result, many brokers become aware of the owner's willingness to sell and make contact. Where brokers don't have any particular image or special service to sell, they may be tempted to compete for the listing by offering to list it at a higher price than another broker. This may sound quite good to the sellers because they are under the impression that they will actually receive this higher price. However, it is usually nothing more than listing bait used by the competing broker. A limited market study by the author of the effect of overpricing of residential listings on the actual required selling time is summarized in Table 5 – 4.

Table 5 – 4		
LISTING OVERPRICING -vs- ACTUAL SELLING TIME (Residential Listings)		
No of Properties	Sale Price Compared to Listed Price (Difference)	Number of Days on Market (Median)
38	0	27
22	-1%	25
42	-2%	27
37	-3%	41
12	-4%	46
17	-5%	47
9	-6%	70
5	-7%	49
9	-8% to -15%	64

This summer of 1996 study involved 191 single family homes, all in the $80,000 to $100,000 selling price range. They were all located in three major sections of a large midwestern city and in four adjoining suburbs, all in the same county. These transactions involved many different brokers in a combination of in-house sales as well as co-broker sales. Combined, all of these brokers had a conversion ratio of about 60% . . . that is, about 60% of the listings sold during the initial listing period.

These figures indicate that the degree of overpricing has a corresponding effect on the length of time it takes to sell the property. Assume a property has a realistic market value of $90,000. If the property is listed at or very near to market value, it should sell in about 30 days. If the property is listed at 6 percent over the market value, based on these averages, it should take twice as many days to sell. It appears as if the undesirable effects of overpricing rapidly multiply even with what appear to be small percentage increases in asking prices above actual market value.

By overpricing the property the broker has deliberately reduced the chances of sale and will have to do a double selling job. It is going to be harder to induce an offer from a prospective buyer and harder to undo the high-price promise that was made to the seller when a lower offer is presented. The broker is going to have to sell the seller as well. Brokers employing this "list 'em high, sell 'em low" philosophy will soon develop a very undesirable image in the real estate market. There is a price to be paid for over-pricing.

For Sale by Owner

The number of for sale by owners seems to increase year after year. This is due to the fact that turnover is occurring more frequently in the residential real estate market. As a result, sellers are gaining more knowledge of the workings of the real estate market and developing a higher degree of confidence. This is particularly true of people in business and professional categories who feel that they are able to handle the transaction on their own. In some markets for sale by owner transactions account for as much as 20 percent of the residential transactions in a given year. This doesn't speak well for the real estate industry because the sellers are saying that they possess equal or better knowledge than the real estate broker. They feel they can do the job equally well or better.

There are some serious questions that need to be asked.

- Do the sellers know the true market value of their property?
- Do the sellers have adequate market information to negotiate properly?

- Do the sellers have access to the various sources of financing in order to complete the transaction?

Many homesellers have full-time occupations and may find it difficult to commit the necessary time to properly handle each phase of their sale. Further, lack of instant sales success usually brings them to the stark realization that there is much more to real estate marketing than putting up a for sale sign on the property and placing an ad in the newspaper. With this in mind, is it possible that the sellers may make a serious economic or legal error in the process of sale? While it is true that the sellers may by-pass the real estate broker and save a commission, they may also be taking on a risk that may be much greater and may have a greater financial impact than the amount of money they think they are saving. However, the for sale by owner movement parallels the do-it-yourself fad present in the country today. It is generally recognized that any do-it-yourself project, on average, represents lower quality of performance than that of a professional. More observations on this point will be a part of a later chapter dealing with the future of the real estate industry.

Older Homeowners

As life expectancy in the United States increases, "overhousing" will become far more significant in motivating housing turnover. Mature households living on retirement incomes are finding it increasingly difficult to shoulder the cost of maintaining three or four bedroom detached single family homes. While this size home was necessary when they were raising their families, now the total cost of occupancy is beginning to become somewhat burdensome . . . higher real estate taxes . . . higher heating and utility bills . . . and no return on the large equity in a mortgage-free home. To these people, some return on their "tied up" equity and lower occupancy costs are more desirable trade-offs even if they have to live in a smaller housing unit than they now occupy.

The Internal Revenue Code provides some relief in making such decisions. Effective for sales after May 7, 1997, couples filing a joint tax return can exclude up to $500,000 of gain on the sale of their principal residence. Single return filers can exclude up to $250,000. Gains in excess of $500,000/$250,000 are taxable at the capital gains rate. The home must be used as a principal residence for two of the preceding five years. This exclusion does not apply to vacation or second home properties.

The age 55 requirement has been eliminated, therefore this exclusion provision is available to qualifying home owners of any age. This tax-free benefit has no requirement to roll over the proceeds nor to reinvest.

It is important for the real estate broker to know of these income tax provisions, but it is recommended that the sellers be referred to their lawyer or tax advisor to utilize any of these tax relief measures.

CHAPTER 6 — YOUR CLIENTS – THE HOME BUYERS

"... 'Caveat emptor' ... let the buyer beware ... has no place in the vocabulary of a real estate professional." *Charles Goldberg*

The Changing Market

In 1995, census estimates indicated that nearly one half of the population of the United States was under the age of 34. This in part accounts for the fact that a younger buyer has been entering the real estate market ... the "Baby Boomers". Traditionally, the age of the head of households of first time home buyers falls in the range of 33 to 40 years. However, the impact of this pronounced change in population mix has reduced that range to 25 to 33 years. This is a clear cut indication that young couples are not waiting as long to enter the home buying market. Examination of home buying patterns over the past three generations indicates that buyers usually saved their money for a down payment. Six decades ago many lenders talked in terms of 70 to 75 percent mortgages. This made it necessary for prospective buyers to accumulate a relatively large down payment, representing their 25 to 30 percent initial equity. Now that financing terms have been liberalized, there is an opportunity to enter the real estate market much sooner. Today many of these same lenders are willing to accept a 5 or 10 percent down payment on conventional loans provided that the risk is backed up by private mortgage insurance. Also, since World War II, lenders have increased their willingness to make low down payment FHA and VA mortgage loans. This also facilitates entry into the real estate market for first time home buyers.

It isn't financing alone that induces young couples to enter the home buying market. Today's young people, on average, are better educated than previous generations and therefore are able to command a better income. A continuing increase in the standard of living has also created a desire for new, modern innovations in housing. Further, because of the increasing acceptance of the use of credit they don't have time honored reservations about going into debt. "Buy now, pay later" has become a common practice in American society, as opposed to the old "save and then buy for cash." This all suggests that the "savings lag" that preceded home buying in our American society for so many decades has been fast disappearing. Increased income has produced increased confidence and has resulted in an earlier age at marriage and an earlier start in raising families. These young people also have observed how financial leverage is employed in real estate investments. They note how a developer is able to build a project with 10% equity; thus trading on the mortgage money, as is common place in the real estate market. In effect they have carried this same leverage concept over into the area of home ownership. They realize that with a small down payment, say 10%, they are able to command 100% utility of their "dream" home and in the process improve their standard of living. They too are trading on equity. The willingness on the part of these young couples entering the market at this early stage demonstrates a confidence in home ownership and implies a long sustained demand for owner occupied houses.

In addition to the young group of buyers there have been other significant demands for owner occupancy. The propensity to move appears to be a function of age and income as illustrated in the following chart:

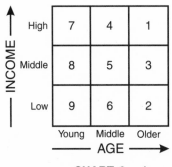

CHART 6 – 1
PROPENSITY TO MOVE
(Degrees of Mobility)

The relative propensity to move is indicated by the numerals, one through nine. The higher the number, the greater the mobility. The number "nine" is assigned to low income, young people. Their length of tenure is the shortest, hence the highest tendency to move. At the other end of the scale, number "one" is assigned to high income, older people, indicating low mobility. It must be recognized that this analysis relates to all residential households, owners and renters. The real estate broker will readily realize that the number "nine" category is dominated by renters rather than by buyers.

As stated in Chapter 2, according to Census Bureau figures, 17 percent of all U.S. households moved every year between 1985 – 1991. Within this framework, the mobility rate was highest for people in their early 20s (35 percent) and lowest for those aged 65 and older (5 percent).

Since the broker depends on turnover, it is imperative to know who is likely to be a mover. As a general statement, older people move less. This is because older heads of households place a higher value on the importance of family ties and stability. As a group, low income families move more frequently than families in the middle income bracket. There is evidence that the tendency to move decreases as income increases. In spite of the fact that older households tend to move less frequently, growth in the size of families and the growing up of children often create a demand for space that outweighs other objections. Therefore, the propensity to move also increases with the number of persons in the household as was described in the previous chapter.

The Younger Market

Reasons for moving are usually practical such as a job change, a change in space needs for the growing family and a motivating force, most noticeable in the post World War II period, that is strong enough to induce households to move simply because they have a compelling desire to own their own homes. This desire is strongest among families with school age children. There is a counterpart to this in the rental category. A more recent factor entering the scene is the desire of post-high school age family members to be emancipated from the household. Although they may be a part of a family household in the same urban area, they have a desire to live on their own. However, in most cases, they lack the financial qualifications to live by themselves. As a result they pool their resources with other young people in the same age bracket having the same housing objectives. By pooling their rental resources several young people are able to chip in and enjoy a housing or rental facility of a higher standard than they would be able to command on their own. In some rental markets this new kind of demand accounts for about 20% of the occupancy in recently constructed apartment buildings. The following table summarizes the characteristics of first time versus repeat buyers.

TABLE 6 – 1 PROFILE: FIRST TIME VS. REPEAT BUYERS - 1992		
CHARACTERISTICS	FIRST TIME BUYER	REPEAT BUYER
Average Age	31 Years	41 Years
Married	66%	72%
Average Family Size	2.5	2.9
Household Income	$51,200	$66,200
Price of Home Purchased	$122,400	$158,000
Average Down Payment	14%	28%

The above characteristics were selected from "WHO'S BUYING HOMES IN AMERICA", The Chicago Title and Trust Family of Title Insurers' 17th Annual Survey of Recent Home Buyers, January 1993.

The Desirability of Home Ownership

Real estate, as a subject of this book, can be viewed in several sets of characteristics. In one sense, real estate in the marketplace is of two kinds . . . a *product* (land and building) as well as a *service* (brokerage). In another sense real estate may be described as having tangible and intangible characteristics. . . physical features (length, breadth, height) and ownership features (rights).

In the term real estate the *estate* portion refers to a collection, or "bundle of rights". These rights might include the right of possession, the right of use and the right of disposition. On the other hand, these rights are not perfect or absolute. The government has four important rights over land: taxation, police power, eminent domain and escheat. The government in effect is saying, "Your rights end where our rights begin." This is much like the concept of freedom in our society where one citizen may be reminded that his or her freedom ends where another's rights begin. It is these rights associated with real estate that are sought after and give the product value in the marketplace.

Real estate market reports in the 1980s might have led one to believe that there was a major shift in preference from home ownership to rental status. It cannot be denied that the number of new units added to the housing inventory was dominated by accelerated construction of rental units. But bearing in mind that total new units increase the existing stock by only two or three percent each year, the impact on the percentage of home ownership has not been dented. A look at housing figures would indicate that both segments are still increasing in absolute numbers. In the rental and home-ownership sections, however, the percentage increase in the 1980s was in favor of rental units.

During the 1980s, rental units comprised more than one out of three new units built. As a result, home ownership ratios dropped a full percentage point from 64.8% to 63.8%. After a decline in the rate of construction of new rental units in the 1990s, to about one out of seven units built, home ownership ratios recovered to their previous highs.

That earlier swing of the pendulum of market demand in favor of renting was a sign of the times. It represented a response to the changing age structure of our population. One of the characteristics emerging from our present day society is the individual quest for time. . . more time. . . in order to be able to do more things and thereby enjoy a better standard of living. New housing can be more easily found in suburbia or the new in-town apartment houses being built. It stands to reason that alternatives to new owner occupied units in suburbia will be introduced into the marketplace. We see evidence of condominium units, town-house units and cluster type developments. Mature cities experiencing redevelopment in the central area are bound to provide both rental and owner occupancy opportunities for those returning to the city.

Back in 1994, President Clinton appealed to Realtors for help with a new initiative to raise home ownership to an historic high by the end of the century. His announced goal: to raise the home ownership rate to at least 66 percent by the year 2000. By the end of 1995 home ownership in the United States reached the 65 percent level.

Owning vs. Renting

Some renters view their non-owner status as a "missed opportunity" in certain respects. To them, renting is a bargain if the landlord charges less than market rent. . . the landlord is subsidizing the tenant. If the landlord is charging market rent. . . the rent then must cover all operating expenses plus a profit. . .in that case the tenant is subsidizing the landlord. The key word appears to be "IF" and it can be used as the focal point in this non-technical summary diagram:

"IF" represents the two classes of benefits of home ownership . . .
. . . intangible and financial

"I-F"

INTANGIBLE
(psychological)

FINANCIAL
(monetary)

Taste of
the "Good Life"

**S
I
P**

Getting your share
. . . of the "Pie"

**P
I
E**

1. **S**ecurity (no need to fear "notice to move")
2. **I**ndependence (no landlord setting the rules)
3. **P**ride of Ownership (enjoying part of one's success)

1. **P**ossible Appreciation (inflationary effect)
2. **I**ncome Tax Advantages (expense deductions)
3. **E**quity Build-up ("forced savings")

**CHART 6 – 2
OWNING vs. RENTING
(Advantages vs. "Rent Receipts")**

The above chart is an outgrowth of the tenant's lament, "If only I had the courage to make a buying decision ten years ago. . . if only I had purchased that two family home when prices were low . . . if only I had purchased that vacant lot and built a home on it back then". Yes, it is much like a litany of missed opportunities.

It is not an overstatement to say, "Home ownership is still the American dream". In the early 1990s, the Federal National Mortgage Association (FNMA) conducted a survey that highlighted the fact that for many Americans owning a home is basic and fundamental to their lives. For the average American, home ownership is one of the most important ways to accumulate wealth over his or her lifetime. It is quite interesting to note that this survey indicates that most Americans would go to extraordinary lengths to own a home, including the following statements:

- 75 percent indicated they would be willing to work 10 years longer in order to own a home
- 80 percent indicated they would rather own a home with a longer commute to work than rent with a shorter commute
- 80 percent indicated they would rather own a home than take a better job in a city where they could only afford to rent
- 66 percent indicated they would own even if it meant getting a second job to pay for the home
- 71 percent indicated they would give up two weeks of vacation a year to be able to own a home

On the other hand, there were some realistic statements. Four out of five respondents stated that they would forego home ownership if they had to overextend themselves financially. Two out of three indicated that home ownership would not be worth it if they had to place a child in day-care because both parents were forced to work in order to afford a home.

A 1994 report from the Bureau of the Census disclosed that American households had a median net worth of $36,623 in 1991. Of that total, home equity represented the largest portion, at 42 percent of the total household net worth.

1995 statistics reveal that 65 out of 100 American families live in an owner-occupied unit. This represents an overwhelming vote of confidence for this type of occupancy. It is important to examine the reasons why families would rather buy than rent their housing unit. It is a mistake to treat all home buyers in one single group, since there are significant subclassifications. The two major groups of home buyers can be classified as follows:

1. First time buyers
2. Repeat buyers

The range of motivations of people in these two categories is rather wide. One can identify general categories such as use and occupancy, investment, speculation and financial advantage. However, motivation tends to be more specific as indicated in the following list:

- Job transfer or promotion
- Living space may be too large or too small
- Desire to get away from urban congestion
- Chance to share in inflation
- Relief from landlord's rules
- Improved security
- Owning is a good investment compared to renting
- A forced savings plan
- Need for more storage space
- Housing related stress
- Need for more space for recreation and entertaining
- Pride of ownership
- Present rent out of proportion to perceived benefits
- Need for more privacy
- Ethnic tradition
- Improve children's opportunities
- Part of long range financial plan
- Desire to express individuality
- Establish a stronger credit rating
- Upgrade family quality of life
- Keeping up with the neighbors
- Urging of relatives (that provide funds)

The above list is admittedly long and certainly does not apply in its entirety to each of the general categories. However, each individual household is affected by several of these motivations, with some packages being more comprehensive than others. The com-

bination of factors that apply to each particular home buying decision from the above list might be termed the "motivation mix."
Such individual mixes indicate that there are other dimensions to
preference for home ownership than those concerning pure economic reasons. The above list includes psychological, social and
physical factors as well. In any case, the motivation must be accompanied by economic capabilities.

Price Range and Monthly Payment

In examining the economic ability of a motivated prospective
home buyer, there are two important factors: 1) the size of the
down payment; and 2) the prospective buyer's income as it relates
to the monthly payment required to amortize the mortgage. But
before determinations of this type can be made there is a more
basic issue to be faced and that is the price to be paid by the prospective buyer. In both of these cases there are widely used rules
of thumb. It is often quoted that one should buy a house two to
two and one-half times one's annual income. This, at best, is an
average of all buyers in the marketplace. This general statement
ignores the impact of the size of the down payment which may
vary from buyer to buyer. Consideration of Schwabe's Law adds
some insight to the situation. The law states that as family incomes increase, the percentage of income used for housing decreases. This means that the proportion of family income used for
housing purposes decreases as families move up the income ladder. However, there is no one single relationship of income to
housing expenditure that applies to every family. Annual income
is not the only determining factor. Other rules of thumb that are
approximately the equivalent of two and one-half times annual
income are:

 a.   100 times the monthly housing payment
 b.   one week's pay equals one percent of the total
      purchase price
 c.   one week's pay equals one month's housing cost
 d.   monthly housing costs times 100 plus down payment

It would seem the more realistic procedure would start with the
prospective buyers' examination of their household operating budget. After considering all of the different kinds of demands on their

148

monthly housing budget, the family should decide how much they can comfortably afford for housing. This then represents the monthly expenditure that they can comfortably use to amortize the mortgage on a house they are considering to purchase. This monthly payment should include principal, interest, real estate taxes and hazard insurance. It might be the equivalent of the cost of comparable housing obtained in the rental market. The debt service portion (principal and interest) of this monthly expenditure can then be translated into a capital amount equal to a mortgage. Therefore, the mortgage that can be handled comfortably plus the available down payment equals the upper price limit for these particular prospective buyers since it is consistent with the family budget. An illustration of this procedure follows, assuming the buyers have a cash down payment of $5,000 and can afford to make monthly housing payments on a 30 year, 7½% mortgage. Property taxes and hazard insurance are estimated at $255 a month.

TABLE 6 – 2 HOME LOAN QUALIFIER		
Buyers: John Jones has an annual gross income of $24,000 ($2,000 per month) Mary Jones has an annual gross income of $12,000 ($1,000 per month) They have these other installment payments: Automobile — $200 per month Furniture — $100 per month Real Estate Taxes are estimated at $2,700 per year Insurance premium is estimated at $360 per year		
	No Installment Debt	Some Installment Debt
Total Gross Monthly Income	$ 3,000	$ 3,000
times lender's upper limit factor	$ X 28%	$ X 36%
Available for Housing Expenditure	$ 840	$ 1,080
Less: Estimated Monthly Escrows for		
Real Estate Tax $ 225		
Insurance $ 30		
Monthly Total $ 255	$ – 255	$ – 255
Less: Monthly Installment Payments	$ – 0	$ – 300
Affordable Monthly Payment (Principal, Interest, Taxes & Insurance)	$ 585	$ 525
Mortgage Loan Factor: 7½% 30 years = $ 7.00 (rate per thousand dollars/mo.)		
(Affordable Monthly Payment divided by Mortgage Loan Factor) x 1000	$ 83,571	$ 75,000
Affordable Mortgage Loan (rounded)	$ 83,500	$ 75,000
Plus: Down payment	$ 5,000	$ 5,000
AFFORDABLE HOUSING AMOUNT	$ 88,500	$ 80,000

Notice that the size of the down payment becomes critical in the determination of the upper limit of the buyer's price range. A buyer with no down payment and no installment payments would be limited to $83,500; a buyer with a $5,000 down payment could handle a $88,500 house as illustrated; while a buyer with $10,000 down could handle a $93,500 transaction.

It should be observed that in the process of selecting an amount for housing as part of the family budget it may be that housing is not rated number one as far as a given family is concerned. Commitments for other kinds of expenditures, such as automobile payments, short term loans, and other forms of consumer credit may reduce the amount available for housing expenditure. Hence, to meet a fixed current and unforeseen expenses the scale of values may be different from household to household since some families are willing to sacrifice more for home ownership than others. It can be demonstrated that 2½ times annual income may be too high in some cases and too low in others. In the case of the household with an annual income of $36,000 a year the rule of thumb suggests that they are capable of handling a $90,000 home. Referring back to the $80,000 house with a $5,000 down payment and a 7½% 30-year mortgage, the manner in which a level monthly payment is calculated is illustrated in Table 6 – 3.

TABLE 6 – 3
BUYER'S MONTHLY PAYMENT ESTIMATE

Principal and Interest ($75,000 Mortgage ÷ 1000 x $7.00)	$525.00
One-twelfth of annual property taxes ($2,700.00 ÷ 12)	225.00
One month's Homeowners coverage insurance ($360.00 ÷ 12)	30.00
Total	**$780.00**

The principal and interest payment is calculated by using the level monthly rate of $7.00 per $1,000 to amortize a 7½% mortgage in 30 years. The $7.00 factor can be found in standard mortgage payment tables. The real property tax amount of $225.00 per month represents one-twelfth of the annual real estate taxes of $2,700.00. The monthly insurance amount of $30.00 represents one-twelfth of a one year hazard insurance policy having a total premium of $360.00.

In general, the majority of buyers are not acquainted with the detailed process of calculating a monthly payment. Therefore it is a definite service for the broker to do so for his or her client. The rule of thumb — monthly payments should not exceed one week's earnings — is more commonly stated as the "four times" rule wherein the monthly earnings should be four times the monthly housing payment. Here again, we are dealing with averages. Examinations of many transactions indicate that Schwabe's law applies. Households with incomes less than $20,000 appear to be using one third of their annual income for housing expense. Households in the lower middle income bracket, $25,000 to $30,000 a year, use about 25% of their income for housing expense. Those in the $40,000 a year bracket use about 20% of their annual income for housing expense. So it can be seen that in the low income groups the ratio is 3 to 1; the lower middle income groups, the ratio is 4 to 1; which appears to be typical, and in the higher income groups the ratio can increase to 5 to 1 or more. Therefore, the 4 to 1 rule must be adjusted in line with the level of income, except in cases where you are dealing with the average category. It seems as if typical buyers are more concerned with net cash flow than with the detailed dimensions of the transaction in which they are engaging. The buyers appear to be more concerned with the size of the monthly payment, the cash outflow, rather than the dimensions of interest rate, the amount of interest, the rate of principal reduction and the like. A term of 25 or 30 years brings minimum reaction since they feel they will resell the property long before that period. But as long as real estate prices hold steady or increase they have no special problem. As a matter of fact it turns out to be a form of forced savings, an opportunity for them to build up equity.

A closer look at the impact of interest rates reveals the following: The $525.00 a month level principal and interest payment referred to earlier related to a 30 year mortgage. This means that the buyer will pay $525.00 a month or a total of $6,300.00 each year. Over a 30 year period total level payments amount to $189,000.00. Subtracting the original amount of the $75,000.00 mortgage which is totally repaid at the end of 30 years, leaves a difference of $114,000.00. This represents the total interest paid for the 30 year period or an amount greater than the original principal repaid. This is a cost of home ownership that is not often identified by the buyer. It does suggest that if the buyers are concerned with the size of the interest to be paid, they can offset it by increasing the size of the down payment, thereby reducing the mortgage and reducing the interest. However, it should be observed that this kind of reasoning falls within the realm of opportunity costs. The buyer paying interest on a mortgage is no better off than the buyer who pays cash, because the buyer paying cash is in effect foregoing the interest that one could have earned on the money. In short, if the buyers have an opportunity to invest at the mortgage interest rate they should be indifferent to whether they pay cash or use a mortgage.

Not to be overlooked is the matter of normal price appreciation. In 1949, a well-respected midwestern university professor predicted that "if you are waiting for residential real estate prices to come down, you are going to have an eternal wait!" Of course, there have been short-run price corrections, but in the long run residential real estate prices of well maintained properties have trended upward. Stock market observers are acquainted with the notion of what goes up can come down. . . what about housing? There are two main factors that could drive down the price of existing housing:

1. If new houses become cheaper to build than resales with comparable features, and
2. If severe unemployment causes a significant number of mortgage delinquencies in a local market.

It should be noted that even a seemingly harmless average inflation rate of 4% a year will cause prices to double every 18 years. In 30 years, and at the same annual rate of 4%, prices would be increased 3¼ times!

It generally follows that most households experience an increase in income during their productive years. This would mean that they have a greater capability of handling housing expenses in later years as opposed to earlier years. Therefore, it might be advisable for families needing larger housing facilities to seek a longer term mortgage loan in order to spread the payments out for a longer time period. If at some time in the future they are able to handle larger payments, the pre-payment privilege would give them the opportunity. It follows that the higher the down payment the lower the amount of the mortgage loan. The greater the equity in the house, the smaller the monthly mortgage payment, the lower the total interest cost over the years and the easier it becomes to obtain a mortgage loan. Of course, in an inflationary economy, present dollars have greater value than future dollars, therefore each household must make its own value decisions in allocating present money for present benefits. It has been observed in the housing market that the younger group of buyers is not buying for as long range of occupancy as previous generations. They accept the notion that they may make several moves during the course of their household cycle rather buying a single home that will serve the needs of the household over an extremely long term.

Resistance to Increasing Interest Rates

There is evidence that some buyers display a special kind of resistance to increasing interest rates. The resistance seems to build up at even rate levels of interest. By that it is meant that while the interest rate increases by fractions above the whole number, like 6¼%, 6½%, 6¾%, the consumer seems to accept it. But as soon as it hits the next highest whole number, in this case 7%, consumers tend to display resistance. This might be compared to the kind of stock market resistance that is seen at even 1000 levels of the Dow Jones Industrial average, such as the 3000 level, 4000 level, 5000 level. There tends to be a resistance on the part of the participants in the stock market as the Dow attempts to pass these particular significant marks. And so it is in the real estate market when the interest rate approaches the next highest level. As the rate approaches the next full percentage point, noticeable consumer resistance sets in. But this is usually temporary in nature and perhaps of only a few months duration. After this initial period, consumers become accustomed to the higher rate and then resume regular buying habits. In 1996, interest rates in midwestern markets ranged from 7.5 percent to 8.4 percent for residential mortgages on owner-occupied properties. There was ample evidence of consumer resistance to these higher interest rates. However, it is somewhat difficult to explain this resistance when one realizes that at the very same time the consumer was paying $4.50 on a hundred dollars for an automobile loan – the equivalent of paying 9 percent a year. The same consumer was paying 1 percent per month on an unpaid balance at a credit union – the equivalent of 12 percent a year. Some charge card accounts, both for department stores and banks, were getting 1½% per month on the unpaid balance – equivalent to an annual rate of 18 percent. Local loan companies were charging even higher rates of interest. In summary, the consumers were paying 9 percent on their automobiles, 12 percent at their credit union, 18 percent on charge accounts and as high as 24 percent on short term loans to local finance companies. On that basis one wonders why there was any resistance to 8 percent real estate mortgage loans. This 8 percent was in fact one of the more attractive interest rates to the consumer in the overall money market. However, there are other dimensions to these interest rates that are not exactly comparable. For instance, the automobile loan and the charge account at a department store are short term commitments, most of them running from 12 to 36 months. The amounts in general were below $10,000; therefore the consumers felt they had the financial capabilities to liquidate them during this period. On the other hand, with a real estate loan, the consumer is looking at terms of 25 years and 30 years, and of course much larger dollar amounts, perhaps 4 to 5 times the upper limit of consumer loans. Because of the longer duration of real estate loans, there may be a greater reluctance to make a long term commitment at a relatively high interest rate. On the other hand, experience tells us that the average length of the real estate mortgage is only 7 or 8 years. If this is the case, then, the average consumer, in fact, is not making a long term commitment. The real test is not so much in the interest rate itself but the size of the monthly payment on that mortgage loan. Consumers look at it on a cash outlay basis. If they feel they can handle the payment in spite of the interest rate, they then compare it to the comparable cash outlay for renting similar quarters and make judgment accordingly.

The Broker's Role – Agency Disclosure

The broker is in a unique position as a marketer. While he or she does not take title to the property, they act as an intermediaries. The broker is the person whose services are usually needed as much by the buyer as the seller. Thus it might be said that the broker has one hand on the selling strings and one hand on the buying strings of most transactions. The broker uses the tools of knowledge, experience, sound judgment and a sense of fairness toward all parties concerned to pull these strings together and thus bind the seller and buyer in a successful transaction. Just like the sellers, the buyers often find themselves engrossed in what seems to be an unmanageable and confusing situation. The successful broker recognizes this. Although he or she is the agent for the seller, the listing broker shows empathy toward the buyer and makes a concerted effort to remove this shroud of confusion so that the buyer is able to make a sound purchase decision which will result in satisfaction for the seller as well as the buyer.

The lack of understanding of the broker's legal role in a developing transaction was revealed in a 1978 survey conducted by the Federal Trade Commission. The survey showed that over 70% of the buyers thought they were being represented by the selling broker. Also, nearly 80% of the sellers thought the selling broker represented the buyer. Since then most states have enacted some form of agency disclosure laws. It must be emphasized that disclosing agency relationships has become an extremely important part of doing business. In general, the law requires all licensees to make agency disclosures *before* showing a property, *before* taking pertinent information, *before* getting into negotiations. The law also requires that a written disclosure be signed *before* the buyer makes an offer on the property. The various forms of agency . . . seller agency, buyer agency and dual agency . . . will be discussed in much greater detail in Chapter 12 – Your Career: Professional Status.

Buyers may be confused individuals since the residential market has limited comparability among properties. Most buyers lack adequate knowledge of market prices and property values. To add to this confusion, the housing desires and needs of the buyers are often at variance with each other and the household's pocketbook.

Thus, with proper disclosure, the successful broker acts in the interests of the buyer as well as the seller. In doing so he or she will educate and assist the buyer in selecting the most suitable property. The professional tends to counsel rather than to sell. After complete agency disclosure, the position of the broker is loaded with genuine responsibility. To act in the interest of both parties requires the highest ability as negotiator and judge. The broker must be certain that both parties are honest and fair with each other. A good transaction is one that benefits all parties concerned. In short, each participant — the buyer, the seller and the broker — achieve their desired objectives. There really is no shortcut to a sale, but doing a competent and professional job at the time of listing certainly eliminates unnecessary work at the selling stage. As a professional, it is the broker's obligation to be well informed of market information. The professional broker is an expert rendering information to non-experts who are genuinely in need of his or her service. The buyers are faced with the monumental task of scanning thousands of lines in the classified section of the newspaper in order to find a property that may suit their needs. As an alternative, buyers can consult a broker who will provide convenience and efficiency in finding suitable properties. This is an important aspect of the broker's service and function. Integrity is important since, in many cases, the buyer will look to the broker for advice. Buyers characteristically develop a state of uncertainty when it comes to critical decision making time. Therefore, they often turn to the broker for advice and guidance. It should be recognized that the costs of owning are more than just the purchase price of the house: continuing maintenance, standard of living commensurate with the neighborhood and gradual escalation of housing costs due to normal inflation. Marginal buyers with fixed incomes may find home ownership impossible as they take on these increasing costs and therefore may be forced into a selling situation in short order. If it is expected that housing costs will rise through the passage of time or the development of a given neighborhood, then there should be accompanying prospects of increase in income on the part of the buyer in order to offset these future increases. The total function of the broker is to help the buyer to focus on a decision that will give consideration to price range, size to suit the family needs, style of housing to suit the family living standards and other features including neighborhood. A composite of all of these dimensions makes up the final decision. In the purchase of existing homes, not all of these objectives may be achieved. While there must be some kind of trade-off, there should be some kind of ordinal ranking of these requirements to insure that the most important factors are met or satisfied. In this respect, counseling does not emphasize salesmanship but works toward a goal of "satisfying" the needs of prospective buyers in accordance with the relative importance of those needs.

The broker should never discourage the buyer from attempting to obtain legal counsel. Only qualified attorneys are legally able to render legal advice. Experience indicates that transactions where buyers and sellers are represented by legal counsel tend to flow more smoothly toward a successful completion. For a broker to give legal advice is to attempt to practice law without a license, but he or she should have sufficient legal background to recognize those situations that require them to recommend legal counsel. Regarding the earlier statements made as to the limited knowledge of the buyer, it should be pointed out that these characteristics generally applied to buyers of generations past. Today the trend is toward more rapid turnover in home ownership. Whereas in generations past people lived in a house for 20 or 30 years, now the average occupancy time is perhaps 7 or 8 years. As a result, the buyers in today's market are upgrading their experience because of more exposure and are better qualified than buyers in previous generations.

However, the level of information which buyers possess is still less than complete and in some ways unsatisfactory. Therefore buyers definitely need the service of a real estate broker.

This shorter turnover period does suggest that housing needs should be interpreted accordingly. In other words, a buyer should be looking for housing needs for the next 10 years rather than the next 20 years because the normal expectancy is that he or she will move about every 5 to 10 years rather than every 20 years. Even though buyers are becoming more knowledgeable as compared to their predecessors they still display a great amount of hesitancy in making the final decision. This is where the broker can be extremely helpful. Analysis of the motivation, financial qualification, household needs and a reasonable range of alternatives set the basis for making an intelligent recommendation.

Sources of Buyers

The volume of prospective buyers varies with the state of the real estate market. In a seller's market they are plentiful, in a buyer's market they tend to be more scarce and much more independent. In most communities the classified section of the local newspaper serves as the source of market information. This seems to be the most common form of attracting prospective buyers. A second source is the for sale sign. In addition, there is direct mail advertising, radio, television, public transportation, advertising and direct referrals. The quality of the buyer might be related to the degree of effort that the buyer spends on coming in contact with the real estate broker. Obviously the prospect uses less effort to contact the broker by telephone than if one pays a visit to the broker's office. The broker has less control over a prospective buyer inquiring by telephone as opposed to the buyer who pays a personal visit to the office. Other forms of contact could be at open houses, or by the broker paying a visit or contacting a prospective buyer by telephone. The broker could also search for buyers via direct mail. There is no set pattern for analyzing the quality of buyers as to source. However, one survey of buyers showed that 80 percent of home buyers came from an area within a radius of one-half mile of the listed property. This suggests that in this particular case a search either by telephone, mail, or by direct contact could be quite fruitful if limited to a one-half mile radius around the listing.

Where do buyers come from? Obviously there are many sources. According to research in the early 1990s by the National Association of Realtors, seven of the most important ways that prospective buyers first come in contact with the real estate sales associate who assisted them with a purchase are as follows:

- Agent was referred by a friend or previous customer   26%

- Agent was a friend or neighbor   19%
- Ad call   14%
- Sign call   11%
- Met agent at open house   11%
- Walked into office   7%
- Former client or customer   5%

Relocation of families is becoming more important in our American way of life. Relocation can take place as a result of a job transfer, urban renewal project, expressway construction or other public or private improvement. Such sources can readily be identified through stories and announcements in the local newspapers.

Other studies in cities across the country indicate that buyers come from three major sources in equal proportions. In general, one third of the buyers respond to classified newspaper advertising. Another third contact the broker as a result of a for sale sign on the property. The remaining third can be attributed to personal referrals and other forms of contact. Referral business is perhaps one of the highest forms of business compliment to a broker. The well known, competent broker in a community will always find a certain amount of natural buyer attraction because of the reputation he or she has developed from past satisfied customers. This will result in referral from previous customers or the return to the market by past customers who have entered a new phase of their household cycle and thus have had their housing needs and financial means altered. Also, it is often very rewarding to communicate with renters and newcomers in the community. There are many different ways of attracting or finding buying prospects. It would seem that it would be easier to find buyers than sellers. But in general, the buyers' level of motivation is more intense than the sellers'. Buyers are aggressively focusing on a clear and definite objective. In a way, sellers seem to play more of a defensive role. Buyers focus all of their energies and try to satisfy their desires by looking at a specific property. They are going from the general to the specific. Once buyers have narrowed down their choices, their level of enthusiasm runs rather high as they take positive aggressive action. They are in pursuit. On the other hand, sellers faced with this kind of enthusiasm are relegated to a defensive position where they try to justify price. When sellers hold out for their price, the negotiating battle starts. The charged-up buyer tries to change the mind of the defensive seller who holds out for a price. Buyers seem more excited about the possible transaction because they expect to convert the house into a home. Sellers think in terms of leaving their home and accepting dollars in exchange. The buyers will experience benefits over the long run while the sellers will receive benefits in the short-run. Buyers pursue expected utility and future enjoyment while sellers seek immediate dollars. Because of the nature of the real estate market it is easy for buyers to find out who sellers are since sellers readily declare themselves by advertising. On the other hand, sellers have to play a waiting game since they cannot identify who real buyers are until they come forward with an offer to purchase.

Buyer Psychology – Consumer Behavior

National averages indicate that one out of thirteen households will buy a new or existing home during the current calendar year. These are qualified buyers having the determination to enter the marketplace and make a housing decision. The characteristics of the typical buyer can be described in the form of a "profile," representing an average or composite of the characteristics of all home buyers within a given year. A profile for a recent year is illustrated in the following chart, using the same data source as in Table 6 – 1 earlier in this chapter.

TABLE 6 – 4 PROFILE OF A TYPICAL HOME BUYER (Conventional Financing)
Median Price of Home Purchased $141,000
Loan to Value Ratio .... 69% or more
Initial Mortgage Amount $97,000
Total Monthly Housing Expenses as a Percent of Monthly Income (debt service + real estate tax + fixed charges) 33%
Length of Mortgage .... 28 years
Type of Home .... New 20%
.... Older 80%
Age of Buyers .... First Time Buyers 31 years
.... Repeat Buyers 41 years
Two Income Families 81%
Household Income $58,800
Marital Status .... 69% married
Average Family Size 2.7
Period of Time from Look to Buy .... 5 months
Number of Houses Looked at 16

160

It should be noted that the characteristics depicted in Table 6–4 relate to the average home buyer in the United States in 1992, but with the qualification that the financing had been arranged on a conventional basis. This implies that the buyer had a down payment anywhere between 5 and 30 percent of the transaction price, with a first mortgage complementing it in order to spell the total purchase price. The range of age of head of household in this category is about 30 to 40 years. This is in sharp contrast to transactions that are financed through government insured and government guaranteed loans, such as FHA and VA loans. Profiles of buyers in these categories indicate that the age of the head of household is between 25 and 30 years. An important observation is that purchasers of residential properties, for the most part, consist of family groups and related members of a household, compared to a noticeable number of non-related households in the rental category.

Experienced real estate sales people will testify to the fact that the prospective buyer's initial preference for location is not too deeply rooted. They may express a preference for one area of town and end up making a purchase in another area of town. This is not to say that they changed their minds but that the submarket in which they were shopping was fragmented. In other words, their submarket was not concentrated in one specific area but scattered about in different sections of town. On that basis they were able to consider alternate properties of the same price range, offering about the same utility. They were indifferent as to whether they purchased on one side of town or another since their qualifications for housing limited them to a particular bracket. The consumer may have expressed preference by stating a kind of property in a specific area without being aware of similar properties available in other parts of town. The prospective buyer may discover that they have other alternatives, consider those alternatives, and select from among them. Perhaps the buyers can best express their desire for the kind of property they seek by citing an example, like "a colonial on the northwest side of town." Buyers who are also present property owners tend to use their present property as a basis for comparison when shopping for a newer home. Renters don't have this opportunity because their comparisons are made against the rental facilities that they now occupy. Many marketing surveys indicate that "area" is the number one factor of importance to home buyers.

Price does not give buyers many alternatives since they are locked within a specific price range commensurate with the size of their down payment and income. Buyers have little range of choice with regard to price. A second constraint in making a purchase would be the needs of the household members, in terms of number of bedrooms, number of baths, eating areas, recreational areas, yard space and garage space. These minimum standards are set by the present conditions and needs of the household members. There is little "trading" that can be done in this regard. So price and physical facilities offer a limited range of alternatives, while the greatest range of selection may be in the category of area. If households are interested in new housing, they most likely will have to consider suburban areas where new subdivisions are developed. That is where the vacant land is and where most new homes are built.

Home purchases are made by adults. During the course of their normal life expectancy, they may enter into real estate transactions three or four times. This means that they have limited opportunity to accumulate real estate experience. We have also seen that the tendency to move in the residential area, among other reasons, is affected by seasonal variation. Greater numbers of people are willing to move during warmer months than in colder months. This variation occurs on an annual basis. Variations related to longer time periods are affected by the household cycle — the change in household status from formation to growing to maturing to contracting. Of course, other factors enter into the picture as well. Economic factors, such as change in income or change in employment could bring about a decision to buy or to acquire another kind of housing.

The buying process is a drawn out one. Studies show that the typical buyer is engaged in the home buying process anywhere from four to five months at varying levels of intensity. This kind of market exposure helps to acquaint the buyer with market values, availability and prices. It seems as if buyers are hesitant to make their final decision until they have had ample opportunity to shop the current market, become acquainted with it, and have a basis for making a decision.

Another side of why and when people buy houses can be associated with the psychological stages through which the head of the household passes in the course of one's natural life. The process might be compared to the raising of grapes in the vineyard as often cited in the bible. Years 15 to 28 might be described as the "fertilizing stage." During this time period there is a tendency to go "where the action is," to get involved in popular activities and popular issues of the day. Because of this extensive commitment to outside activities there is a low desire to get involved with the responsibilities of home ownership. As a result, people in this category are likely to be renters, particularly in apartment buildings where the amount of housing care is at a minimum. Ages 28 to 44 might be labeled the "pruning stage." The psychological drive in this stage compels the head of the household to play the role of being the good provider. He or she has a strong desire to provide a detached single family home, a good car, education for the children and perhaps start some kind of security program. Ages 44 to 58 are called the "harvesting stage." At this point the head of the household has a strong desire to rule and to impart his or her wisdom to others. Having attained financial success, he or she has a feeling of security and desires to pass on some of this goodness to others. Being long on experience, he or she has a success story to tell, and as a result can enhance one's status by doing so. In most cases the head of the household has a captive audience with school age children to listen to his or her wise words. The final stage is 59 and older. This stage might be labeled as the "wine tasting period." This is the time when retired people enjoy recollecting their past experiences, pleasures and successes. It perhaps is the least productive stage of the life cycle. People have a tendency to withdraw from society more so than before. They tend to associate with people in their own age category. Senior citizen groups are typical of this state. This is in sharp contrast to the historical pattern in our American way of life where relatives provided for retired people by permitting them to become a part of the household of the younger couple. The growth of nursing homes and retirement homes is ample evidence that retirees are becoming disassociated with members of their families and are congregating in groups. The housing habits of people in the reminiscent category tend to be somewhat stable as the retirees attempt to hang on to their present housing facilities, extending the memories and experiences over past years. Only when they face a financial or physical problem are they willing to surrender what appears to be an overly-large housing facility far beyond their needs. It is in the pruning category from 28 to 44 that we find most of the major decisions are made. This is when heads of households buy homes, make their major investments and acquire significant insurance programs.

The desire for special features in a home is qualified by the type of housing selection considered — new or existing. In the case of a new house to be built, the features or the desire for features can be satisfied as long as they are within the financial reach of the prospective buyer. On the other hand, it is more difficult to satisfy desires for specific features in an existing home. Chances are that the prospective buyer will have to rank features in order of importance and may have to make some sacrifices in order to get the best combination of features that will satisfy their needs. Seldom does a buyer of an existing home find all of the features that he or she had searched for originally. As in the case of new home purchases, the number of features is limited by financial capability.

At times it appears as if some buyers are playing the role of actor, as they participate in the home buying process. They take on roles that appear to be inconsistent with their character. For example, inexperienced buyers are at times reluctant to admit their inexperience. Accordingly, they take on a role of being a suspicious buyer, doubting facts and representations, or they may take on the role of a defensive buyer, deliberately procrastinating and taking a lot of time before arriving at a decision. Inexperienced buyers are in the greatest need of counseling, but they may resist counseling by their decision to play the role of a suspicious or defensive buyer. Therefore, it is imperative for a real estate broker to make an extra effort in communicating and in building a warm relationship with inexperienced buyers of this type. In such cases, it would be advisable for the broker to explain things in as simple terms as possible and avoid using the jargon of the trade, since the inexperienced buyer may not understand technical terms. Rather than admit one's ignorance, this type of buyer withdraws partway from the conversation. The buyer finds out that it is easier to say "no," or "we'll think it over," simply because they don't understand the terms of the transaction. On the other hand, the experienced buyer welcomes information, cooperation and assistance from the real estate broker because they have gone through the tedious process and realize that the most convenient way of acquiring information, getting assistance and completing the transaction is by working along with the real estate broker. From a long-range point of view it makes good sense for the real estate broker to treat all prospects in a professional manner. The successful broker realizes that today's buyers will eventually become tomorrow's sellers and a source of future business.

Creating Buyer Interest

The key to creating buyer interest is to gain the buyer's confidence. Because of the infrequency of real estate transactions the buyer may hesitate following the broker's suggestions. But once an aura of confidence has been established, a good deal of resistance melts away. Residential real estate is not sold over the telephone. In order to effect a transaction, the buyer, the broker and the house have to be at the same place in order to develop some degree of interest. Therefore, it is imperative for the real estate broker to "sell the showing" first. In answering a prospect's call on the telephone the prime objective is not to sell the house over the telephone, but to create a sufficient amount of interest that will cause the inquirer to agree to see the property in person. There is little room in real estate selling for the so-called "hard sell." The long term implications of professional conduct suggest that "soft sell" or counseling is much more advisable and will turn out to be more profitable. It is important for the broker to understand the motivation and the needs of the buyer. In fact, the broker must visualize living in the house, but under the conditions of the prospective buyer. Brokers cannot look at the property through their own eyes, but through the eyes of the buyer. Each buyer has his or her own image of a castle. The diversity of motivations, buyer types and the broker's own personality forbid forming any generalized method for handling prospects. Proper information, sound advice and professional guidance will set the stage for a logical conclusion. In many cases, the buyer says "no," and stalls for time simply because he or she wants more information than what was given. That buyer lacks confidence. Perhaps the broker has not properly assessed the needs of the buyer. Perhaps the prospect's finances have not been properly qualified. Perhaps the broker had not properly presented the property in that he or she has not identified all of the advantages. Perhaps the broker has failed to properly answer the objections raised by the buyer. Or, in a common error, the broker tries to outguess the behavior of the prospective buyer. Here again it is strongly suggested to avoid cliches and other special language of the real estate field, since these terms may not be completely understood by the buyer. In summary, the real estate broker should serve as a source of information, provide answers to questions deemed important by the buyer, give advice and guidance where requested and assist the buyer in the real estate decision making process.

The Offer to Purchase

When the house hunting process has reached the stage where the broker confidently feels that the buyers would be well housed within their financial capabilities, then it is proper to move toward the preparation of an offer to purchase. The time to prepare the offer to purchase can be ascertained through a series of easy questions, often referred to as "soft closes." These questions give an indication of the thinking of the prospective buyer. For example, the broker might ask, "Do you think the distance from this house to the school is too far for the children to walk?" If the prospective buyer gives a sincere answer it indicates that he or she has given thought to actually living in this house. Another kind of question would be, "Is the distance from this house to your place of employment too far?" Still another would be, "Will your bedroom furniture fit into the master bedroom?", or "Will your family be able to take most of its meals in the kitchen?" The basis of all of these questions is to determine whether or not the prospects have given serious thought about actually living in this house. If the answers sound comfortable and not strained, then one can assume that the buyers are favorably disposed toward the particular property. On the other hand, if the answers seem strained or the prospects seem alarmed and react in a defensive fashion, it would appear that the broker is pushing the issue too far and had better give more information before trying to close to the point of drawing up the offer to purchase.

When the opportunity presents itself, it is much more advisable to draw the offer to purchase in the real estate office. This is an accepted place of doing business and there is no misunderstanding between the broker and the prospective buyer as to what is taking place. In cases where the prospective buyer is reluctant to discuss an offer to purchase it indicates that he or she has been inadequately informed or is not interested in the property. Market studies indicate that brokers show about 15 or 16 properties on average to each prospective buyer. The buyer is interested in alternatives and is interested in viewing the available selections. In cases where one or two properties have been shown, some resistance might be related to the buyer's feeling that he or she has not seen an adequate segment of what is available for sale. A buyer may entertain doubts that perhaps something better is available that has yet to be seen.

The offer to purchase is in writing and it is a legal way by which buyers and sellers can start the negotiation process. The fact that the document is called an offer to purchase indicates that some negotiation would take place. Market statistics show that 7 out of 10 offers are accepted and result in completed transactions. This indicates that 3 out of 10 are unsuccessful efforts in completing a transaction. It is important for the broker to appreciate the position of the prospective buyer in completing the offer to purchase. For the broker this is routine and it is done regularly, but for the buyer this is something he or she hasn't done in perhaps five or ten years, or ever. Therefore, the buyer may feel insecure and show signs of lacking assurance. The broker should not hesitate to encourage the buyer to take the completed offer to his or her lawyer for review and recommendations prior to presenting it to the seller. This helps to condition the buyer's thinking in a positive fashion. It also reminds the buyer of the seriousness of the transaction into which he or she is about to partake. Typically, asking prices are above market value. Correspondingly, the buyer's offering price tends to be lower than market value. Broad based statistics from one midwestern state's multiple listing systems show that transaction prices are about 93 percent of asking prices. This reveals that a certain amount of bargaining takes place. One of the unusual characteristics of the real estate market, particularly the bargaining process, is that there seems to be some reliance on the trite statement of "Let's split the difference." There doesn't seem to be any logical basis for this kind of psychology in bargaining. There could be if both parties were bargaining from realistic bases. However, the asking price is subjective in nature and may be a fabrication of the seller. It may have no precise relation to market value. By the same token, the buyer in the process of trying to sound out the lowest possible offer that the seller will take starts at a subjective level as well. Therefore, the difference between the asking price and the offering price is not related to a common base. However, market behavior is such that it seems fair and honest to meet halfway, to split the difference. As a result, a good number of transactions are completed based on this weakly grounded approach. However, if this is a kind of psychology employed in the marketplace then it has market relevance because it represents actual consumer behavior. It seems ironic that buyers and sellers should bargain so aggressively with each other with regard to the price and pay much less attention to other important dimensions of the real estate transaction. They may be willing to commit themselves to the purchase of a $125,000 or $150,000 house, yet skimp on other kinds of expenditures such as a professional appraisal, updated title evidence, surveys, or legal advice. The cost of the last four items is relatively low when compared to possible losses that could arise in a real estate transaction.

It is the broker's responsibility to present all offers in writing to the seller. It is the seller's privilege to counter, accept or reject offers. In cases where the seller thinks the price or any other feature of the offer is unsatisfactory, he or she can proceed to set forth terms desired in the form of a counteroffer. But the seller should be apprised of the fact that once he or she inserts a counteroffer, they are then changing the offer to purchase, automatically nullifying the original offer made by the buyer. In effect, the counteroffer is an offer to sell that is tendered to the buyer. The offer to purchase takes on special significance when it is accepted in writing and signed copies are delivered to both parties. At this point the offer ripens into a binding contract. Failure of either party to carry out the contract doesn't affect the right of a broker to collect a commission. It is assumed that the broker is familiar with the closing procedures that would involve extension of the title evidence to date, the proration of taxes and insurance, or the cancellation and acquisition of new insurance, the recording of the satisfaction of the existing mortgage, the acquiring of financing, the passing of title by means of a deed and recording of the deed, mortgage and other papers attendant to the transaction. All of these services — the title search, the insurance matters, the survey, etc. — are services rendered by professionals in the field. It is expected that the real estate broker will not be a "do-it-yourselfer" but turn to these professionals for services in connection with completing the transaction. The transaction is not completed at the time the deed is transferred and the commission is collected. Professional service implies a continuing relationship. There may be other questions that are asked by both the seller and the buyer long after the transaction is closed and the broker should be available to answer such questions. It is good business to render such services on a continuing basis because this too provides a source of renewal business as well as referral business.

CHAPTER 7 — YOUR CLIENTS –
THE INVESTORS

"The right investment is equal to a lifetime of toil." *Charles L. Paine*

The typical real estate broker enters the field via the residential route. This is understandable since the residential segment of the real estate business is the easiest to learn and is the one that which most people have the highest degree of familiarity. The residential field is also the most active segment of the real estate market. For these reasons the residential area is a natural point of entry. As the real estate broker gains more knowledge, experience and success in the residential area, he or she begins to identify additional opportunities in the real estate investment field. Dealing in investment properties represents a challenge on a higher plane since it involves much more knowledge than the residential sector. The residential sector, as referred to above, relates to residential-owner occupancy. There is also a residential sector in the investment field, namely apartment houses. The average transaction price in the investment field is considerably higher than the average transaction price in the owner occupied residential field. Investment real estate also represents a higher status in the hierarchy of real estate brokerage. The fact that it does represent higher status implies that the broker needs a higher level of education and a higher level of experience in order to operate effectively in this field.

Anyone purchasing real estate is, in fact, investing in real estate. Real estate investment value represents the present value of future benefits. In the residential occupancy field these benefits are measured in terms of utility and other intangible values that are

170

rather difficult to quantify and are determined by each user. Some examples of these benefits are listed below:

1. Use and occupancy
2. Security (certainty of tenure): no worry about renewing a lease
3. Eventual ownership (free and clear): forced savings through debt service
4. Source of future capital needs (remortgaging the property)
5. Pride of ownership (the great "American dream")

On the other hand, investment real estate returns are measured in dollars and cents. Therefore, the benefits can be measured more accurately. The investor in real estate has three main objectives:

1. return *on* investment
2. return *of* investment
3. income tax advantages

These major benefits, as well as others, are listed in Chart 7–1 on the following page.

As can be seen in the previously mentioned chart, there are sub-areas of these major objectives. The return on investment can take the form of realized periodic income that may be in the form of the excess of cash received over cash paid out – net cash flow. It can also be expressed in the form of net income as determined by normal accounting procedures. Another kind of return on investment is the unrealized periodic increase in equity that results from gradual amortization of the mortgage. This equity increase can also take place as a result of increase in market value appreciation. However, in both the case of amortization and appreciation the gain will not be realized until the property is sold in the marketplace.

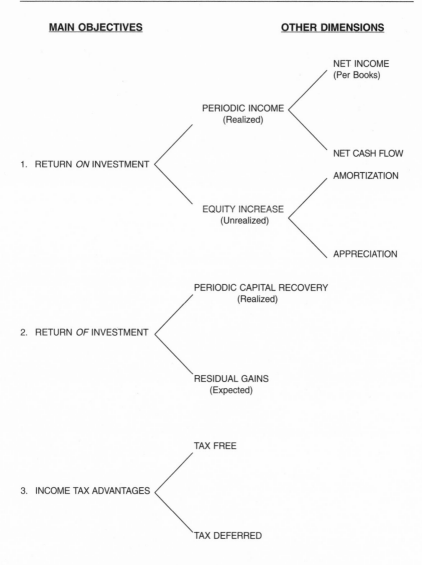

MAIN OBJECTIVES

OTHER DIMENSIONS

NET INCOME
(Per Books)

PERIODIC INCOME
(Realized)

NET CASH FLOW

1. RETURN *ON* INVESTMENT

AMORTIZATION

EQUITY INCREASE
(Unrealized)

APPRECIATION

PERIODIC CAPITAL RECOVERY
(Realized)

2. RETURN *OF* INVESTMENT

RESIDUAL GAINS
(Expected)

TAX FREE

3. INCOME TAX ADVANTAGES

TAX DEFERRED

CHART 7 – 1
REAL ESTATE INVESTOR'S – RETURNS AND BENEFITS

Return of investment takes the form of periodic capital recovery or residual gains. Periodic capital recovery can be realized as a portion of net cash flow received. The building improvement portion of real estate is a dissipating asset. The investor expects to be compensated for the return on the investment plus a portion of the investment, a kind of capital refund. Expected residual gains might be the equity portion of the reversion; that is the liquidated sales price over and above actual capital inputs.

Income tax advantages fall into two broad categories: those that are tax free and those that are tax deferred. Tax free implies that no income tax need be paid on the particular income or gain. In the case of tax deferred income, the payment of tax is put off until some future date.

This summary of the terms and objectives of investors includes the reasons why individuals are willing to come into the real estate market and invest. It may be all or some of these objectives depending upon the financial standing and tax position of the investor. Obviously, high income investors are more concerned about tax advantages than low income investors dealing in smaller properties.

Kinds of Investors

Individual investors combine objectives in different size packages. In the process of combining investor objectives one can identify four distinctive kinds of investors:

Kinds of Investors:	Objectives:
1. Investor for use	Occupancy, utility, inflationary hedge
2. Short term investor	Capital gains, net cash flow
3. Long term investor	Regular income, possible long term gain
4. Creditor-lender	Interest, fees, recovery of capital

The owner-occupant can be found in all classes of real estate. Such an investor could be the owner-occupant of a detached single family home; the owner-occupant residing in a unit of a duplex or four-family; or the owner-occupant of a retail store. A corporation that purchases and operates a manufacturing plant is an owner-occupant in the industrial area.

The short term investor is more popularly known as a developer or speculator. Traditionally, he or she has entered into real estate ventures with a low down payment and relies heavily on mortgage financing. The same is true of the smaller investor buying residential income properties.

The long term investor is typified by a larger institution, such as a life insurance company, pension fund or university. Long term investors tend to purchase real estate and hold it over the long term, relying on the periodic income that the property provides. While they are not speculating in the market, they would hope that the investment would not lose value but rather appreciate and therefore have some hope of eventually realizing a long term gain.

The creditor-lender is looking for the periodic collection of interest on the mortgage loan and the orderly amortization of that debt thereby recovering the capital lent out. It is important to identify the four kinds of investors in order to be aware of the objectives for each category.

There is a relationship between the physical real estate and the kind of investor. For example, a developer may build a four-family apartment building. This is an example of a short term investor. That developer in turn may sell it to an owner-occupant who lives in one of the four units and rents out the other three. This is an example of an investor for use. In the process of purchasing it, the owner-occupant may turn to the creditor-lender in order to acquire the necessary financing. And finally, the owner-occupant may decide to sell the property to a real estate investment fund, a long term investor.

It is also possible for an investor to move from one category to another. For example, a developer might put up an apartment building and having failed to find a buyer, or being impressed with the productivity of the apartment building, decides to keep the building for the long term. In that case he or she switches from a short term to a long term investor. In view of these investment objectives it can be seen that the nature of motivation in buying investment real estate is quite different from buying real estate for owner occupancy. The motivation is centered around periodic income as well as the gain at the time of sale, ordinary income plus capital gain. These benefits are measured in dollars.

The objectives of the investor take on more meaningful form when one looks at the 3 major steps involved in the real estate investment process. They are:

1. acquisition
2. management
3. disposition

The real estate broker is involved in all three steps. In the acquisition stage the broker is involved in the selling of the property to the new owner. In the management step he or she advises, assists and renders service to the owner of the property. In the third step, disposition or disinvestment, the broker comes back into the marketplace and again performs the selling function. It is the marketing function which we are primarily concerned with in this book. Therefore, it follows logically that it is the broker's function to match the objectives of the prospective buyer with the advantages of a given piece of investment real estate. The broker must identify the financial capability of the prospective buyer since this limits the size and value of the investment that the investor is capable of handling. In presenting an investment opportunity to a prospective buyer, more time and emphasis is usually placed on financial analysis than on the physical characteristics of the income producing property. It is essential that the real estate broker develop extensive preparation prior to presentation of an investment opportunity to a client. This is over and above the description of the physical characteristics and locational characteristics of the property. The major items of interest to most prospective real estate investors would be the series of income statements related to the property, the depreciation status of the building, the rate of return and the tax shelter. The features of these four elements provide the basis for the investment decision.

Income Statement

There are four major parts to the income statement for real estate investment purposes. They are revenue, allowances for vacancy and collection losses, operating expenses and replacement reserves. The general format of the income statement is organized as follows:

TABLE 7 – 1 INCOME STATEMENT (Periodic)		
Gross Revenues (at 100% occupancy)		$XXXX
Less: Estimated vacancy & collection losses		- XX
Effective Revenue		XXXX
Operating Expenses	$XXX	
Replacement Reserves	+XXX	
Total Expenses		-XXX
Net Income Before Depreciation		$XXX

Revenues are usually stated at 100 percent occupancy at current market rentals. While listings were described as being like merchandise on the shelves and a source of revenue, rent from a real estate entity is comparatively perishable. Today's unsold listings may be sold tomorrow, but a day's rent lost is gone forever. Vacancy allowances are stated in terms of "typical" for a particular type of building and neighborhood. Some estimation of vacancy allowance must be made regardless of the past performance of the building. There is bound to be some level of tenant turnover in buildings not completely under long term leases. Turnover causes interruption. Interruption results in vacancy and loss of rent. Collection losses represent inability to collect rents when due. This could be due to the tenants' serious decline or loss of income, personal misfortune, or dissatisfaction with the space being rented. The difference between revenue and allowances for vacancy and collection loss is referred to as effective rental revenue. Operating expenses include normal items such as maintenance, insurance, real estate taxes, repairs, etc. Replacement reserves include annual estimates for items within the building that have shorter lives than the physical structure itself. This would include items replaced at regular intervals such as the roof, water heaters, heating units, etc. A second kind of replacement reserve relates to the furnishings within the building such as carpeting, stoves, refrigerators and the like. Effective rental revenue less operating expenses and replacement reserves produces net income before depreciation. This is one of the peculiar characteristics of real estate accounting. Depreciation is not considered among the operating expenses. Instead depreciation is treated as part of the capitalization rate which will be explained later. In analyzing income statements it is important to look at a series of income statements covering several sequential years. This enables one to identify trends of rents and expenses and to identify abnormal items. It is possible that items may be over-expensed one year and under-expensed another. Consider the case of buying a three year insurance policy where the entire three year premium might be charged against a single year for a tax-payer reporting on a cash basis. In this case the following two years show no insurance expense at all. The revenue reported and the expenses reported should realistically reflect market conditions typical for the property. It may be that the rents are not at the proper level because of certain concessions given to friends, relatives, or employees. It may be that expenses are low because of lack of maintenance. Expenses could also be high because of inefficient management. In order to measure the reasonableness of expenses it is advisable to compare the operating ratios with the standards in the field. A reliable source would be the Apartment Owners Experience Exchange or those reports issued by the Building Owners and Managers Association. Performance above or below these standards certainly should be questioned and explained. It is not uncommon in the residential field to find owner-occupants doing some of the work themselves, especially maintenance and minor repairs. They often fail to pay themselves a salary and as a result the operating expenses may be materially understated. The owner might attempt to explain the situation as being a normal thing, since he or she may have the free time available. However, if the owner-occupant is replaced by an absentee owner the expense then must be incurred in order to have the work done. So in some cases actual expenses must be adjusted for items of this type. It was pointed out that depreciation is not a part of the operating statement. It should also be added that the net income before depreciation is net income before income taxes are considered.

The net income calculated in this fashion can be adjusted to other meaningful and useful forms by means of the following procedures:

TABLE 7 – 2
SPENDABLE INCOME (NET CASH FLOW)

I.	Net Income before Depreciation	
	<u>Subtract:</u>	<u>Depreciation</u>
	Result:	Taxable Income
II.	<u>Subtract:</u>	<u>Federal Income Tax; State Income Tax</u>
	Result:	Net After-tax Income
III.	Subtract:	Mortgage Amortization Payments;
	Subtract:	Cost of Capital Improvements (not deductible)
	<u>Add:</u>	<u>Depreciation (Step I)</u>
	Result:	Net Spendable Income
		(Net Cash Flow or Cash Overage)

It is obvious that "net" can be stated in several different ways. It is paramount to know which "net" the client has in mind when discussing the purchase or sale of investment real estate.

Depreciation

There are three kinds of depreciation related to investment real estate:

1. Depreciation for accounting purposes
2. Depreciation for income tax purposes
3. Depreciation for valuation purposes

The accounting depreciation is a cost allocation process wherein the acquisition costs of the asset are spread out over the estimated life of the depreciable portion of the asset. There is no necessary relationship between the income tax depreciation procedures and the market value of the property. In accounting, the cost of the asset minus accumulated depreciation equals book value.

For income tax purposes the book value (cost of the property minus depreciation to date) represents the basis for calculating long term gain or loss. For real estate valuation purposes depreciation represents the loss in market value from all causes. While it can be estimated in various ways, the best measure of this loss in value can be determined in the marketplace. The replacement cost new, at current prices, is compared to the realistic market value. The difference is the experienced depreciation or loss in value. It should be pointed out that in the valuation process, the possibility for appreciation also exists which represents increase in value, a factor not treated in the other two depreciation methods.

In real estate investment analysis depreciation enters into the picture in two significant ways. First, it is looked upon as recapture and becomes part of the capitalization rate. And, secondly, the amount of the depreciation deducted for income tax purposes affects the net cash flow. The former has a direct impact on the capitalization rate while the latter affects the size of the cash income stream. The selection of a depreciation rate for income tax purposes is determined by the Internal Revenue Code.

The code permits a deduction of a reasonable allowance for the wear and tear on a property held for the production of income. This does not include land apart from its improvements. Real estate placed in service by its owner after 1986 must be depreciated under the Modified Accelerated Cost Recovery System (MACRS). There are two classes of real property under these regulations:

a. 27.5 Year Residential Rental Property. This includes buildings or structures of which 80% or more of the gross rental income is from dwelling units.

b. Non-Residential Real Property. The cost of non-residential real property placed in service by the taxpayer after May 12, 1993 is recovered in 39 years. For such property placed in service after 1986 but before May 13, 1993, cost is recovered over 31.5 years.

For income tax purposes depreciation is scheduled over the estimated useful life of the property. The estimated useful life as determined by the Code provides the basis for the selection of a depreciation rate. The rate is applied to the depreciable portion of the property. Land values cannot be depreciated. A common problem is the allocation of a purchase price into the components of land and improvements. One useful basis for dividing the asset into depreciable and non-depreciable portions is the assessed value.

Assessed value of land	$22,000
Assessed value of building	78,000
Total assessed value	$100,000

$$\frac{\$22,000}{\$100,000} = 22\% \text{ portion of purchase price assigned to land}$$

$$\frac{\$78,000}{\$100,000} = 78\% \text{ portion of purchase price assigned to building}$$

The assessed value of the land is added to the assessed value of the improvements to get total assessed value. This provides a basis, in percentage form, for allocating the total purchase price into land and buildings. This procedure is fairly well accepted for income tax purposes. Another kind of procedure that would be acceptable is an appraisal made by an independent fee appraiser, establishing the market value of the land and the building at the time of acquisition, thus providing a basis for applying depreciation rates. Depreciation for income tax purposes can only be applied to properties that are held for investment or business purposes. Depreciation cannot be deducted on properties that are wholly owner-occupied as a principal residence or portions of the property that are owner occupied as a principal residence. Strategies that are related to the use of depreciation are discussed in a later section dealing with income tax.

Components of Value

Expressions of value appear in the marketplace in the form of prices. They represent the end estimate. Underlying the value are some rather important dimensions as illustrated in Chart 7 – 2 on the following page.

CHART 7 – 2
DIMENSIONS OF VALUE

Basic to this sequence is the matter of convenience. Convenience is expressed in terms of accessibility and transportation costs to use a given piece of real estate. Costs are described in terms of expenditures, time and inconvenience involved to get to the property. Intangibles might be expressed in the form of favorable and unfavorable exposures. A combination of positive characteristics will result in a site being described as a favorable location. A favorable location is desirable. This, in turn, creates demand. Competitive demand for the desirable location is expressed in the form of bidding up rents. Gross rents are adjusted by operating expense to provide net income. Net income, in turn, is capitalized as an expression of value.

This form of logic makes sense to the real estate appraiser since it generally follows the customary procedures that the appraiser employs during the course of one's professional activity. The real estate investor may not pursue this particular route of logic. Another way of explaining how these factors combine to produce real estate value is by means of an illustration involving solid geometry. It could be referred to as the "Cone of Value." Starting with location as a fixed point, one can identify a certain site within an urban area. Though its physical dimensions are such that one can describe the shape of this lot, it is much more important to consider the site's "positional complexities", its relationship to other land uses. Value-wise, location represents an untapped potential until such time as it is committed to a higher and better urban use. In the model of value, location and land use combine to form a circular plane, infinitely small in area. Without the stimulation of market forces, this value potential remains in a latent state. However, when affected by increasing intensity of effective market demand, the circular plane expands outward and upward, taking on a solid conical shape. The solid volume of the cone represents real estate value and increases as successive layers of effective demand are laminated on the growing cone. Good property management is the adhesive that binds the layers together and holds them intact.

Should circumstances change and demand fall off, layers are peeled off, reducing the size of the cone, and total real estate value. It should be remembered that the market expression of the level of demand is partially in response to the changing quality of the location. Since location is half of the basic circular plane in this model, it is necessary for the other half, land-use, to be upgraded in line with the improvement in locational status. Failure to maintain the land at its highest and best use produces a situation of underdevelopment, hence, an imperfectly formed cone . . . less in total value than under optimum conditions. Over-improvement also produces a distorted configuration. Distortion of the basic circular plane (location and land use) will be reflected in a lesser market demand, hence, less dynamic expansion of the cone in the vertical direction.

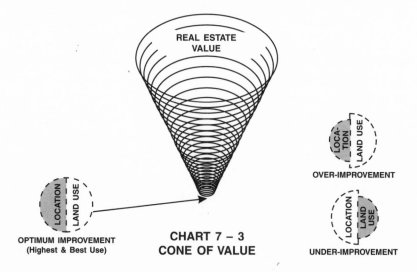

REAL ESTATE VALUE

OVER-IMPROVEMENT

OPTIMUM IMPROVEMENT
(Highest & Best Use)

CHART 7 – 3
CONE OF VALUE

UNDER-IMPROVEMENT

Rates of Return

For the most part real estate investors are not organized into professional groups for practicing their expertise. They tend to operate as individuals or in small groups. Very few of the market participants are bound together in institutes or societies. As a result, terminology is not very precise. In fact, clients may not be able to adequately differentiate between rate of return and capitalization rates as they are known to the professional. Aside from the standard operating practices of real estate investment funds, life insurance companies and other large investors, there are no rigid standards or guidelines by which to operate as a real estate investor. This does suggest that the decision making process is extremely subjective in nature and may vary from investor to investor. However, there is a kind of commonality in that they are all participants in the marketplace and as a result influence each other according to the degree of competition that may exist in each investor's own sub-market area. Many investors are attracted to the real estate because of the higher returns that may be gained from this type of investment. It has been observed that in most markets good real estate investments would yield several percent more than the going interest rate in the prime mortgage money market. But just how is this rate of return calculated? Newcomers to the field are under the impression that there is *a* rate of return. However, after talking to a cross section of active investors, one soon finds out that many different interpretations of rates of return are employed. Rates of return are structured to the objectives and circumstances of the individual investors. The basic formula is as follows:

$$\text{Rate of Return} = \frac{\text{Income}}{\text{Capital}}$$

There are many possible combinations for both numerator and denominator in this simple formula. The numerator could be stated in terms of:

> net income after depreciation
> net income before depreciation
> net income before income taxes
> net income after income taxes

        net income before debt service
        net income after debt service
        net income + equity increase

and many other combinations of the above components. The numerator might even include such intangible values as status, business image, and other kinds of satisfaction such as "monument" value. Monument value refers to an over improvement that gives identity and satisfaction to the owner but does not test out as an economic enterprise.

The denominator could be stated in terms of:
        initial cash or equity investment
        initial investment free and clear
        initial investment with mortgage financing
        initial investment + equity build-up
        present market value of the property

The specific behavior pattern of a given investor will determine which combination is applicable. It is not the objective of this book to attempt to explain the appraisal process but it is recognized that certain tools and certain portions of tools in the appraisal process can be used in real estate investment analysis as well. In considering the components that could be included in the numerator and denominator it is recognized that in view of the number of variables involved many combinations are possible.

Another example of the variations in rates of return is illustrated in what is called the "Hierarchy of Residential Investments" where investments are ranked by typical rates of return:

    1. Single Family
    2. Two Family
    3. Four Family
    4. Eight Family
       etc.

In most situations, the tenant occupied single family investment has the lowest rate of return as compared to other types of residential structures. Due to the economies of scale in management, the larger the number of units in a building, the higher the rate of return. Therefore, the two unit building has a higher rate of return than the one family; the four greater than two, the eight greater than four, etc.

Simple Investment Models

The simple capitalization process capitalizes net income by dividing the property's annual net income by a rate of return. For example, a $10,000 a year net income divided by a 10% rate of return produces a capital value of $100,000. While this procedure deals with net income, it is recognized that there is no time limit on that net income stream. To be realistic one would have to admit that the income stream will not flow forever. Perhaps it is possible on the land but certainly not on the building. It is accepted that the building, without major additional capital inputs, will deteriorate in due time either physically or due to obsolescence.

Assuming that the property has a remaining economic life of thirty-nine years, the basis for recapture or depreciation is 2.56% a year on a straight line basis. If the investor's subjective rate of return on investment is 10%, then an increment for return of investment must be added. This is the depreciation factor which in this case is 2.56%. The sum of the two provides a combined rate of 12.56%. The $10,000 net income divided by 12.56% produces a value of $79,618. This procedure provided for a recapture of both building and land. This calls for a closer look at depreciation since land is not depreciable. Assume that the land has a value of $22,000 and the building cost $78,000 new. On a straight line basis depreciation is $2,000 a year or 2.5641% times the building cost of $78,000. One of the purposes for considering recapture is to compensate the investor for dissipation of capital due to depreciation of all kinds. A conservative way of looking at it would be to actually fund the annual depreciation in order to assure the investor that one will be financially able to replace the building at the end of its economic life. The question might be asked whether or not straight line depreciation would be able to do this kind of job. On a straight line basis with no interest it appears to do so, since $2,000 a year for 39 years equals $78,000 – the cost of the building. If one assumes that the investor is able to reinvest the recaptured funds at a safe rate, say 5% at a savings institution, there is an opportunity for greater accumulation. Annual deposits of $2,000 compounded at 5% for 39 years amounts to over $228,000, or nearly three times that accumulated in a non-interest bearing fund.

This conservative technique suggests that an annual amount, considerably less than $2,000, only needs to be deposited at 5% compound interest in order to accumulate the replacement cost of the building in 39 years. However, not to be overlooked is the possible impact of inflation over the 39 year period. This leads to more sophisticated forms of analysis such as sinking fund techniques, annuity methods and other forms of capitalization including mortgage-equity methods with before and after-tax positions. However, in view of the objectives of this book, it seems inadvisable to treat such technical forms of analysis at this time.

At times the objectives of the investor are not as sophisticated or orderly as one might be led to believe from viewing the previous examples. Take the case of the novice investor or one who is pyramiding his or her real estate investments. The overall objective may be to acquire a real estate portfolio of a given size. The initial acquisition may involve a limited down payment and a high percentage mortgage loan. In such cases one's real estate analysis may be relatively simple as illustrated in the following chart:

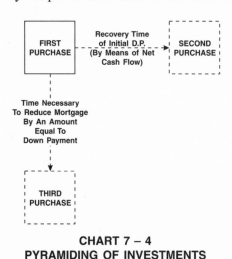

CHART 7 – 4
PYRAMIDING OF INVESTMENTS

The kinds of questions that this investor wants answered to meet his or her investment objectives are these: "How soon can I recover my initial investment through the process of net cash flow accumulation?" The first objective is to recover one's initial down payment as soon as possible in order to use it as a down payment in the acquisition of a second property. Another kind of question that may be asked is, "How long will it take to reduce the balance of the mortgage by an amount that will equal the initial investment?" This will give this investor the opportunity of increasing the mortgage balance back up to the original amount thus providing the down payment for the acquisition of the third property. In such cases a rate of return expressed in the form of a percentage is not very meaningful. The emphasis is on the employment of cash, cash flow and mortgage reduction. This investor's habits, in effect, make him or her appear as if they were a short-term investor or speculator. However, these actual objectives are longer term in nature.

Market experience tells us there are gross rent multipliers for each class of property. In this instance, one is dealing with gross revenues and the inherent assumption that all properties within the same class have similar vacancy and operating expense ratios. It is realized that an estimate of net income for each property would be more meaningful than dealing with gross revenues alone. One might ask which of all these models is most appropriate? Bear in mind that all sales and acquisitions of income property have a common denominator. They all involve a business decision making process. Results of these decisions are real estate transactions in the marketplace by many different decision makers with varying degrees of expertise. One measure of these transactions is the end figure — the transaction amount and its components. The more the broker understands about rationale employed in arriving at completed transactions, the more effective will be the ensuing analysis. This represents a continuing upgrading of the level of sophistication of investment analysis. Over the years, as displayed by these evolving models, more significant variables will be introduced. The most appropriate technique to employ would be that approach that comes closest to the rationale actually employed by the decision makers in the marketplace. This decision maker is the broker's client. It might be an insurance company, a real estate investment trust, a real estate syndicate, isolated private individuals, or even first time investors. It should be remembered that the various calculations in these investment models enable one to arrive at the upper limit of investment value. The investor will attempt to bargain below this limit. Beyond this limit the investor will not be able to achieve the investment objectives as the broker has interpreted them.

Investment Leverage

There are few other types of investments that allow a greater use of borrowed funds. In recent years the margin requirements for the purchase of securities has been in the area of 50 percent with the opportunity of financing the remaining 50 percent. In real estate it has been just about the opposite. In fact a good number of transactions have been consummated with as little as 5 percent or 10 percent down, or even less in some cases. The use of debt financing in the purchase of investment properties is known as leverage. The effective use of mortgages or borrowed funds increases the rate of return on the investment over the return which the investor would receive if he or she purchased the entire investment with cash. In effect, positive leverage is the process of borrowing funds and earning a rate of return on them that is higher than the rate that the borrower must pay for the use of such funds. However, if an investor borrows funds at a higher rate than he or she earns on them, the return on one's own investment is reduced. The lower the ratio of equity to total value, the greater the effect of leverage (or equity return) but also the greater the amount of risk. Consider a simple example of leverage using the same property under two different situations:

TABLE 7 – 3	
Situation A	**Situation B**
Investor uses 100% Equity	Investor Uses 6% Mortgage and Part Equity
Purchase Price $10,000	Purchase Price $10,000
Income 1,000	Income (1,000 - 360 Interest) 640
Equity 100% or 10,000	Equity 40% or 4,000
Return on Initial Equity	Return on Initial Equity
$= \dfrac{\$1,000}{10,000} = 10\%$	$= \dfrac{\$640}{4,000} = 16\%$

The investor in situation B is earning a higher rate of return on the investor's initial equity because the lender's money is put to work at a higher rate of return than the rate that is being paid to the lender for the use of the money. As the following diagram illustrates, investor B is effectively using leverage because B is not only receiving all of the return on B's equity investment (E) but also the differential (L) between the 10 percent rate that the borrowed money (M) is earning and the 6 percent rate that is being paid for its use.

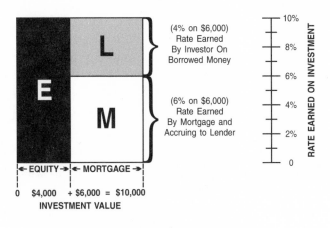

CHART 7 – 5
INVESTMENT LEVERAGE

It must be remembered, however, that leverage can work in both directions for the investor. While the investor can control large investments with small amounts of equity capital and thus have a greater opportunity for larger percentage gains, there is also the chance of losses. As a result, the investor must carefully consider the margin between debt service and the property's cash flow. This difference represents the margin of safety or degree of risk involved in using leverage, for the larger the dollar margin the more likely it will be that debt service payments can be met. All other things equal, as shown in the illustration below, property D with a $1,000 annual cash flow and an annual debt service of $600 has a greater margin of safety ($400) and thus a lower degree of risk than property C with the same $1,000 annual income but an annual debt service of $800.

TABLE 7 – 4				
	Property C		**Property D**	
	Expected Net Income	Actual Net Income	Expected Net Income	Actual Net Income
Annual Cash Flow	$1,000	$800	$1,000	$800
Debt Service	– 800	– 800	– 600	– 600
$ Margin of Safety	$ 200	$ 0	$400	$200
% Change in $ Margin of Safety		-100%		-50%

Only small changes or errors in estimating income have a tremendous impact on the risk of the investment when leverage is used. The greater the amount of leverage used the greater the degree of risk and the lower the margin of safety but the higher the rate of return. As can be seen in the illustration, only a 20% drop in income results in a 50% drop in the margin of safety for property D and a 100% drop for property C. For emphasis, perhaps another way to state this is that with a 20 percent decline in net income, property D's degree of risk increases 50 percent and for property C the degree of risk rises 100 percent.

The question that may now come to the broker's mind is, "How can this knowledge of leverage help me to price investment property?" The answer lies in the fact that leverage or the use of borrowed funds is found in the majority of sales transactions involving investment properties. Also, as previously illustrated, the use of leverage results in higher percentage returns to the investor, based on equity rather than the total value of the property. There can only be one market value and that is created by competitive bidders in the marketplace. If the probable demand for the income producing property in question includes a substantial portion of leverage-minded investors, then their particular buying behavior must be taken into account. Within this context, the starting point for the broker would be to estimate the maximum mortgage loan that the property is likely to carry.

MARKET PRICE
Less: <u>MAXIMUM MORTGAGE</u>
<u>EQUITY GAP</u>

The "equity gap" then provides the basis for calculating a return on equity since initial equity plus mortgage equals acquisition price. The rates of return on equity so calculated must fall within range of alternatives in the market in order for the asking price to be deemed reasonable.

Income Tax Aspects of Investment Real Estate

It appears as if most real estate brokers and salespeople are neither sufficiently trained nor duly licensed to give income tax advice on the intricacies of investment real estate. To give professional income tax advice implies the assumption of responsibility to those who have relied on such advice. Income tax matters should be referred to competent professional tax consultants, properly qualified attorneys and certified public accountants. These professionals are adequately trained, experienced, qualified and licensed to perform such service and since they hold themselves forth on this basis, they then assume the responsibility for the consequences of their advice. Most real estate brokers and salespeople lack such specific training and therefore should step aside for the professional in the field. On the other hand, the real estate broker cannot avoid being drawn into income tax discussions. As a result, he or she should be prepared to identify tax situations and be ready to recommend consultation with the proper tax advisor as the situation warrants. On this basis the clients have the assurance of receiving individual and expert treatment and thereby have the full opportunity to maximize their objectives in the real estate transaction.

There are a number of terms that are basic to understanding income tax problems related to real estate transactions. The more prominent terms are these:

1. Capital asset
2. Adjusted basis
3. Capital gain or loss
4. Installment sale

5. Tax free exchange
6. Like kind
7. Tax deferred exchange (Starker type)

A brief definition of each of these terms follows. The reader is cautioned that these are non-technical definitions for the purpose of a general understanding of the concepts involved. Legal definitions and attendant specific limitations can be found in the Internal Revenue Code and published professional interpretations.

1. *Capital asset* – real property being held for investment purposes. Property held for resale in the ordinary course of business is not considered to be a capital asset for tax purposes. The same is true of real property subject to depreciation and used by the taxpayer in one's business but in the latter case the gain or loss of the sale of such property may receive favorable tax treatment as "Section 1231" assets. Personal residences are capital assets and the gain on their disposition may qualify for special tax treatment as explained in Chapter 5.

2. *Adjusted basis* – the acquisition cost of the property to the taxpayer adjusted for capital additions and subsequent accumulated depreciation. The adjusted basis is deducted from the net proceeds of the sale in order to determine the amount of gain or loss.

3. *Capital gain or loss* – the resulting gain or loss from the disposition of a capital asset. To qualify for a long-term gain, the taxpayer must hold the asset for more than 18 months. If held for less than 18 months, the gain or loss is considered to be short-term. For federal income tax purposes, long-term gains are taxed at a maximum rate of 20% for individual taxpayers.

4. *Installment sale* – a sale of property where one or more payments are received after the close of the tax year in which the transaction takes place. Gain on the

sale is reported only as payments are received. The amount of the gain that is taxable in a given year is calculated by multiplying the payments received in that year by the gross profit ratio for the sale. The gross profit ratio is equal to the total gross profit divided by the total contract price. (See Internal Revenue Form 6252). While the term, "Installment Sale", is used in the Internal Revenue Code, similar type transactions in the marketplace are called "Land Contract" or "Contract for Deed", depending on the geographical area in which the transactions occur.

5. *Tax free exchange* – trading equity in one property for equity in another property of like kind, that is real estate for real estate whether improved or not. Title to all properties involved passes at the time of closing.

6. *Like Kind* – refers to the general type of property exchanged rather than the property's specific grade or quality, that is, real property for real property. Real property used in business can be exchanged for investment property; unimproved land may be exchanged for improved land; rental real estate may be exchanged for a farm; and urban real estate may be exchanged for a rural ranch.

7. *Tax Deferred Exchange* (Starker type) – all titles need not pass at the time of the closing of this special type of exchange transaction. However, these important qualifying steps must be followed:
   a. The replacement property must be identified within 45 days after the taxpayer transferred the relinquished property.
   b. The maximum number of replacement properties that a taxpayer may identify is three.

    c. The replacement property must actually be received by the taxpayer within 180 days after the transfer of the relinquished property.

    d. The net proceeds are to be turned over to a qualified intermediary and are to be held for reinvestment in the replacement property per written instructions agreed upon at the initial closing.

It is strongly recommended that your clients seek accounting and/or legal advice in structuring a tax deferred exchange.

A summary checklist is provided in the following chart, showing the applicability of capital gains, capital losses and deductible expenses for four major classes of real estate.

TABLE 7 – 5 CLASSIFICATION OF REAL ESTATE FOR INCOME TAX PURPOSES				
CLASS	CAPITAL GAIN	CAPITAL LOSS	EXPENSES DEDUCTIBLE	DEPRECIATION ALLOWED
INVESTMENT OR PRODUCTION OF INCOME	✓	✓	✓	✓
USE IN TRADE OR BUSINESS	✓	*	✓	✓
PERSONAL RESIDENCE	✓	***	****	******
HELD FOR SALE TO CUSTOMERS	**	*	✓	*****

*	LOSS IS ORDINARY LOSS
**	GAIN IS ORDINARY GAIN
***	LOSS IS NON-DEDUCTIBLE
****	EXPENSES NON-DEDUCTIBLE EXCEPT INTEREST, PROPERTY TAX & CASUALTY LOSSES
*****	DEPRECIATION NOT ALLOWED UNLESS PROPERTY PRODUCES INCOME
******	DEPRECIATION NOT ALLOWED

Participants in the investment real estate market are most often motivated by the anticipation of profit. These expectations are tempered by the degree of certainty that the potential profit can be estimated, as well as the timing and availability of acceptable financing terms. Net cash flow and equity income (equity build-up) become more significant when interpreted in terms of tax shelters. The monetary significance of tax shelters vary from investor to investor, depending upon individual income tax positions. This sets the stage for the real estate broker to play an important role in matching seller's and buyer's needs.

In an attempt to integrate some of these points, consider the limited example of a single property. Assume that this real estate investment was acquired for $137,000 ($117,000 for the building and $20,000 for the land). Cash payment was $37,000 and a 30-year, 6½ percent mortgage was secured for the balance of $100,000. Annual payments on the mortgage are $7,600 including principal and interest. Rental receipts are $18,000 per year and operating expenses, including insurance, repairs, real estate taxes and management, are $7,500. The remaining economic life of the building is estimated at 39 years, setting straight line depreciation at $3,000 a year. Two statements showing the impact of depreciation on net income and net cash flow and its subsequent effect on tax-free distributions to the owners of a real estate investment are given in Table 7 – 6.

TABLE 7 – 6		
PROFIT AND LOSS FOR INCOME TAX PURPOSES		
Rental Receipts		$18,000
Expenses:		
Mortgage interest (6½% of $100,000)	$6,500	
Depreciation (straight-line, 39 years)	3,000	
Operating Expenses	7,500	
Total Expenses		17,000
Net Income		$ 1,000
NET CASH FLOW STATEMENT		
Rental Receipts		$18,000
Disbursements:		
Mortgage Principal and Interest	$7,600	
Operating Expenses	7,500	
Total Disbursements		15,100
Balance Available for Distribution (7.8% on Equity)		$ 2,900

As can be seen, here is a property which made only $1,000 net income based on regular accounting procedures with the use of straight line depreciation. The real estate investor will pay federal income tax on the $1,000 of taxable income. However, due to the favorable net cash flow of $2,900, the investor is in a position to draw off a sizable amount of cash. The rate of return on a cash basis would be $2,900 divided by the initial equity of $37,000, or 7.8%. The first year's increase in equity would be $1,100 ($7,600 payment less $6,500 mortgage interest). Therefore net cash flow ($2,900) plus equity income ($1,100) produces total annual income of $4,000. The total income, based on initial equity, then becomes 10.8% ($2,900 + $1,100 ÷ $37,000). This, of course, is based on the first year only. It would be advisable to make a series of year by year calculations covering a normal holding period of time.

There are many different techniques by which to estimate investment value . . . from the very simple capitalization formula to the sophisticated Internal Rate of Return (IROR) that deals with discounted cash flows over time. However, one should recognize that investment value is not created in financial tables but rather in the marketplace by the interaction of buyers (investors) and sellers (dis-investors).

As a reminder, the broker should not try to impress the client with his or her investment knowledge and jargon, but rather discuss real estate investments at the client's level of comprehension. If a potential investor fails to understand, he or she will most likely fail to act.

CHAPTER 8 — YOUR COMPANY
OFFICE AND OPERATIONS

"A well laid foundation provides the proper base for
a sound structure." *Walter Hilton*

The material in Chapter 3 on market changes dealt with seasonal, cyclical and irregular change as well as long term trends. These forces influence the course of operations of a real estate business and therefore must be given appropriate attention. Planning ahead becomes vital in the successful operation of any business. Therefore, several aspects of business management are given proper consideration in the next three chapters as they relate to the real estate enterprise. This chapter will discuss five sub-areas dealing with decision-making as it applies to certain real estate business operations. These areas cover operating functions, type of business entity, company name, office location and management of the firm.

Operating Functions

There are relatively few real estate businesses that operate in "pure" form; that is, having the single business function of brokerage by itself. Nearly all real estate companies engage in a range of activities. The most prevalent type of activities can be classified into two general categories as listed in Table 8 – 1 on the following page.

TABLE 8 – 1	
FUNCTIONS PERFORMED BY REAL ESTATE COMPANIES	
Volatile	**Stable**
1. Brokerage	5. Insurance
2. Speculation	6. Mortgage services
3. Development	7. Property management
4. Exchanging	8. Rental service (leasing)

The volatile group of functions includes those that are subject to marked volume fluctuation and consequently involve noticeable degrees of change and higher risk. For the most part, the four functions in the volatile group are highly dependent upon the availability and terms of mortgage money and the public's confidence in the future of the local and national economy. These functions are generally characterized by one-time transactions. In the brokerage area a property may be sold and a commission is earned. This commission is usually a percent of the contract price in most urban markets. These rates are negotiable between the seller and the broker. However, vacant land sales in both urban and rural areas often bring a higher percent selling commission. In the speculation area the broker may take an option or even buy property outright; take title to it and then hopefully sell it at a profit. This procedure requires investment capital, financing and risk-taking during the time the property is held in inventory. In the development area, the broker may buy vacant land, subdivide it and then sell the lots thus created at a margin of profit. This process not only entails the steps involved in speculation but also requires effective planning, design, governmental agency approval and additional capital inputs. In the area of exchanging, the broker may effect a mutually beneficial exchange of real estate equities and thereby earn commissions on the properties involved. While there is economic opportunity in each case, it is also common to all four of these functions that the frequency of continuing contacts with the same client is generally low. It is possible the client may come back as a repeat customer but it may be five or seven years later, on average. The time lapse between transactions with the same client may be relatively long.

The stable group includes those activities for which there is a steadier demand. They are less subject to the swings of the real estate market. The characteristics of these two groups of activities are summarized in the table below.

TABLE 8 – 2 CHARACTERISTICS OF REAL ESTATE FUNCTIONS		
	VOLATILE	**STABLE**
Remuneration Factor	(individual transaction)	(continuing service)
Amount	large commission or profit	smaller commission or fee
Frequency	periodic, usually one-time	continuing, over longer term
Stability	subject to ups and downs of the real estate cycle	more regular, usually based on a fixed arrangement or contract

The significance of different combinations of these functions becomes more obvious upon further analysis. Assume a real estate business concentrates on the four volatile functions only.

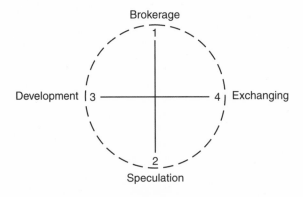

CHART 8 – 1
THE REAL ESTATE FIRM – VOLATILE FUNCTIONS ONLY

The identification numbers employed in Chart 8 – 1 correspond to the numbers used in Table 8 – 1. Such a combination implies that the company may be large in size and subject to a high degree of risk. It also suggests that capital requirements may be high and that its activities may be significantly affected during the low ebb of the real estate cycle. As an alternative, some of the possible ill affects that may occur during a generally slow market could be offset by becoming more competitive. This kind of company must get more than its usual share of the market in order to compensate for the general drop in market activity.

On the other hand it is possible for a company to concentrate on the four stable functions: insurance, mortgage services, property management and rental service. This is more typical of the mature, well-established real estate organization that for various reasons has decided to curtail the real estate brokerage function. In many cases, though, originally it was the brokerage function that enabled them to develop the company to its present size and range of activities. The graphic form for a business entity of this type takes on the following appearance:

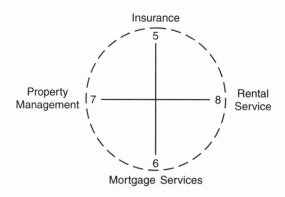

CHART 8 – 2
THE REAL ESTATE FIRM – STABLE FUNCTIONS ONLY

It will be readily recognized that the absolute dollar amounts involved in transactions in this category are generally smaller in size than those in the volatile category. The average size of an insurance premium, a mortgage payment, rental collections and short-term leases usually does not approach the dollar-size of transactions in real estate brokerage, speculation, development, or exchanging. Most insurance commissions fall into a range of about 10 to 30 percent of the annual premium with the exception of some life insurance policies. Although these commission rates appear relatively attractive, the typical annual insurance premium may be several hundred dollars a year, if that high. Mortgage services include mortgage loan referrals, completing mortgage loan applications and mortgage servicing. Mortgage servicing, the periodic collection of mortgage payments on behalf of the lender, may produce revenue for the real estate agency in the range of ¼ percent to ½ percent of the amounts collected and transmitted to the mortgagee. Property management fees are negotiable and may fall in the range of 5 to 6 percent of rents collected except in cases of smaller properties where the fee is necessarily larger. Rental service, referrals of clients to income property owners, may produce fees equivalent to one-half to one month's rent on short-term occupancy. The handling of longer term leases may produce commissions comparable to brokerage fees in the sale of real estate.

The larger company may be able to offset the risks of volatile functions by expanding its range of activities to include all eight of these functions, presenting the following well-rounded kind of characterization.

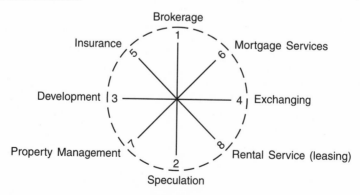

CHART 8 – 3
THE LARGE REAL ESTATE FIRM –
VOLATILE AND STABLE FUNCTIONS

The presence of both volatile and stable activities provides the opportunity for profit maximization as well as the built-in defense of continuing income during periods of market distress.

While ideally desirable, this does not mean that above average income and stability are limited to large firms alone. The medium sized and small firms can employ much the same philosophy, except on a more limited scale. For example, a smaller firm might have this combination of functions:

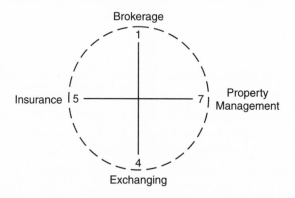

CHART 8 – 4
THE SMALLER REAL ESTATE FIRM – BALANCED FUNCTIONS

Limited investment capital would not necessarily impede a good level of activity in brokerage and exchanging, providing two excellent sources for sizeable commissions. Stable functions such as insurance and property management seem to complement the volatile functions very well. The insurance and management activities provide continuing contact with property owners that constitute an excellent source of listings as well as potential buyers whose real estate needs may be changing with the passage of time. It can be seen that insurance and property management functions not only provide a steady income flow but enhance the expansion of brokerage and exchanging.

An aggressive company will tend toward the functions in the volatile group whereas the defensive or conservative organization may rely on more of the functions contained in the stable group. However, the aggressive company that avoids the stable functions completely may be overlooking a logical source of additional income as well as lacking a natural line of defense against the seasonal variation that occurs each year in the real estate market. The stable functions also serve as a kind of hedge against cyclical fluctuations.

It should be noted that there may be more than the mere selection of a function to a broker's array of services offered to the firm's clients. For example, the sale of insurance as well as mortgage services may require a separate license in most states. Also, the Real Estate Settlement Procedures Act (RESPA) sets down the regulations under which licensed real estate firms may receive fees for "one-stop shopping" services connected with mortgage lending, title insurance and home warranty protection. These regulations have been issued by the U.S. Department of Housing and Urban Development (HUD) and are subject to change from time to time. The main thrust of these regulations is that to receive fees of this type the real estate firm must meet HUD's "for *services rendered* test". Note the emphasis on "services rendered". Receipt of such fees without meeting the attendant service requirement may be a violation of federal law.

Advance planning on the part of the broker in the development of his or her company will serve as a kind of insurance against some of the market hazards that are most likely to repeat themselves in the future. It should be noted that the emphasis is on *advance* planning in order to prevent undesirable situations in the future. Lacking such planning, should such detrimental situations develop, it may be too late to take corrective action.

Form of Business Organization

More common forms of business organization of real estate firms:

Sole Proprietorship
General Partnership
Limited Partnership
"C" Corporation
"S" Corporation
Limited Liability Company

Considered attention should be given to the proper legal and operating structure of a real estate company. The type of entity selected is affected by such considerations as capital requirements, need for managerial talent, degree of control desired, extent of possible liability and the tax position of the company. All of these factors have an impact on the operating efficiency as measured in terms of growth, profit, stability and continuity. However, there appears to be no standard method for selecting one form of business organization over another since the individual goals of business owners are extremely subjective in nature. At best one may want to rank the various organization characteristics in order of importance for purposes of facilitating a selection decision. This can be illustrated by considering the five characteristics previously cited and weighing their relative importance.

1. *Capital requirements*

   All other things remaining equal, it is logical that two partners would be able to raise more investment capital than one of them acting as a sole proprietor. Since most corporations consist of multiple ownerships, it follows that a more broadly based stock ownership arrangement should provide the opportunity for raising more capital than a partnership. However, a real estate firm specializing in brokerage and service functions does not have very large capital requirements compared to most other kinds of business activities. It would carry no inventory and may lease office space rather than purchase a building; therefore its capital needs would be primarily related to furnishings, equipment and an amount of working capital sufficient to cover normal operating expenses such as salaries, advertising, rent, insurance and the like. In such cases a sole proprietor may have the ability to raise the necessary capital without seeking help from other investors, be they prospective partners or stockholders. On the other hand, a real estate firm dealing in buying for its own account and reselling or engaging in some form of development may have rather high capital needs and therefore might have to seek additional capital from outsiders, causing them to consider the partnership form or the corporation.

2. *Managerial talent*

Management planning and leadership are important to all real estate firms but tend to become more critical factors with increasing firm size. The sole proprietor must operate within the constraints of his or her managerial abilities. It is somewhat unrealistic to think that such an operator would hire a primary manager and play a secondary role unless the broker was a top producer. It is probably a drive for independence and the desire to "be one's own boss" that has motivated the broker to start his or her own business. Any managerial talent hired would most likely be subordinate to the sole owner and report directly to that broker. A partnership provides for co-ownership and the pooling of talent at the top level. Ideally, one might seek out suitable investor-talent that would tend to complement one's own. In the corporate form, ownership and management may be one of the same or separated. The combination of policy-making directors and operating officers provides the basis for hired management. It should be pointed out that corporations may be established with relatively few stockholders. In some states there can be a single stockholder for the entire corporation providing there are several directors. This form of corporation enterprise tends to approximate the managerial status of a sole proprietorship.

3. *Degree of control*

The investors in the real estate business may favor certain degrees of controlling the business in order to enhance the achievement of their particular objectives. Obviously, the sole proprietorship should provide the highest and most direct degree of control. A wholly owned corporation may be an equally effective device but this is dependent on a compatible board of directors and a set of officers working in consonance with the objectives of the owner. The partnership arrangement usually results in the sharing of the control of the business decision-making processes.

4. *Extent of liability*
    The sole proprietor has unlimited liability. The same is true of members of a general partnership. Under certain conditions, partners may limit their liability. However, at least one of the partners must be subject to unlimited liability. While a broker/owner may have one or more partners to help raise capital and share in the management of the business, if that broker is a general partner (not a limited partner) there may be no limit on his or her personal liability for partnership bills. If one of that broker's partners uses poor judgment in making decisions within the scope of that partner's authority, the general broker could lose everything he or she owns, including one's house and one's car. In the corporate form the stockholders are usually liable only to the extent of their investment. Such limited liability represents a line of legal defense for the investors in the firm.

5. *Tax position*
    For federal income tax purposes current earnings and capital gains are given the same treatment for sole proprietorships and partnerships. The partnership as such does not pay any income tax but income is passed through automatically to the various partners in proportion to their profit or loss sharing agreement. The standard form of domestic corporation is subject to a kind of double taxation. The corporation itself must report and pay income taxes on current income and capital

gains. Then any dividends passed on to the stockholders, whether ordinary income or capital gains, must be reported and taxed once again. However, it may be important for real estate firms to explore the possibilities of establishing a so-called Sub-chapter "S" corporation which has distinct advantages over the standard form of domestic corporation. To qualify the corporation must be a domestic corporation with only one class of stock and have 35 or less shareholders. It is further required that the corporation have shareholders who are citizens or residents of the United States. Non-resident aliens cannot be shareholders. The qualifying corporation under this section pays no corporate income tax and the annual profits pass through and are reported in partnership-like fashion. Capital gains and losses are passed through as well. It is advisable for real estate firms to have their professional tax consultant explore this possibility as it may relate to one's own firm. Another tax aspect deals with the relationship of the owners to the business entity. In the case of the sole proprietor and the partners, they are considered to be owners sharing in the profits and not paid employees. However, in the case of the corporation, the officers are considered to be employees of the corporation and are treated as such for compensation and tax purposes even though they may be stockholders . This becomes a critical matter in the handling of earnings subject to federal unemployment taxes and withholding federal income tax. Companies employing individuals in non-exempt employment on each of 20 or more days during a given calendar year, each day being in a different week, are subject to the federal unemployment insurance tax. Obviously, employees come under these regulations. Sole proprietors and partners are not considered to be employees of their business. It is also important to note that real estate sales associates are not employees for purposes of federal unemployment taxes and federal income tax withholding under the internal revenue code where the salespeople have an independent contractor-like relationship with the broker. A test case upheld by the courts determined that real estate sales associates were not employees based on certain conditions. Such conditions included a written contract wherein the real estate company agreed to make available to the sales associate its facilities and its listings of properties for sale; the company agreed to assist the sales associate with advice and cooperation; the company would provide the necessary forms, stationery and business cards; the company would divide commissions earned by the salespeople on a fixed schedule; and the company furnished a policy manual for operating procedures. The sales associates, in turn, procured the required real estate license, paid their own dues in the local trade association and agreed to work diligently for the company. The sales associates provided their own transportation and were responsible for all expenses they personally incurred in connection with their listing and selling efforts. The sales associates reported to the office regularly and attended weekly sales meetings, but this was not mandatory. They were not required to keep fixed hours but took turns in holding the office open on weekends. Sales associates were not permitted to sell real estate for other brokers; all sales had to be made in the company name only. Sales were closed in the name of the company, commissions were collected and distributed according to agreement once a month. This tax matter, as can be seen, is interrelated with company policy which will be discussed later in this chapter. The very technical nature of employee status is such that it should be thoroughly explored with legal counsel rather than making an independent determination.

LLC: Limited Liability Company

As a result of a 1988 Internal Revenue ruling, closely held businesses have had an opportunity to avoid personal liability and corporate income tax by forming a limited liability company (LLC). The LLC is a general partnership with special protections. For one, it eliminates the partners' unlimited liability aspect of the general partnership for all of its members. As a result, the personal assets of "innocent" partners and their spouses are safe from liabilities due to another partner's negligence or misjudgment. Further, the LLC can qualify as a partnership for income tax purposes with a pass through tax provision, thus avoiding the so-called, "double taxation".

The LLC vocabulary is somewhat different as well. Investors in an LLC are called "members" rather than partners or shareholders. Ownership in an LLC is called a "membership interest" rather than shares of stock as in the case of a corporation. The leadership direction in a corporation is the responsibility of the president whereas in an LLC the leadership counterpart is the manager.

In order to qualify for the avoidance of corporate income tax liability, the LLC must follow certain rules, the most important of which are:

1. The business must be called a limited liability company (LLC).
2. The company must have at least two members but with no minimum percentage ownership requirements. (A member could own a mere one percent of the total membership interest and still qualify.)
3. All members (investors) must approve the sale of the business.

This is in sharp contrast to the position of corporate shareholders. Compared to the corporation, the LLC requires less paperwork and fewer forms. It is suggested that existing general partnerships look into the advisability of converting to LLC status.

This brief summary of organization characteristics treats some of the major issues and in no way is deemed to be complete. It does bring some of the more important issues to the attention of the real estate broker and thus provides the basis of initiating an exploration of the circumstances with a professional advisor.

Even though great care may be taken in the process of initially selecting the most appropriate form of business organization, the broker should give some attention to the future as well. Partners' ideas may change over time. . . growth and expansion may pose new kinds of problems. . .second generation family members may want to come aboard, however qualified. . .marital problems may present new issues not present at the outset of the company's founding. While long term precautions are important, they tend to be overshadowed by the urgency of problems of the present.

The Company Name

At the outset the selection of a company name may seem to be a rather simple task but nevertheless, if thoughtfully and properly chosen, it could make a positive contribution toward the success of the company. An appropriate name can impart confidence, create an image of soundness and dignity and have the ability to remain in people's minds. Of course a name cannot create qualities that are not actually present in the firm. On the other hand, poorly selected company names can easily become the basis of ridicule or the butt of jokes. If the choice is available, it is suggested that a short name would be preferable to a longer one. A short name is better for advertising purposes. It looks better on a "For Sale" sign. It can be more effectively presented in capital letters in the classified section of the newspapers. It has greater flexibility and may be easier to pronounce and remember. But there are cases wherein the use of a longer name could be an advantage. This is especially true of a well-known and well-received family name, the name of a sports celebrity, or the name of a former public official. Names of this type almost always impart confidence. In such cases there appears to be no need to put any restrictions on the length of a company name. But once a company name has been selected, it is advisable to stay with it and not change. Consistent advertising, promotion and high quality service tend to be cumulative in nature and build on the improving image of the company as the years wear on. Switching names is the equivalent of nullifying a good deal of the past goodwill and may be likened to a new start in an attempt to establish effective identity.

Slogans attached to the company name can be meaningful if they are realistic and in professional taste. Sheer bragging and self-asserted acclaim can hardly have a lasting affect on discriminating clients. Some examples of short, but effective, phrases attached to the company name are listed below:

"Recommended"

"Since 1943"

"Always Reliable"

In cases where the broker is a bona fide member of a local board affiliated with the National Association of Realtors®, it is strongly recommended that the designation, "Realtor®," be used. This is a term that can be used by qualified members only. NAR's bylaws prohibit the use of any additional words or phrases with the term, "Realtor." It is a service mark registered with the U.S. Patent Office and the "R" in Realtor should always be capitalized.

A noticeable number of business people strive to obtain a telephone number ending with several zeros, since it is usually an easier number for clients to remember. A novel approach can be used in connection with telephone exchanges. Telephone companies assign seven digit telephone numbers. The first three digits represent the particular exchange and the last four digits are for individual identification. Real estate firms that are fortunate enough to have a seven letter name corresponding to an existing telephone number might make arrangements to obtain that number and advertise as follows:

Call J O H N S O N Realty

Dial: 5 6 4 - 6 7 6 6

Each number corresponds with the letter as it appears on the telephone. The caller, in effect, dials out the name, letter by letter. It may be easier for the client to remember the broker's name rather than his or her telephone number. Alternate uses for this idea would be to select a meaningful seven letter slogan illustrated as follows:

To sell your home
Dial: F O R   S A L E
3 6 7 - 7 2 5 3

Many combinations are possible, depending on the emphasis the broker would like to place on his or her own business. Combined with the selection of a name, this telephone novelty could have some significance in establishing the identity of a new firm entering the field.

Office Location

There seems to be a natural tendency on the part of the real estate brokers to attempt to keep their occupancy costs down to a minimum. This is understandable since it is a fixed operating expense that remains fairly level regardless of the swing of the seasonal sales variation during the course of the year. Effective control of operating expenses is an integral part of net income production. Controlling the size of an expenditure is but one dimension of financial control. Extracting maximum benefit from the expenditure is another. The latter might be particularly applicable to the real estate company's occupancy costs. Low rent in itself might not be the best budgetary goal. Higher rent at a more efficient location may prove to be more productive in terms of maximizing profits from the business. Quality of the space and efficiency of layout may be other factors entering into the picture as well. Employee and client attitude toward the facilities must also be considered. The very nature of the real estate brokerage business provides some insight about a decision of this type. How often does the typical client enter the real estate market? Recalling the information presented earlier about the workings of the real estate market, it is reasonable to assume that this client may come into the market two. . .three. . .or maybe four times during the course of one's lifetime. This indicates long periods of absences from the market that may be six or seven years, on average. A well located real estate office can serve as one of the effective vehicles to remain in contact with the client. Company identification can be maintained in several ways and a favorable exposure to the public may be one of the least expensive avenues. A ground floor level office with an attractive street exposure provides an informal means of communication with the public. Hundreds or thousands of people may walk by or drive by the broker's office day after day, week after, week, month after month, year after year. They are bound to become familiar with the company's name and its specific location. The company's image has been established in their minds and this identification has been reinforced with the passage of time. While they may not have come in direct contact with the real estate company, they are fully aware of its existence and physical appearance. Continued favorable exposure of this type reminds the public that the broker has been at a particular location for an extended period of time. This, in turn, imparts the notion that the broker must be successful because continued operation connotes success since an unsuccessful operation would have closed up and moved away. This kind of rationale suggests that a favorable exposure is a feature of a good location and is a secondary benefit of occupancy expenditures. Proponents of this type of thinking maintain that a portion of such office rental could be treated as being a part of the advertising or promotional costs of doing business.

Where should a real estate brokerage office be ideally located, given freedom of choice? Should it be in the central business district, a local business district, or in a residential area? A simple answer would be to locate at a site where the office will be seen by as many people as possible, but the kind of people who are likely to patronize the broker's business. Locations of this type might be across from a church that is well attended, near a supermarket, or next to a bank or savings institution. The kind of exposure must take into account the type of people the brokerage business (or other functions) is trying to attract. A downtown location may attract crowds of passers-by, but numbers may not be too significant if they are made up of young people working in the offices in the immediate area. Residential real estate brokerage offices must make contact with people who are interested in selling and buying homes. Contacts represent the initial step along the road of opportunity. Real estate is primarily sold out in the field for the most part. The probability of generating an offer is enhanced when the prospective buyer, the house and the salesperson are all at the same site at the same time. Nevertheless, an impressive office enhances the probability of such events occurring. Prospective clients tend to judge (or prejudge) a real estate broker by the quality of his or her office facilities.

Application of Management Principles

It is only natural that real estate businesses should be sales oriented. This is particularly true of the smaller real estate office since the brokerage function is usually its main activity. But the dominance of sales activity can easily overshadow the necessity for the proper company management. There are brokers who resort to the simple philosophy that "sales cures all problems." The deteriorating morale of the sales staff is arrested by an increase in sales; excessive advertising expenditures can be offset by an increase in sales; or high selling commissions can be overcome by an increase in sales. It is comparable to saying that inefficiencies can be tolerated if covered by adequate revenue. However, it should be recognized that sales attainments represent the achievement of a short-range objective. While it is a critical factor in managing the firm, it is not the only function. If a firm is to be viable, if a firm is to grow, if a firm is to have continuity, it must have some basic and workable form of business organization. Unfortunately many basic textbooks and fundamental courses on business management deal with the larger corporate structure and give little or no attention to the smaller business organization, let alone a smaller real estate brokerage firm. It is generally accepted that there are four basic management functions: planning, organizing, directing and controlling. These broad principles have direct applicability to the real estate brokerage firm, regardless of size and along with certain sub-areas are illustrated in Chart 8 – 5.

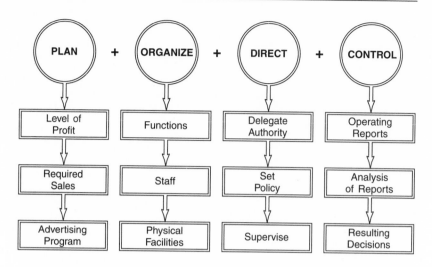

CHART 8 – 5
FOUR BASIC MANAGEMENT PRINCIPLES

The preceding chart represents a rather condensed version of generally accepted management principles. This is done in an effort to relate them to the small real estate firm. All four of these management principles are continuous in operation but some functions have shorter cycles than others. They can more easily be identified in the larger real estate companies than in the small organization. It may be that in the case of the small organization the sole owner-broker performs all four functions. It is just as important that the sole operator discipline and manage one's self as disciplining and managing others. These four categories of principles will now be discussed as they relate to the individual real estate brokerage firm.

1. PLAN

The economic incentive that induces the establishment of real estate businesses is the opportunity to make a profit. On this score expectations tend to run high. There is little doubt of this being the primary motivating force in nearly all cases. Not to be overlooked are secondary motivations such as independence, prestige, pride and security. Dreams are put to the test as soon as the doors are opened for business. This is where the realities of the marketplace enter into the picture. What realistic level of profit is desired by the owners of the business? What sales volume would be necessary to achieve this level of profit? How much and what kind of advertising program will be needed to sustain sales at this required level? These decisions represent expectations of the future. There are other sub-areas that must be considered as well. For instance, how will the required sales quota be constituted as to new or used homes; single families or multiple family; low, medium or high priced property; particular area of town and so forth? Is the sales policy in line with the type of image that is intended to be created for the firm? Planning is the developing of a workable program consisting of goals that have a reasonable possibility of being attained.

2. **ORGANIZE**

Earlier in this chapter the matter of selecting a combination of real estate functions was discussed. Once that decision is made, then subsequent decisions are in order.

A realistic timetable must be set up in order to introduce and establish the various functions selected for the real estate business. In most cases it would be the brokerage function that was introduced first, followed by insurance, appraisals and rental service as the company's capabilities develop. The establishment of these functions calls for the hiring of a staff. Competent sales people must be hired. In the medium and large size real estate organization the sales staff has to be backed up by supporting office staff. Organizing the physical facility deals with office selection, office layout, obtaining the necessary equipment and arranging it properly.

3. DIRECT

In the smaller organization we find that the owner-manager is involved in nearly every transaction, since he or she serves in the dual capacity as sales manager and office manager. As a result the owner/broker makes continuing contact with most of the clients in the field as well as during the closing process. As the firm grows, the owner-manager must recognize that he or she cannot make all of the decisions in the organization. The broker generally runs out of time and spreads oneself so thin that the quality of his or her work begins to suffer. Should he or she pursue such a course one will find that the growth of the organization will be distinctly limited. If this is the case, it may be that members of the organization may have difficulty in finding the owner-manager available when he or she is needed. A sensible way of overcoming this limitation is through the delegation of authority. This enables the owner-operator to magnify the company's growth potential. Capable subordinates should be given both the opportunity and the privilege to make the lesser decisions in the organization. The owner-broker can still be involved in the major decision-making processes.

It is important to spell out the company policy in written form. Company policy includes such subjects as selling techniques, advertising, conduct of open houses, dealing with the public and other brokers. It should also include commission policy, protection of prospects and a code of ethics. Given the proper authority, managers below the top level can then proceed to supervise the staff based on such established policy.

In this day and age of consumer protection, it is imperative that the real estate firm recognize the absolute need for risk management. Consumers are becoming more sophisticated and along with their increasing knowledge comes more litigation. Aside from the direct complaints to the real estate firm, complaints are filed with the state licensing agencies, real estate trade associations, consumer protection groups and law offices. As a basic requirement, a risk management program should deal with education, dispute resolution and liability insurance. The basic part of the education portion can be incorporated in the company policy but should be supplemented with relevant periodic releases in printed form as well as the appearances of well qualified guest speakers at company meetings. The real estate firm should implement an internal system of dealing with disputes in a prompt, fair and courteous manner. Usually, there are two sides to most disputes and they should be heard objectively. For financial reasons, the firm should carry Errors and Omissions insurance coverage. Small settlements can be handled in the ordinary course of business. However, it is the large settlement risk that should be covered by insurance. The balance between the two can be achieved by means of a reasonably sized deductible limit on the E & O policy.

4. CONTROL

Evaluating the progress of the company is a continuing process. Basic information is derived from the various kinds of reports related to sales, budgets and financial conditions. Detailed and meaningful analyses of these reports set the stage and provide the basis for further decision making.

Specific applications of these principles are illustrated and discussed in Chapters 9 and 10.

Chapter 9 — Your Company – Staff and Procedures

"Success Breeds Success. . . ." *Charles Young*

"What is Success?"

The standard definition of the word success is the accomplishment of something planned or attempted. The level of success may be related to the level of achievement or importance of accomplishment. Success in an educational career may be the attainment of the degree or diploma. Success in the business world might be measured in terms of level of income, accumulation of assets, or obtaining a prestigious title or position of authority. There seems to be a relationship between success and satisfaction, the need to satisfy one's desires. Such desires are personal in nature and vary from person to person. Desire combined with drive adds to the probability of achieving the goal. In the real estate business there are three sides of success. There is success from the point of view of the owner-operator of the business and from the point of view of the managerial and sales staff. The owner-operator might conclude that because the business is successful, he or she as an individual is also successful. This might be carried forward to be applied to the sales associates. Based on the fact that they may be earning above average incomes, the owner-operator might conclude that the sales associates are successful, therefore satisfied. Such a conclusion could possibly be misleading with respect to the attitude of the sales staff.

Another kind of success would be the respect one receives from competitors. It would be a serious mistake on the part of the

219

real estate broker to be concerned only about one's own business, with the attitude that the competitors can take care of themselves. This may be an effective philosophy in the short run but in the long run it may have some damaging effect. By virtue of their very numbers alone, the competing brokers have a much larger exposure to the public in general than one individual broker. With this kind of communicating advantage the competitors provide the market with information about other brokerage firms. It is almost a form of public relations. The broker operating on a high plane of ethical conduct and integrity is bound to make a favorable impression on the competitors. When questioned about the characteristics of a particular broker, the competition is practically forced to give a favorable recommendation. This represents unsolicited, unpaid advertising and promotion for the benefit of the broker. On the other hand the broker who pays little attention to ethical standards will soon be found out. Bad news travels fast. Respect from competitors is earned by displaying a high level of conduct in the handling of business transactions.

There also is a measure of success in the quality of the broker's public image. A favorable image breeds confidence. Confidence overcomes public resistance in doing business with a particular firm. In general, the public prefers to deal with successful companies simply because they don't appreciate and don't want to deal with unsuccessful people. Therefore, a real estate broker holding a favorable public image has a better chance of getting a larger share of referral business. Both buying and listing prospects gravitate toward this broker as a natural process. Just as in the case of respect for one's competitors, this matter of public image is something that has to be earned. It is developed by years of good service, years of honest dealing and years of hard work. It accrues to those who exhibit these qualities.

Generally speaking, top notch sales people with very high earnings are not very security conscious because these high earnings provide for present as well as future needs. On the other hand, the average or marginal salesperson whose earnings are mediocre are very security conscious since their earnings provide for present needs only, thus leaving their future in doubt. In most offices the top notch earners are few in number and, as a result, the typical sales staff is long on people in the mediocre category. Number wise this latter group exerts the strongest influence on management policy. This group is very security conscious; therefore they are concerned with such things as the continuity of the firm, retirement plans, leisure time, income insurance. No real estate firm can expect to have a sales staff of all top notch personnel. There simply aren't that many to go around. Furthermore, the attrition rate of those in the top category is rather high. Realistically, management may rely on average salespeople to maintain the going concern. Therefore, consideration must be given to insurance plans, retirement plans and other forms of security. Periodically the sales manager should make an analysis of production totals and corresponding ages of members of the staff. An increasing average age of the sales staff may show a high degree of correlation with factors such as a growing concern with security type measures in the organization.

Why do Sales Associates Leave an Organization?

Personnel studies of real estate organizations reveal a strikingly high turnover rate. What causes sales associates to leave? Some of the more obvious reasons are these: (1) ambition of the sales associates; (2) friction with new employees; (3) dissatisfaction with the owner; (4) ambition of spouses. The majority of real estate brokers are former real estate sales people. In the usual case the salesperson inwardly compares his or her talents with those of the owner. If he or she deems one's talents to be equal or better than those of the owner, he or she develops a frame of mind that produces confidence that in turn provides the basis for entertaining thoughts of going into business on one's own. If this person is ambitious, willing to take the responsibility, ready to make the investment, ready to assume the risk, then this person appears to be ready to go out on his or her own. The sales associate may also be motivated by the fact that he or she may have reached an intellectual plateau. This associate may think that he or she has learned everything there is to know about the residential real estate business and assumes to be in a rut. Daily work has become repetitive in nature. This associate knows how to get listings, sell houses, write up offers, get the financing, close the deal and this is getting kind of monotonous. He or she may feel they have greater capabilities that go beyond direct selling. It is at this point that the broker should be able to provide greater challenges like inviting the sales associate of this type to sell more complex types of real estate such as investment properties or participate in the purchase and resale of properties or equity exchanging. New fields offer excitement, new challenges and a new lease on life and a new attitude on the part of the sales associate toward his or her work. Such revitalization is necessary from time to time. Lacking this kind of revitalization the sales associate may become discouraged and leave.

The adding of new persons to the sales staff may cause frictions. It is possible that the present members of the sales staff resent the addition of new sales people. They may resent the addition of part-time people to the staff. In general, they may feel this kind of resentment and have it build up in their minds. They may feel that more sales associates results in the pie being cut in thinner slices and the individual shares become smaller. It would seem logical that if a broker intends to expand the sales staff, the broker should simultaneously expand the advertising and sales promotion program as well. Introducing some type of sales development tool will assure the people in the company that the firm is reaching for a higher sales total and that they will share in the increased sales. There may be some comfort in the old sea captain's observation, "A rising tide lifts all boats." It is possible that the expressed resentment toward new members, part-time members or more sales personnel, may be convenient excuses to cover up a real underlying reason for leaving.

A spouse's ambition can be a strong motivating force in driving the sales associate to higher heights or to opportunities elsewhere. It is natural that the spouse would want the partner to get ahead. It may be for social reasons or perhaps the desire to have a better home, better car, better clothes or to send the children to better schools. These are natural reactions but the spouse may keep prodding the partner. Basically the spouse wants the partner to be successful in order that other members of the family can share in this

222

success. This is a form of motivation that can be effectively utilized by a real estate firm. The spouse should be made to feel that he or she is a part of the selling team. Spouses should be invited to company functions whether they are social or business meetings. In some cases it may be advisable to encourage spouses to get real estate licenses in order that they may help their partners more effectively. However, this last recommendation must be used in a qualified manner, particularly in cases where there are children of school age in the family. With the present day availability of personal computers, fax machines and the like, it may be more convenient to have the spouse assist at home, rather than in the office. The important thing is to maintain communication between the real estate office and the spouse. This communication need not be very direct but adequate to let him or her know what is going on in the office. This may be in the form of an occasional letter, a periodic publication, a social gathering or informal visits to the office.

The Size of the Sales Staff vs. "The Cycle of Effort"

The cycle of effort refers to the varying levels of momentum displayed by a real estate sales associate. The top notch sales associate stays at a relatively high level throughout the course of a year. His or her potential is directly related to the seasonal variation. This associate is a consistent performer. On the other hand, the average producer tends to have more ups and downs in his or her pattern of production. This producer may list and sell two properties each month or list one or two properties and sell two other properties. This level of volume has some important management implications. There is a significant psychological dimension associated with this type of performance. Let us assume a salesperson lists two properties and sells two other properties. This means he or she has been involved in four different transactions, two listing contracts and two selling contracts. Assuming that each one of these transactions occurs on a separate day, we come to the conclusion that in the course of an ordinary month, this salesperson has experienced four days of success and 26 days of failure. This kind of reinforcement of the failure syndrome may have a depressing effect on the salesperson. If he or she is a member of a four person sales staff, the sum total of success of this salesperson and the other three on the staff amount to sixteen days of success and fourteen days of failure, again assuming that all transactions occurred on separate days. This suggests that in order to avoid this sort of depression, that there is a minimum workable size of a sales office. From a listing point of view it would mean 30 listings per month or 30 sales per month from a selling point of view. For a combination of the two it would amount to 15 listings a month and 15 sales a month. In the latter case, a total of 30 transactions and again assuming each salesperson has a capability of four transactions a month, suggests that the minimum size of sales staff should be seven or eight people in order to accumulate this kind of volume. Where higher production levels per person are required, obviously the sales staff has to be increased proportionately in size. These concepts are displayed in the following chart:

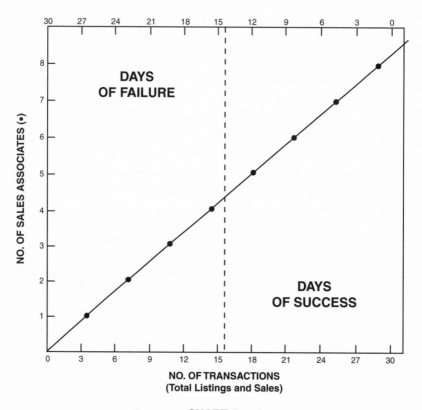

CHART 9 – 1
FREQUENCY OF SUCCESS vs. FAILURE

The progressive sales manager will readily recognize that although a salesperson may suffer 26 days of defeat, confidence is restored and reinforced by the positive performance made by other members of the sales staff. Therefore, it is necessary to maintain a sales staff of a minimum size in order to generate this kind of positive atmosphere. Witnessing other sales associate's success in listing and selling assures each salesperson that there is activity in the current market and that there is positive evidence that it is occurring.

Recruiting and Training

Who are the prospective sales associates that the firm is trying to recruit? Based on national averages here is an overview of a typical recruit:

- Average age will be 45 to 50 years
- About two-thirds of them will be women
- About one-half of them will have had some college training
- Nearly all of them will want to start in residential real estate

Of the women who apply, a noticeable number come from households that have recently entered the "empty nester" stage. The children have gone off to college, got married, or decided to have their own apartment. Now these women are free to pursue other options such as re-entry into their professional field, second career training, or completion of a college degree.

A second substantial group is made up of men who have had involuntary career changes due to corporate "down-sizing", "right-sizing", or "re-engineering". Both groups possess the maturity and motivation to succeed in the residential real estate field. It should be noted that of all income sources, nearly 80% of licensee's income is derived from the residential field.

What is the usual source of contact with these incoming recruits?

- Real estate career seminars.
- Real estate license training schools.
- Newspaper help wanted classified ads
- Guest speaker appearances at real estate schools.

- Referrals from present sales staff members

In the case of recruiting experienced sales associates, the approach needs to be different. Consider this basic management equation:

GOOD PEOPLE = GOOD COMPANY
MORE GOOD PEOPLE = BETTER COMPANY

The recruiting appeal can be made through the existing full-time sales staff. The firm's rationale can be stated as follows:

"We need *your* help to build a better company."

"It will be good for you . . . and it will be good for us."

"Let's work together — you help us . . . we'll help you!"

"We would like to move up a level in our real estate market. That's a big challenge that requires a bigger team . . . but we don't want to lose sight of quality!"

"You'll have to agree that it's great to have good people working next to you."

"You'll have to agree that it's great to have our associates help sell your listings."

"You'll have to agree that it's great to have our associates help service your listings by holding them Open for Inspection."

"You'll have to agree that it's great to have our associates help service your listings by showing them by appointment."

"You'll have to agree that it would be great to have more competitive listings to show to your good buyers."

"You'll have to agree that more competitive listings will bring in more incoming floor-time calls."

"You'll have to agree that by putting all these things together . . . that you will be bound to earn more money."

This appeal to the present sales associates is then followed by awards for their participation in the recruiting program. Bear in mind that they will be involved in the selection of new colleagues but with these qualifications:
1. Recruits must be licensed.
2. Must be full-time (capable of handling floor-time)
3. Experienced (rather than newly licensed)
4. Acceptable to the company

The awards given must be substantial in view of the benefits to the company. For the first qualified recruit obtained, give the sales associate a paid registration to a real estate convention, or something of equivalent value. Other awards, in steps, may include air fare and/or hotel accommodations. To encourage more than one qualified referral per associate, it may be advisable to include the spouses for a free weekend vacation.

What is being said to the present sales associates is that they are encouraged to be involved in the expansion process. They are wanted to help determine and control the quality of their real estate sales team. They are wanted to help maintain the reputation that they have built up over the years. The appeal is to work together and succeed together.

Pareto's Law

The Italian born Swiss professor and economist, Vilfredo Pareto (1848-1923), although known more for his social reform ideologies, produced a simple observation about the concentration of wealth in Italy. His research demonstrated that about 80% of the wealth in that country was owned by only 20% of the families.

This 80% - 20% concept was rather broadly applied by other various sectors of society.

In the United States, we often hear these adapted versions:
- In churches, 80% of the annual contributions are made by 20% of the member families
- In non-profit organizations, 80% of the volunteer work is done by 20% of the members
- In sales organizations, 80% of the sales volume is attributable to 20% of the sales staff

Whether these adaptations of "Pareto's Law" are valid or not, the fact remains that this 80% - 20% concept is quite widely used and repeated. This stresses the importance of adding top-producers and further raises the question of the cost of carrying sub-marginal producers.

Enthusiasm

All human beings are subject to emotional highs and lows. In the real estate field, a sales associate experiences an emotional high right after his or her offer is accepted. That same sales associate experiences an emotional low right after his or her offer is rejected without even a counter-offer.

Emotions affect your attitude of the moment. It certainly would be preferable to be on an emotional high all of the time. One dimension of an emotional high is a positive attitude. Enthusiasm, in part, is an expression of a positive attitude. Many psychologists maintain that enthusiasm can make the difference in attempting to make things happen.

Enthusiasm generated during a one-time training session of several hours duration has a "shelf life" of about 48 hours. Without a continuing program to ensure follow-up and renewed commitment, it takes on the characteristics of a skyrocket . . . spectacular . . . a great high . . . excitement . . . but no depth . . . and a gradual fade out . . . and soon forgotten.

Engendering enthusiasm is a significant start toward developing a change in one's attitude plus getting and keeping motivated.

Most lectures eventually become boring and cause the mind to wander rather than thinking along with the speaker. A day long seminar may be somewhat cost effective but the rate of retention of the subject matter is not very impressive. A series of shorter interactive learning sessions over several months may prove to be far more effective. A longer series of sessions of shorter duration provides the opportunity for reinforcement of important parts of the training program.

There should be ample time for participants to try their classroom ideas in actual practice and then report their experiences back to the group for critique. The participants will be more interested and receptive to actual everyday experiences in the field rather than hypothetical examples given in lectures.

Here is an illustration of self-generated enthusiasm that evolves into motivated selling activity. It's an actual experience that has been proven to be successful over the years. It is called the "Charlie Young Story".

Charlie Young was a sincere, hard-working sales associate with well above average sales success. His personal appearance was quite average, nothing out of the ordinary. However, he did, on occasion, have a slowdown or slump in his sales production. He devised a simple system of regenerating his enthusiasm within a sales stimulating framework. He was a believer in the notion that "Enthusiasm makes things happen!" But the real challenge was . . . . how does one develop enthusiasm? . . . real, sincere enthusiasm? . . . not artificial or superficial. His procedure was very practical and it seemed to work each time he tried it. As a matter of fact, it worked for others who copied his technique as well. Here is the procedure, step by step:

1. Set aside a few hours for several days, take time out to study *all* of the listings in the company's property book (or other system).
2. Study the picture of each home or building . . . reread the description very carefully, noting the value features.
3. Then select the *ten best buys* in the whole book . . . based on overall value features
4. Next, narrow the ten best buys down to the *five* best buys.
5. After that, narrow the five best buys down to *three*.

6. Finally, select the *one best buy.*

   Now that the sales associate has done his or her work diligently, one can honestly say, "In my opinion, this is the best buy in the book!" It's not the company's opinion. It's not the sales manager's opinion. It's the sales associate's own independent opinion. That's why he or she honestly believes it. That's what generates true enthusiasm.

7. Now that belief must be put into action.

   Granted, it's much easier to talk convincingly about something one believes in. Further, the enthusiasm is being generated naturally – from within.

   a. Schedule an Open House for that outstanding property — even if it's someone else's listing.

   b. Check out the available financing on the property.

      1. Call one or two lenders

      2. Get the current mortgage interest rates on fixed rate and ARM financing

      3. Assume minimum down payments and calculate the monthly payment (PITI)

   c. Call people in advance and tell them about this unusual Open House *and* exactly how this "best buy" status was arrived at.

      1. Call your buying prospects and invite them to the Open House.

      2. Call people in the immediate neighborhood, tell them about the best buy Open House, asking them for help in telling others.

      3. Tell other associates in your office all about it.

   d. Spread the good news at the Open House.

   e. The visitors to the Open House are bound to get as excited and interested as the sales associate. Enthusiasm is contagious!

In the process, aside from motivating oneself, the sales associate has become better acquainted with all of the firm's current listings and is obviously more knowledgeable.

This approach is generated from within and therefore has greater credibility with the sales associates. It is suggested that sales associates start on this program while on floor duty . . . instead of just waiting idly for the next incoming call. What's more, they may become better prepared to handle that next call.

Sales Manager's Role

The prime goal in a real estate firm that cuts across all levels of activities is simply this: *Make the salespeople successful!* This applies to the company, the sales manager and the salespeople themselves. After all, the company's success is the sum total of the individual sales associates' success, embodied in the statement, "Your success is our success!" There should be unanimous support for these ideas from the top down to the operating level. Success is a very desirable concept as far as everyone is concerned. However, there may be varying degrees of commitment toward achieving success by the firm, the sales manager and the sales associates. The firm is the largest risk taker in view of its capital investment. The firm measures its success in terms of net profit, continuity, growth and reputation. The sales manager measures his or her success in meeting sales quotas, recruiting effectiveness, training sales people and the satisfaction of helping agents to become successful. Sales associates measure their success in terms of high earnings, their degree of independence and personal recognition for their achievements.

The leadership role focuses on the office sales manager. After recruiting and training, the sales manager's job is to keep the sales associates sufficiently motivated to perform in a satisfactory manner. Ideally, the challenge is to motivate each sales person to utilize his or her talents to the best of each one's own ability.

The sales manager must keep in mind that, in general, people are all somewhat alike even though their physical appearances, talents and personalties may vary.

- Our day to day attitude is never perfectly consistent
- We all have our moods ("ups" and "downs")

- We tend to respond to the influences of our environment — the weather, general business conditions, the people around us, our relatives, friends, business associates, even the progress of college and professional sports teams.
- Our actions tend to reflect the tempo or the mood of what is happening around us.
- Life, in general, seems to be much more enjoyable when we are in the midst of a winning or positive situation. Most people enjoy the pleasant feeling that one experiences on being connected with a winning team. At such times the world seems great, you have a positive attitude, you are "up", you are smiling and you seem to see nothing but "sunshine and roses".

Take, for example, Baltimore Oriole's Cal Ripken approaching the immortal Lou Gehrig's record 2,130 consecutive games played. You may recall how it dominated the news . . . a very high level of excitement in the newspapers as well as on television and radio. But as soon as the record was broken it all came to a sudden halt. The magic electricity in the air, all the excitement, all the enthusiasm suddenly dissipated. That is the nature of these mystical changes of human behavior that are ever present in our daily living. Psychologists, economists and other observers of such changes in human behavior describe these highs and lows as phases of cycles . . . a sort of roller coaster-like ride through life.

Things are much the same in the real estate field . . . we see sales volume vary with the four seasons of the year . . . we see market volume influenced by changes in mortgage interest rates . . . we see buyers' attitudes affected by extreme weather conditions.

Obviously, we like the "highs" but we don't particularly like the "lows". It is the basic responsibility of the sales manager to coach and motivate members of the sales staff to higher heights of achievement. There appears to be a parallel of real estate production to the comments made by an old southern preacher at a funeral service. His words were plain and simple but had a great depth of meaning . . . "seems like everybody wants to go to heaven, but nobody wants to die!" These words might be paraphrased in the real estate context . . . "seems like everybody wants to be successful, but too many are afraid to make a genuine commitment." For some sales associates making a genuine commitment may be a quantum leap. However, this goal of success cannot be achieved by wishful thinking alone.

The successful sales manager knows how to take an annual sales goal and divide it into achievable segments. Due to seasonal variation, the first and fourth quarters of the calendar year present more of a challenge, production-wise. One way of meeting this challenge is by introducing the "First 100 Days Theory". It is based on the notion that what one does in the first hundred days of a given year will set the pace and tone for that year. A good start, especially in the first quarter of the year, should give one great momentum into the improving market of the second and third quarters . . . thus being well on the way to a successful year.

The initial step is to get a "jump-start" on the first sale of the year. This is where commitment comes in. The sales associate should start planning on how he or she is going to sell that first property in January. The sales associate should picture that event occurring . . . thinking about it continually. The plan should be shared with the sales manager . . . just how it is going to be done. To reinforce the commitment, the plan should be explained to the sales associate's spouse on how it is going to be done. It may be the special promotion of an open house or promoting one of the associate's listings. It may involve asking friends, relatives and business acquaintances to help. It may also involve asking one's social friends and/or fellow church members to help. Above all, the associate should pass out business cards and literature to let people know that he or she is really in the real estate business. This certainly causes an aura of sales excitement. Once that first sale is achieved, the sales associate is beaming with enthusiasm and should be on the way to the start of a successful year.

In the matter of training recruits, bear in mind that such salespeople are new only once. In that stage they are most likely to listen to and respond to training advice and procedures. They must be trained properly in the beginning, otherwise the broker will have a double job down the road. First of all, newly acquired bad habits must be eliminated before basic training can be restarted. Trainees may be more skeptical the second time around. Lack of productivity on the part of new salespeople cannot be ignored by means of the argument that no sale means no pay, hence nothing lost. In reality, no sales means no profit but it also means being strapped with the related expense.

It is also important that the sales manager provide proper direction for the newer salespeople because selling on a straight commission basis can be very stressful. As a result, during a sales slump, a newer associate may become easily discouraged and may look to other fields of employment if proper guidance and encouragement are not provided.

Selecting a Sales Manager

Being a top producer in real estate sales does not necessarily qualify that person to become a good sales manager.

Here are some of the important qualities that prove to be valuable in performing the role of a good sales manager:

a. Willingness to be an enthusiastic team player
b. Patience, listening skills and concern for others
c. Understanding of the need for policy and planning
d. Appreciation for intangible benefits such as enjoying progressive improvement in people

It is said that the best business managers are good forecasters. This is true in the sense that they have good, workable plans (forecasts) that are self-fulfilling as they implement them successfully. There seems to be a tendency for sales associates having the above mentioned qualities to become a sales manager by informally conveying such aspirations to the owner of the firm as opportunities arise. It is also important that the owner of the firm be on the continual lookout for sales associates having the necessary qualifications so when the time comes to hire a sales manager, the names of qualified prospects will come to mind. One of the inherent challenges in selecting a new sales manager is that it is difficult to expect a top selling agent earning an annual six figure income to be excited about a sales management position that may pay less. This is where the appreciation of intangible values comes into play

. . . such as the position of title, prestige, experience, career path and coach-like satisfaction in seeing people develop. Not all persons exhibit this broader outlook on life. A famous professional basketball coach once said, "Pay me one dollar a year more than the highest paid player on the squad and I would be willing to coach that team." If that were the typical case, there would be very few coaches hired.

It is up to the owner of the company to put together a compensation package that may include salary, bonuses based on achievements, profit-sharing, fringe benefits and even options to buy into the firm at some future date. Allowing sales managers to compete with the sales associates they supervise should be done on a very reserved and controlled basis. In most cases, if the sales manager is doing a good job, there is little or no time available for personal listing or selling.

The field of biological science identifies three well defined circumstances within which different species exist together. These three categories seem to have some interesting relationships to categories of sales associates in the real estate field.

1. *Competitive interaction* – when grain vs. weeds or grass vs. weeds compete with each other for moisture and sunlight.

2. *Symbiotic interaction* – when two species help one another as in the case of the bee and the flower. The flower provides nectar for the bee and the bee carries pollen to the flowers for pollination.

3. *Parasitic interaction* (or partial interaction) – when moss grows on the trunk of a tree, attaching itself to the bark, exploiting the host.

The first category typifies the top producers who enjoy the competitive arena and thrive on the challenge in search of listings and sales. The second group consists of the real team players who understand mutual interdependence and the need for cooperation with others within the real estate market. The third category would include those marginal sales associates who wait for the incoming calls on floor time in order to sell other agents' listings. It is no coincidence that the annual income of sales associates in these three categories rank in the top one-third, the middle one-third, and the low one-third, respectively.

Economies of Scale

As firms grow in size, there is a tendency for sales associates to specialize in listing or selling. This provides for more effective utilization of equipment, office space and the Multiple Listing Service. This, in turn, produces more co-broker sales as well as more in-house sales. The larger firm, due to its larger volume, can readily absorb such specialization. The smaller firm finds it more difficult to cope with increased costs per unit due to an imbalance between listings and sales.

Management studies often refer to the size of supervisory staffs. At one end of the scale is the size of the staff in the controlled society, as was found in the Communist nations. They required ten to fifteen percent of the work force for complete regulation of the workers. The comparable number for the United States is about three percent of the work force to be engaged in supervisory positions. This suggests that a sales office of 33 agents can support a sales manager. As the number of agents increase, the office grows, the work load increases for the sales manager and there may be need to hire an assistant sales manager. However, these are averages and serve as general guidelines.

Antitrust Laws

Alleged violations of antitrust laws can have serious consequences for the real estate broker. The cost of violations can be in the form of damages paid to another party, sizeable attorney fees and even the negative impact of adverse publicity in the media. The purpose of antitrust laws is to preserve competition in the marketplace. It is intended that competitors will be prevented from conspiring together to reduce or eliminate competition. In the real estate field individual brokers may establish their own commission policies with regard to listing rates, agent's share and cooperating broker's share. However, such policy decisions must be made solely by that company and not involve any competing brokers whether through formal or informal discussions. Two elements of the typical real estate antitrust violation are:

1. conspiracy
2. restraint of trade

A violation might include the setting of listing commissions, fixing co-broker commissions or boycotting a competitor or supplier. A supplier could include a newspaper, a lender, a closing service, etc. Note that there must be two or more individuals or companies involved on the violation side of the complaint. Legal experts in this area emphasize that there is no such thing as an innocent agreement among competing brokers about commissions charged sellers or shares paid to co-brokers. Agreement by two or more brokers to act in concert on commission matters, however formal or informal the agreement, is deemed to be price fixing. The same broad tests apply to two or more brokers joining their efforts to injure a third party in the market, be it a competitor, customer, or supplier. Such action is deemed to be a boycott. These antitrust laws are enforced at both the federal and state levels and may appear to be rather stringent to the average real estate broker. However, it is in the understanding of the laws that one identifies the parameters within which real estate activities can operate on a respectable, professional level.

Public Relations

For the most part, the amount of direct contact by a real estate firm with the public is usually limited to prospective buyers and sellers that may become parties to a transaction. That group of contacts may be less than ten percent of the total local population in a given year. The firm's advertising program provides another form of contact with the public, but in a much less direct manner. In order to increase the company's visibility and improve its image, it is recommended that the real estate firm supplement existing efforts with a public relations program. Such a program is a planned and sustained effort to maintain media relations. In one way it can be referred to as "free publicity". But it really isn't free because it takes time and effort to keep the channels of communication open between your company and the media. It is different from paid advertising where the real estate company pays the bill and therefore is in control. With public relations, the real estate firm is at the mercy of the media. Accordingly, news releases should be only at those times that the firm has something important to tell the public. It may be the addition to the sales staff of a well known person. It may be the ground-breaking for a new building. It may be the affiliation with a nationally known network. To be effective, the public relations program must have some continuity. Continuity involves a provision for funding in the company's budget and the assignment of the duty to a specific person within the organization. If that is not workable, consider retaining an experienced outside person on a part-time basis. The latter may eliminate going through a trial and error process in developing a program. To be newsworthy, the real estate firm must have a release with general reader or viewer appeal. Stories about people have the most appeal, particularly when there is an human interest angle involved.

A continuing program will provide the opportunity to get better acquainted with the proper media contacts. It will also provide a better understanding of what kind of news is most acceptable. A suggestion is to provide the media with observations about the local real estate market that are not published elsewhere. Such information would most likely be appreciated by the media as well as the public. It could even develop into a regular feature each month or so.

CHAPTER 10 — YOUR OFFICE: MANAGEMENT AND BUDGETS

". . . using non-current statistics to run your business is like driving your car by using your rear view mirror." *Erwin Gaumnitz*

Many real estate brokers assign the highest priority to listing and selling activities and the lowest priority to record keeping. The reason is obvious . . . the former produces income while the latter is classified as overhead expense. It is only natural to think that if sales are increasing and bank balances are on the positive side, the business is doing fine. This kind of thinking may hold up during the more active second and third quarters of the year, but what about leaner first and fourth quarters? Some brokers subscribe to the "6 – 3 – 3" rule of real estate brokerage office operations. This rule is based on the belief that of the twelve months in a calendar year, six will be profitable, three months will break even and three months will produce an operating loss. Combined, the twelve months will be operated at a profit. This thinking appears to be based on the seasonal variation that reappears in each calendar year. If a real estate broker is going to be subjected to such marked fluctuation, it is logical to prepare in advance for these changes.

Business Plan

The starting step in preparing one's business plan is to become thoroughly acquainted with the firm's operating expenses. The accounting records for recent periods should show the various categories for which money has been spent for operating expense purposes. If annual accounting statements are not available, the next best source may be Schedule C from the Form 1040 of the firm's Federal Income Tax Return, "Profit and Loss from Business" for sole proprietorships. Partnerships use Form 1065 and corporations file on Form 1120. The following table illustrates the different categories of operating expenses in condensed form. Most firms will have a much more detailed list of accounts.

TABLE 10 – 1 OPERATING EXPENSES		
Name of Account	This Past Year	Next Year's Estimate
Advertising	$ 33,000	$ 36,000
Telephone Expense	12,000	12,000
Postage	3,000	4,000
Salaries – Sales Manager	12,000	12,000
Salaries – Office	27,000	28,000
Payroll Taxes	5,000	6,000
Rent Expense	33,000	32,000
Utilities Expense	6,000	6,000
Insurance Expense	4,500	4,000
Office Services	7,500	8,000
Depreciation – Office Equipment	6,000	6,000
Miscellaneous Expenses	1,000	1,000
Totals	**$150,000**	**$155,000**

In view of the size of the sales staff, assume that the Sales Manager is paid $1,000 a month for managerial services and is allowed to list and sell as well. That manager would occupy one of the ten desks in the office. The firm is owned by a retired third party formerly active in the business. A listing of accounts in this form will give the broker the opportunity to track expenses from year to year. In this case, there are seven full time sales associates besides the manager in this office. Not to be overlooked is the business risk of a sales staff of this size. If two salespeople decide to take vacations at the same time, the firm could lose one-fourth of its production for a few weeks. The same would be true in the case of illness. A single sales office with eight or ten could present a somewhat fragile situation for the management.

One of the first revelations of reviewing the firm's operating expenses is what it actually costs the company to maintain a desk for a full-time salesperson. A simple procedure would be to count the number of salespeople in the office. A full-time person is counted as one while part-time salespeople are counted in terms of full-time equivalents, with two or three part-time sales associates being equivalent to one full-time associate. In the previously illustrated operating expense schedule it was assumed that there were ten sales desks in the office. Seven of the desks were occupied by full-time associates while four part-time sales associates shared the other two desks. With total operating expenses for the year at $150,000, each desk costs the firm $15,000 a year to operate, on average, before any profit is realized. That means that each full-time associate and the manager must produce at least $15,000 in company dollars per year in order for the firm to break even. The four part-time sales people would need to produce $7,500 each, using the same standards. Company dollars for this purpose are defined as the total gross commissions earned less sales commissions paid to the firm's sales associates as well as commissions paid to co-brokers. This is one kind of measurement that can be used to evaluate the performance of individual sales associates. It serves as a reminder to the broker that the "no sale – no pay" logic that sometimes provides a weak excuse for keeping low producing part-time salespeople on the sales staff is an incomplete statement. This prorated share of operating expenses per desk brings to light another dimension of the total cost to subsidize submarginal producers.

Break-even Analysis

A budget is a plan. It provides goals for revenues and expenses. It affords the opportunity to evaluate the firm's performance on an ongoing basis by comparing actual revenue to budgeted revenue and actual expenses to budgeted expenses. Differences are referred to as "variances". Each variance needs to be examined to understand why and how it occurred. This enables management to take corrective action where necessary. One of the constraints is that most budgets are related to accounting records and therefore may have several weeks of lag time in their framework. Larger firms that can afford the cost of computerized service may be able to eliminate a good part of this lag time with daily reporting. In the smaller firm, the concepts of business planning may be incorporated into a procedure called, "Break-even Analysis". It is defined as the volume at which revenue exactly covers the cost of running the business. When the company is at the break-even point, it is neither making a profit nor sustaining a loss.

The next step is to further analyze the operating expenses listed in Table 10 – 1 by considering the fixed and variable characteristics of each of the expenses. Simply stated, a fixed expense does not vary with the volume of revenue production (company dollars). Fixed expenses would be incurred even if business volume would drop to a drastically low level. Examples of fixed expenses would be the office rent, utilities such as heat, air-conditioning and electricity, insurance premiums and non-sales salaries. Variable expenses increase or decrease in proportion to the volume of revenue producing activities. Variable expenses would include such items as advertising, sales promotion, telephone, MLS fees and commissions paid. It should be pointed out that break-even analysis is an estimating tool and therefore should not be considered a precision model. Future expenses are estimates that will hopefully be realistic. Dividing expenses into two distinct categories, fixed and variable, may be somewhat arbitrary at times, since some expenses may contain elements of both characteristics. However, to simplify the procedure, the dominant characteristic will be the basis for classifying a particular expense. On that basis Table 10 – 1 is modified and appears as follows in Table 10 – 2 on page 243:

			TABLE 10 – 2 FIXED AND VARIABLE EXPENSES	

Name of Account	Fixed	Variable	Total	Percent of Gross Comm.
Commissions Paid – 58%		$232,000	$232,000	58.00 %
Advertising		36,000	36,000	9.00 %
Telephone Expense		12,000	12,000	3.00 %
Postage		4,000	4,000	1.00 %
Salaries – Sales Manager	$ 12,000		12,000	3.00 %
Salaries – Office	28,000		28,000	7.00 %
Payroll Taxes	6,000		6,000	1.50 %
Rent Expense	32,000		32,000	8.00 %
Utilities Expense	6,000		6,000	1.50 %
Insurance Expense	4,000		4,000	1.00 %
Office Services	8,000		8,000	2.00 %
Depreciation – Office Equipment	6,000		6,000	1.50 %
Miscellaneous Expenses	1,000		1,000	0.25 %
Totals	$103,000			

At this point the illustration is switching from the company dollar approach of analysis to the standard accounting approach. While the company dollar method may make more sense to the real estate broker, the standard accounting approach provides for more disclosure and facilitates the comparison of one real estate brokerage firm to another, even on a regional or national basis. The percentages in the fourth column, "Percent of Gross Commissions," are based on an assumed annual gross revenue of $400,000.

It will be noted that in addition to the operating expenses, the commissions paid factor has been added. At this point the analysis is broadened and now focuses on the major components of the total company revenue. The total company revenue's major components are commissions paid, operating expenses and net earnings. In general, the commissions paid constitute the bulk of the variable expenses. The operating expenses, except for advertising, telephone and postage are predominately fixed expenses. In this case, the fixed expenses, exclusive of commissions paid, are about twice the size of the other variable expenses. While this may be typical of a smaller firm, this relationship takes on a different magnitude as firms grow in size. Due to the economies of scale, total variable expenses are considerably greater than fixed expenses in larger firms. The gross revenue, fixed expenses and variable expenses are combined in diagram form to produce the chart below:

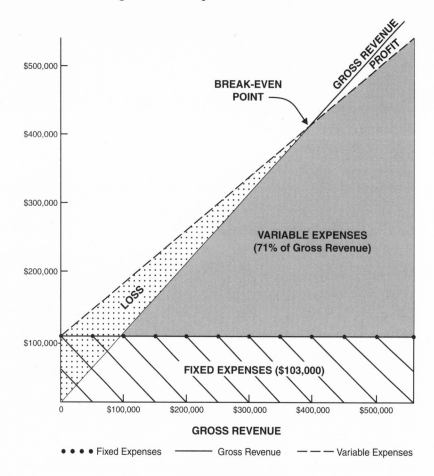

CHART 10 – 1
BREAK-EVEN ANALYSIS

The vertical axis is used to measure total fixed and variable expenses. The horizontal axis is used to measure total revenue. The break-even point is that level at which fixed expenses plus variable expense equals total revenue.

From Table 10 – 2 we see that variable expenses consist of Commission Paid (58%) plus Advertising (9%), Telephone (3%)

and Postage (1%) for a total of 71%. These percentages relate to total estimated gross revenue of $400,000.

In this case, the formula is stated as follows:

Break-even Point = Fixed Expenses + 71% of the Revenue

Break-even analysis can be used to determine the nature of the firm's business risk. It provides an estimate of the total gross revenue needed to cover fixed expenses which in this case is $103,000. Obviously, at zero level revenue, the chart shows a loss of $103,000. By following the upward sloping total gross revenue line, one comes to a point at $355,172 of gross revenue volume that equals the sum of fixed and variable expenses. This is the Break-even Point . . . no profit, no loss. Total gross revenue generated above this level produces a profit . . . and total gross revenues generated below this break-even level result in an operating loss.

Listings & Sales Quotas

Continuing with the previous illustration, it is assumed that it may take about 75 transactions to achieve a total gross revenue volume of $400,000. Some transactions involve the sale of the broker's own listings; others involve the sale of the broker's listings by another broker (co-broker); and a third category is one where the broker's firm sells another broker's listing. The firm's share of the commission may vary from category to category. It is further assumed that the firm's involvement in the 75 transactions was as follows:

TABLE 10 – 3 DISTRIBUTION OF SALES
(a) In 60% of the cases, the firm sold its own listing
(b) In 25% of the cases, the firm's listing was sold by a co-operating broker
(c) In 15% of the cases, the firm sold a co-operating broker's listing

Most residential real estate brokers in the field consider a transaction as having two "sides" — the listing side and the selling side. In category (a) above, the firm would have two sides to these transactions; in category (b) the firm would have one side; and in category (c) the firm would have one side. The assumed 75 transactions would break down as follows:

	Percent of Total	Transactions	Total Sides	Listing Sides	Sales Sides
TABLE 10 – 4 **TRANSACTIONS**					
(a)	60%	45	90	45	45
(b)	25%	18	18	18	–
(c)	15%	12	12	–	12
Totals	**100%**	**75**	**120**	**63**	**57**

A side can be considered a revenue producing source or unit, therefore, in some real estate circles, it is fittingly referred to as a "revenue unit" rather than a side.

If the firm's experience is that about seven out of ten of its listings will be sold, then it will have to list about 90 properties if it wants to have 63 sides in the "listings sold" category. There is no assurance that 7 out of 10 listings will be sold, therefore, a realistic listing quota would have to be set at some level higher than 90, say 100 new listings for the year. On that basis, each full-time salesperson (plus full-time equivalents) would be expected to bring in ten new residential listings during the coming year in order to meet the listing quota for the year.

In order to achieve an annual sales volume of 57 sides in the sales category, it should be recognized that all accepted offers will not result in a closing where a commission is paid. Accordingly, an annual sales quota under these assumptions might be set at 60 sides. This would average out to six selling sides per full-time sales associate (and full-time equivalents) for the sales year.

Based on listings sold and accepted offers closed, the eight full-time associates plus two full-time equivalents (4 part-time salespeople) would have to average 12 sides in order to reach the annual total of 120 sides. Annual listing and sales quotas should not be allocated to the months by dividing the annual total by 12. Instead, attention should be given to the probability of success in relation to seasonal variation over the four quarters of the calendar year.

Market Share

Paraphrasing an old Chinese proverb, "If you are rowing upstream at a rate equal to the flow of the water, you are standing still". In the real estate market, if a firm is satisfied with maintaining sales volume at the same level, year after year, that firm is falling behind in an expanding market. Market expansion could be measured by an increasing number of transactions and/or price inflation.

In order for a firm to ascertain its relationship to the local market, it should be alerted to the trends in that market. Most Multiple Listing Services provide basic information that can be easily charted. Among the numbers that indicate what is happening in the market are the number of new listings, the average number of days on the market, the number of sales, the average sales price, etc. By charting these periodic numbers, the broker is in a position to identify trends in the market. In the event MLS data is not available in the local market, the number of deed transfers may offer some insight into local trends. Deed transfer totals are usually published as county-wide totals rather than by municipalities. Another source of market transfers would be the local tax assessor's office. This may be a laborious process but it may be the only source available in some communities. The effort expended may be well worth being in the unique possession of this valuable and interesting information. Market share is a rather broad term and can be defined in various ways. It could measure a firm's share of new listings in a given time period; it could measure the firm's share of total existing listings at a given point in time. It could measure the firm's share of accepted offers or share of the number of closed transactions. The main purpose of market share calculations is to determine how one's firm is performing in relation to the total local market or a geographical division of it. As an alternative, a firm may want to focus its market share on single family homes or condos or vacant lot sales or some other segment of the local real estate market. The best advice is to not collect data unless it is important enough to use. Keep in mind the cost of collection, storage and processing such data. There's an interesting quip from Mark Twain (paraphrased) . . "Information is much like garbage . . . don't collect it if you're likely to throw it out!"

In the case of MLS information, it may take less than one-half hour a week to compile the necessary numbers related to listings, days on the market, accepted offers and closed transactions. The next step would be to compare the firm's totals to each of these MLS measures. This will enable the broker to find out the number of his/her listings compared to those of the competition. The same would be true of other sales information. There is little doubt that impressive market share statistics can give the broker a competitive edge in the marketplace.

Revenue Pace

Your accounting records will tell what *has* happened, but you may want to know what *is* happening. It is definitely an advantage to be able to track your activities immediately instead of too late to make the necessary corrections. A very important part of running a successful residential real estate business is to have the most current market information available in order to make *daily* management decisions. If the management waits for the monthly accounting statements to be prepared, it may be thirty days or more behind the market. The answer may be in the tabulation of the company's market activity. One such procedure is called "Revenue Pace". Out of necessity, the procedure must be simple, not very time consuming and indicate the company's progress. These component features are necessary to enable management to make almost immediate decisions on selling pace. If sales are not up to expectations, what immediate action should the firm take? Schedule more open houses for the coming weekend? Schedule a Buyers' Forum to explain mortgage financing? Schedule special ads on television or radio? These are short-term efforts that could enhance sales efforts in the matter of days, not weeks. Perhaps it's a shortage of good, salable listings that is slowing down the sales pace. That would call for an immediate advertising remedy as well. Promotional efforts should not be limited to special advertising alone. Other alternatives might include selling incentive awards for the salespeople or a mass telephone campaign on the part of the salespeople to promote specific properties or special financing. The procedures to detect sudden change in sales pace are as follows:

TABLE 10 – 5 DAILY REVENUE PACE (Gross Revenue on Accepted Offers)		
Column 1 LIST & SELL (50%)	Column 2 LIST ONLY (25%)	Column 3 SELL ONLY (25%)

Entries are made on a daily basis, recording the accepted offer price in the appropriate column. It will be observed that each column has a separate percentage of the total commission, representing the company's gross revenue share on each accepted offer. On average, the accepted offers will not become closed transactions where the commission is actually collected until 30 or 60 days after entered. These tabulations serve as a sort of forecast for the closings in the month or two ahead. The quality of such forecasts is related to the number of days' experience connected with the daily pace calculations.

As the entries are made day after day, the form may look like this after 21 days:

Column 1 LIST & SELL (50%)	Column 2 LIST ONLY (25%)	Column 3 SELL ONLY (25%)
$92,000	$84,000	$110,000
	89,000	65,000
	91,000	
———	———	———
$92,000	$264,000	$175,000
Sub-Total (21 days)	Sub-Total (21 days)	Subtotal (21 days)

For purposes of illustration, let's assume that the rate of commission is six percent of the transaction price indicated on the accepted offer to purchase. Calculations for a specific firm would use the actual commission policy of that particular firm. That would include the listing commission rate as well as the commission paid to the firm's listing and selling agent and also to the rate of commission paid to cooperating brokers. Calculations on the twenty-first day would be as follows:

LIST AND SELL:	$92,000 X 6% x 50%	=	$2,760	Company Dollars
LIST ONLY:	$264,000 X 6% x 25%	=	3,960	Company Dollars
SELL ONLY:	$175,000 X 6% X 25%	=	2,625	Company Dollars
	21 Day sub-total		$9,345	Company Dollars

Continuing the procedure...

$$\text{REVENUE PACE} = \frac{\text{Sub-Total}}{\text{No. of Days Tabulated}} \times \text{No. of Days In the Month}$$

$$= \frac{\$9,345}{21} \times 30$$

$$= \$13,350$$

The size of the firm selected for this illustration and the number of its transactions are limited in order to simplify the calculations. However, the concept of Revenue Pace is applicable to firms of all sizes. It is recommended that entries be made daily in the appropriate columns of the form. Revenue Pace should be calculated daily as well. The pace calculated in the first few days of the month may be somewhat distorted but as the days go by, Revenue Pace becomes more meaningful. In the above calculation of Revenue Pace, after 21 days the projected pace for the current month is estimated at $13,350 which is below the previously calculated break-even point of $15,000 for the month. Obviously, this calls for some sort of immediate corrective sales action to stimulate sales before the end of the month. It is said that the best run businesses are those where the owners are close to the day-by-day management. Equal care should be given to the number and quality of the incoming listings also on a daily basis. However, the tabulations need not be as extensive although a similar system could be developed based on the estimated selling prices and probability of sales, using the company's recent past experience.

Budgets

A well prepared budget can serve as a road map toward financial goals. The preliminary planning of a financial budget for the year ahead begins with the operating expense schedule identified in the break-even analysis. Budget totals are set to annual totals. Again, it is not advisable to wait for long periods of time to pass before necessary corrective action is taken. A minimal procedure of budgetary control can be incorporated in the monthly income statement (profit and loss) prepared for accounting purposes. Two extra columns can be added to the standard format of the income statement to provide comparison of actual to budgeted amount. The difference is referred to as "Variance". An example of this approach is listed in the following table.

TABLE 10 – 6 INCOME STATEMENT WITH BUDGET VARIANCE			
	Actual	**Budget**	**Variance**
Total Gross Revenue $400,000		$410,000	– 10,000
Less: Commission Paid – 232,000		237,800	– 5,800
Adjusted Gross Revenue	$168,000	172,200	– 4,200
Operating Expenses:			
Advertising	36,000	35,000	+ 1,000
Telephone Expense	12,000	12,500	– 500
Postage	4,000	3,700	+ 300
Salaries – Sales Manager	12,000	12,000	–
Salaries – Office	28,000	28,000	–
Payroll Taxes	6,000	6,000	–
Rent Expense	32,000	33,000	– 1,000
Utilities Expense	6,000	5,400	+ 600
Insurance Expense	4,000	3,600	+ 400
Office Services	8,000	6,800	+ 1,200
Depreciation – Office Equip.	6,000	6,000	–
Miscellaneous Expenses	1,000	500	+ 500
Total Operating Expense	**$155,000**	**$152,500**	**+ $2,500**
Net Earnings for the Year	$13,000	$ 19,700	– 6,700
Rate of Return on Gross Revenue	3.25%	4.8%	

In comparing the actual revenue and expense figures as tabulated in the accounting statement with the corresponding budget figures, it will be observed that expenditures for advertising, postage, utilities, insurance, office services and miscellaneous expenses were over the targets in the budget. Telephone and rent expense were less than the related budgeted amounts. Gross revenue and commissions paid were also below budget, having a net effect of −$4,200. The operating expenses over budget amounted to +$4,000 while operating expenses under budget amounted to −$1,500, with a net effect of +$2,500. The budgeted net earnings for the year were $19,700 but actual net earnings were only $13,000, with a variance of −$6,700. While this illustration of budgeted amounts and variances deals with an annual accounting statement, it would be far more meaningful to do an exercise of this sort on a monthly basis in order to observe variances while they are still current and management is in a position to make necessary adjustments.

The field of business management is long on esoteric jargon that includes a litany of terms such as:

MISSION STATEMENT
STRATEGIC PLAN
BUSINESS PLAN
SHORT-RANGE PLAN
LONG-RANGE PLAN
TOP QUALITY MANAGEMENT
BUDGET PLAN

The common denominator of all these approaches is to *plan for success*. In order to plan for success, the business owner must thoroughly understand all components of his/her own business as well as the nature of the market in which the business is competing. The most basic management guide can be found in the company's Mission Statement that briefly responds to the questions, "Who are we?", "What do we do?", "Whom do we serve?", "What are our core values?". It does not necessarily have to be a series of sentences. It could simply be a motto or a slogan like

Avis' "We try harder", Dean Witter's "We measure our success one investor at a time", or Ford's "Quality is Job 1".

One of the important dimensions of planning for success is to organize the details of that plan *in writing*. Goals, revenue projections, budgets and company plans need to be in writing to ensure consistent reminders to management of its commitment. In a well organized company, earnings may be planned through effective budgeting. Devotees of budgeting maintain that if one doesn't plan for earnings, they can and may elude your firm. The process begins with a forecast for the coming year. Such a forecast can become more meaningful if one starts with the sales associates on an individual basis. Each salesperson should be encouraged to set a sales goal for the year ahead. Such goals should be well founded, realistic and achievable in relation to the associate's capabilities. The sum total of the sales associates' goals represent an approximation of the company's revenue goal from listings and sales activities. Along with other sources of revenue, this total goal needs to be tempered with judgment by the management. It should be recognized that there is a time lag between the accepted offer and the actual closing date of the transaction. On average, this time lag may be 30 to 60 days after the date of the acceptance of the offer. The revenue forecast for the coming year is then spread over the 12 months ahead. This is not done by merely dividing the annual total by 12, but rather by taking into account seasonal variation and the company's past performance during the various seasons of the year.

It is often said that it doesn't take the genius of Einstein to run a real estate brokerage firm in a booming market. However, when things get to be more competitive, management must have much better control of the situation with good written plans implemented by good management. Goals set on a verbal basis tend to erode and to be altered by easy excuses of conditions of the moment.

What is Your Business Worth?

Aside from one's commissions and annual income, one may on occasion look to the future and wonder what the business is worth. First of all, it should be understood that the valuation procedures of a residential real estate brokerage business does not constitute an exact science. But, nevertheless, one never knows when a "window of opportunity" will present itself. It may be a merger proposal, or a chance to add a partner, or an offer to buy out an existing partner, or simply to make long range estimates in connection with estate planning and retirement. If the broker/owner seeks the assistance of a professional in the field of valuation, that valuator will most likely want to have this kind of information made available for review and analysis.

1. Financial statements prepared by and certified by a CPA or CPA firm. These would include a Balance Sheet (Statement of Financial Condition) and Profit and Loss Statement (Income Statement) for at least two full years as well as recent updates for the current partial year.

2. Copies of Federal Income Tax Returns for the past two filing years.

3. Copies of all leases and service contracts.

4. A written description of the business, the number of sales and office personnel, a brief history and growth pattern, a listing of memberships in real estate and business associations and other important related information.

This, of course, is the ideal set of circumstances. In many cases, the real estate broker may have non-certified financial and operating statements. While they may appear to be somewhat impressive in computer output form, they may contain certain limitations. In the majority of cases, the accounting service uses its software programs to process the data given to it by the client. As a result, a disclaimer is attached to the statements indicating that the records have not been audited and that the compilation is limited to the information presented by management and therefore no opinion or other form of assurance is expressed. For this and other reasons there needs to be some adjusting and/or validating of the financial and income statements.

In an attempt to simplify the understanding of this valuation process, the various methods employed are combined into these two general categories:

1. Net asset value method
2. Capitalized earnings value method

To illustrate the net asset value method, the following financial statement will be used:

TABLE 10 – 7 XYZ REALTY Balance Sheet – December 31, 19XX		
Assets	Accounting Records	Fair Market Value
Cash and Cash Equivalents	$10,000	$10,000
Office Furniture & Fixtures (net)	30,000	25,000
Leasehold Improvements (net)	20,000	15,500
Listing Inventory	–	12,000
Commissions on Pending Transactions	–	12,500
Going Concern Value (Name, staff, etc.)	–	40,000
Goodwill	–	–
Totals	$60,000	$115,000
Liabilities	none	none
Owner's Equity	$60,000	$115,000

The cash and cash equivalents have full market value, therefore, $10,000 is entered into the second column. Based on accounting procedures, office furniture and fixtures are recorded at acquisition cost and those costs are written off over the estimated useful life of each asset. Cost less accumulated depreciation equals book value. However, book value does not necessarily equal market value. The $30,000 figure in the balance sheet represents the total acquisition cost of $50,000 worth of office furniture and fixtures less $20,000 of accumulated depreciation. Based on prices of used desks, chairs, filing cabinets, typewriters, computer equipment, etc., the fair market value was determined to be $25,000. Accordingly, $25,000 was entered into the second column. The leasehold improvements were made to this leased property and paid for by the tenant. The acquisition cost of $45,000 included the interior improvements as well as an outdoor sign. Of that amount, $25,000 had been expensed for accounting purposes, leaving a net book value of $20,000. The fair market value of these leasehold improvements as used in place and the outdoor sign, based on present condition and the estimated remaining economic life, was set at $15,500. In this limited illustration, it is assumed that the business has no liabilities, therefore the owner's equity (assets minus liabilities) amounts to $60,000 under the accounting method used in Column 1.

These tangible assets in Column 1 consist of personal property but do not include intangible assets in this set of accounting procedures. Intangible assets that contribute to the value of this company include the present listing inventory, commissions that will be earned on transactions pending (accepted offers - awaiting closings), the going concern value of the company (firm name, existing sales and office help in place, etc.) and goodwill. Reasonable value estimates can be made for each of these intangible assets.

Listing Inventory

The total of the listed prices of all of the company's current listings amounts to $2,300,000. Local market experience based on MLS statistics, indicates that the average of selling prices to listed prices is 93%. The company's track record of sales of listings is three out of four, or 75%. It is assumed that the gross commission rate is 6% and the company's share of each dollar of revenue is 42%. To translate these numbers into company dollars, the procedure would be ($2,300,000 X .93 X .75 X .06 X .42) or $40,427. This, of course, constitutes adjusted gross revenue and does not take operating expenses associated with this activity into account. Based on previous illustrations in this chapter, this may add less than $12,000 to net earnings. However, looking to another value dimension of the listing inventory, one might ask, "What would be the cost of recreating this listing inventory under present market conditions?" If the inventory consisted of 25 listings, the value as calculated is less than $500 per listing. Such a value appears to be somewhat low. The privilege to sell a co-broker's listing could be considerable higher than that amount, based on commission shared. But based on the calculations, the $12,000 figure is entered into Column 2 opposite Listing Inventory.

Pending Transactions

This category represents accepted offers that are in the process of closing. It is assumed that there are six such contracts in process. However, the financing on one of the six is doubtful, therefore the calculations are limited to the remaining five. The total contract price of the five amounts to $500,000. The company's share of the commission, after commissions to be paid to sales associates and co-brokers, is 2.5%. That amounts to $12,500 for commission earned but not received, pending the closings. Nearly all of the expenses incurred to produce these transactions have been incurred in the past, so the $12,500 is entered into Column 2 opposite Commissions on Pending Transactions.

Going Concern

The company is a profit generating organization in place with a market image and with a sales and office staff that are trained and functioning. There is no special formula to value the company's good name, integrity, or the office and sales staff. One approach is to rely on the cost of recreating this staff and market image from scratch. To acquire, train and develop a comparable sales staff may cost somewhere in the neighborhood of $5,000 per person. This estimate incudes the financial losses incurred during the lower productivity in the development stage. Eight full-time sales staff members at $5,000 each amounts to $40,000. No allowance has been made for part-time staff members. This $40,000 value has been placed in Column 2 opposite Going Concern to cover the fair market value of the company name and sales staff.

Goodwill

As used in this illustration, Goodwill is a value that reflects the extent of net earnings over and above the expected normal return on gross revenue. In the continuing illustration from earlier portions of this chapter, it was determined that the rate of return on gross revenue was 3.25%. This rate of return falls below the average range for real estate brokerage firms, (10-15 percent), therefore there is no premium to be paid for below average earnings. Accordingly, in Column 2 opposite Goodwill, no amount was entered. In the event that goodwill as defined above was present, it would have to be expressed as the value of earnings in excess of average earnings.

So, under the net asset value method, the owner's equity was adjusted upward to $115,000, representing the fair market value of the illustrated residential real estate brokerage business.

There is a noticeable tendency on the part of business buyers to not want to pay for intangible assets, particularly goodwill. They imply, "Why should we pay for something we can't see . . . something we can't touch . . . something that may evaporate into thin air!" A more mundane reason is that future competition may wipe it out. However, there is reasonable basis for pricing goodwill. The prospective buyer has the alternative to buy or lease facilities and equipment, hire and train a staff and start from scratch. On that basis, he/she may incur capital expenditures, operating losses, put in a lot of hours, incur risks and expenses, suffer stress and do some sweating. That's the price that he/she would have to pay . . . and theoretically that total price is the equivalent of goodwill . . . or intangible value. It has been observed that sellers often stress the "potential" of the business that somehow or other they never got around to exploiting. Some negotiators state the situation in a more abrupt manner, "The past belongs to the seller, the future belongs to the buyer!" All of this may lead to the buyer's saying, "We'll pay for the goodwill, if you (the seller) will guarantee it!" This may very well give rise to a "Level of Performance" contingency clause in the sale agreement. It is often said that if one purchases a real estate brokerage business that provides the new owner with only a marginal rate of return, he/she is merely buying nothing more than a job.

In summary, the value of a real estate brokerage business is determined by the value of the net tangible assets plus the estimated value of the intangible assets including goodwill.

Investment Value

This method can best be explained through the logic employed by an absentee owner — the investor. This investment opportunity can be compared to other financial investments having comparable risks. The investor is primarily concerned with return on his/her investment in the form of annual earnings. Therefore, the income stream generated by the business is the focal point of the investor's analysis. One year's net earnings would hardly be indicative of the future pattern of return on investment. A better approach would be to look at the company's earning picture for the past three or five years. A simple arithmetic average of the years may not be representative of what could be expected in the future. Instead, a weighted average gives greater weight to what has been happening in the more recent years. Using this company as an illustration, here is the weighted average method.

TABLE 10 – 8
WEIGHTED AVERAGE OF ANNUAL EARNINGS

Year	Net Earnings	Weight	Net Earnings X Weight
1991	$14,000	1	$14,000
1992	15,000	2	30,000
1993	16,500	3	49,500
1994	17,500	4	70,000
1995	18,000	5	90,000
Totals	$81,000	15	$253,500

Weighted Average (past 5 years) $= \dfrac{\$253,500}{15} = \$16,900$

Weighted Average (past 3 years) $= \dfrac{\$105,500}{6} = \$17,583$

It can be observed that the trend of net earnings over the five year period has been in an upward direction. Perhaps the weighted average of the last three years, $17,583 is more indicative of the company's earning pattern. Considering the limited size of the company, the fluctuations in the real estate market and other risk factors, the rate of return certainly should be higher than commercial mortgage interest rates. In addition to that, because of the lack of liquidity of this type of investment, there should be another increment added to the rate of return for this investor. A rate of 16% appears to be in line with this investment situation. Accordingly,

INVESTMENT VALUE   = $\dfrac{\text{AVERAGE ANNUAL NET EARNINGS}}{\text{RATE OF RETURN}}$

= $\dfrac{\$17,583}{16\%}$

=   **$109,894**

This investment calculation of $109,894 is slightly lower than the net asset value method calculated previously at $115,000. One should be reminded again that these methods result in estimates, rather than precise measurements of value. The motivations of the owner as well as the motivations of a prospective purchaser enter into the picture as well. Value is not generated in financial tables or formulas but rather in the marketplace as a result of interaction between well informed and financially qualified buyers and sellers not under duress to act. At best, it is expected that financial tables and formulas hope to reflect the rationale employed by participants in the marketplace.

Also, the previous discussion merely touches on the basic concepts or highlights of a real estate brokerage business valuation exercise. An excellent, detailed discussion of the subject in booklet form can be found in the 1995 publication of the National Association of Realtors® "Value of a Real Estate Brokerage Firm" by John A. Tuccillo and Frederick Flick with the NAR Research Staff.

Impact of Inflation

In the mid 1990s, the prevailing belief was that inflation was finally under control. With inflation rates hovering around 3% a year, there was a feeling of satisfaction with the policies and efforts of monetary control. On a year by year basis, inflation at the rate of three to four percent was hardly noticed by the public in general. On the other hand, it might be useful to review its future impact over a generation or so.

The following is a table showing what family income and prices might amount to over the following two decades if incomes and prices were to rise at a four percent rate compounded.

TABLE 10 – 9 INFLATION PROJECTIONS					
Year	Family Income	Bag of Groceries	Color TV	Automobile	Home
1995	39,000	$80	$400	$14,000	$110,000
2000	47,449	97	487	17,033	133,832
2005	57,730	118	592	20,723	162,827
2010	70,237	144	720	25,213	198,104
2015	85,454	175	876	30,676	241,024

This could be of interest to residential home buyers, especially to those whose purchase is being financed by a 30 year fixed rate mortgage loan. Consider the increasing ability to meet the fixed monthly mortgage payment for principal and interest as well as the equity build-up due to the inflationary effect.

As far as the owner/broker is concerned, this certainly impacts on forecasts of revenue and expenses. As the average price of a home goes up, so do the commissions that are based on a percentage of sales price, but in the process, operating expenses go up as well.

Management Control

Leadership is also an important element in the successful implementation of plans. While all members of the company should be welcome to offer constructive criticism . . . and make useful suggestions, decision-making authority should rest on the shoulders of one person. Experience demonstrates that in any organization, be it a Communist superpower or a church choral society, committee rule eventually breaks down and a single person has to take charge. As one business leader jokingly said, "If the Lord had appointed a committee instead of Moses, they would still be trying to cross the Red Sea!"

CHAPTER 11 — YOUR CAREER: PROFESSIONAL STATUS

". . . high pay hard work or low pay easy work?" *anonymous*

Is the practice of real estate brokerage a profession? The basic definition of a profession is "a vocation or occupation requiring advanced education and training, involving intellectual skills". In order to elevate that definition to a higher level, one might add, "serving persons in need of such professional service . . . wherein the quality of service rendered is not contingent upon the size of the fee paid". On that basis, the general public has historically accepted the time honored professions of medicine, law and theology (religious ministry). While these three professions, in general, subscribe to the concept of *Pro bono publico* (for the public good), not all members practice this high ideal for a wide variety of legitimate reasons.

Some sociologists prefer to discuss the subject of professions with a two step approach:

(a) EXPERT – one who is very skillful or highly trained and informed in a special field.

(b) PROFESSIONAL – an expert rendering valuable service for a fee to persons in need of such service.

Well qualified and trained real estate sales associates in one sense are "problem solvers". That is one of the reasons that makes their service valuable. There will always be problems in the real estate market of one sort or another. It may be a shortage of existing properties for sale, too few buyers compared to sellers, unattractive financing terms, lack of buyer confidence, etc. If a perfect real estate market ever occurred, buyers and sellers would not need real estate salespeople. If that ever happened, real estate sales people might even be out of business. As Norman Vincent Peale often said, "Thank the Lord for problems!" He went on to explain that problems, in fact, are blessings because they represent opportunities and challenges. He also pointed out that the only people without problems are those in the cemetery . . . what an alternative!

It is estimated that about 15 to 20 percent of all residential real estate transactions are direct sales from seller to buyer without the aid of a real estate broker. So, in every real estate market there are a good number of sellers and buyers who prefer not to be "do-it-yourself-ers". They may not have the time, the experience, the knowledge nor the patience to deal with the demands of prospective customers. They prefer to hire someone to perform these services for them. In these cases, the services are truly needed and very valuable . . . that's why real estate commissions are paid at a professional level. It would seem that real estate sales associates are experts by virtue of the size of commissions they command in serving sellers and buyers. If the average selling price of a residential property is around $100,000, then the typical commission charged the seller may be in the neighborhood of $5,000 to $6,000. Real estate sales associates can render professional level service when assisting their clients in need of real estate related help, especially when applying their training, knowledge and experience in solving their clients' real estate problems. A self-searching test for the sales associate would be to ask oneself the question, "If my doctor . . . my lawyer . . . or my CPA were to send me a bill for $5,000 to $6,000, what amount and quality of service would I expect in return?"

It should be remembered that most clients have had limited real estate market exposure . . . they may come into the market perhaps only two, three, or four times in a lifetime. Therefore, chances are that these clients may be highly dependent on the real estate sales associates for help. Successful associates soon realize that they gain the respect, confidence and loyalty of their clients by sharing their expertise with them.

Aside from the three time honored professions of medicine, law and theology, there are several other groups of practitioners that are making progress toward full public acceptance. The first such group is what might be called the "emerging professions". Included in that group would be dentists, certified public accountants, professional engineers, credentialed teachers, registered nurses, etc. A second group could be called, "aspiring professions", to include opticians, meteorologists, chiropractors, etc. All of these practitioners serve the public and are required to be licensed in order to practice. Nearly all of these practitioners belong to one or more professional associations dedicated to standards of practice, continuing education and public relations. It seems that the respect of the public is one measure that can be used to determine whether a service activity rendered to the public is professional or not. Public acceptance as a profession should be the goal of all practitioners, regardless of what field of endeavor they may be in.

Measures of public acceptance continue to be published as a result of consumer polls taken periodically. The following combined summary is a rank-ordering of adult reactions of several polls taken in the 1990s. These are responses as to the honesty and ethical standards of practitioners in various fields.

- Pharmacists
- Clergy
- Public opinion pollsters
- Journalists
- Politicians
- Lawyers
- Advertising practitioners
- Car salespeople

Those near the top of the list are the most trusted and the level of trust decreases as one goes down the list. Similar polls taken in regard to real estate salespeople vary somewhat, but on average they tend to rank in the middle of the list. Obviously, the frequency of contact by the public with the practitioner puts the public in a better position to render valid judgment of performance.

The extent to which some states go toward regulation and licensing of practitioners is indicated in this portion of the statutes of a midwestern state:

". . . any person who enters into a contract for or engages in any activity designed or intended to affect by artificial means the precipitation of atmospheric moisture in this state shall register each proposed operation with the commission."

The statute goes on to state the fine and penalty for non-compliance. While not specifically stated in the statute, it is assumed that all of these references relate to practitioners known as "rainmakers". Needless to say, both the practice and the statute are outdated.

Education

"For every problem, there is a solution which is simple, neat — and wrong." These are the words of H. L. Mencken, the legendary journalist and satirist. Perhaps, the "and wrong" portion of the statement might be tempered to read, "and *often* wrong". If one were to examine the social and housing programs fostered by the federal government over the past 60 years, it seems that unsuccessful programs outnumbered successful ones. Some may want to defend the government's track record on the ground that there is a very real connection between initiating and risk taking. They would maintain that those who make no mistakes make nothing. In response, critics would summarize that line of thought with a wry remark, "the only way to success is to fail!" This discussion serves to remind us that life is filled with failures which are only natural for less than perfect human beings. Not to be overlooked is that life is also filled with success. Take for example, the performances of professional athletes. In the game of baseball, a ".300 hitter" is considered to be very good, although he has hit safely in only three out of ten times at bat. That level of performance overshadows the seven out of ten times that batter failed to get a hit. The fame and glory bestowed on great home run hitters is even more statistically amazing. A so-called "slugger" who plays every day and who hits a home run once in every ten times at bat would produce a total of about 60 home runs for the season. That would be a monumental achievement in the field of baseball, but on the other hand the success rate would be 10% while the rate of failure would be 90%, based on simple statistics with no regard for other factors involved.

Natural talent, education, training, motivation and attitude all enter into the total personal development picture. It is said that active real estate salespeople receive "No" for an answer about 90 percent of the time. It is the eduction, the training and the experience that gives the successful sales associate the confidence to carry on toward his/her goal. Education is a lifelong process. The dedicated professional has no other choice than to be a continuing student in his/her area of practice. Universities have no monopoly on knowledge. Knowledge may be acquired from a wide variety of sources ranging from public libraries to on-the-job training; from correspondence courses to organized adult education course work. It is possible that a good portion of the present descriptive materials may be taught via programmed texts or other self-teaching devices such as videos or audio tapes.

Higher education seems to play a different role in the real estate field. Having a four year college degree or having being involved in graduate work offers no direct reward in real estate as compared to many other professional fields. A part of this is due to the fact that only a minor portion of schools, colleges and universities offer real estate subjects for course credit toward a degree. While most college course work may be helpful in the business world, it is not specifically related to the field of real estate brokerage. It is the community colleges, the technical and vocational schools, that have directly related real estate programs. There is little doubt that a solid eduction, wherever acquired, is very helpful in forming a good base upon which a real estate career can be built. Most real estate practitioners are of the opinion that the skills that are needed are not taught in educational institutions but learned through experience and repetition. The learning process can be enhanced through training seminars and on-the-job training.

In general, there are two major ways to learn outside the classroom. The first is through personal experience but the time and cost may be prohibitive. The second way is to learn from the ex-

266

perience of others. In most cases, intra-company sessions prove to be beneficial because management is well motivated to help the new sales associate become successful. The concept of sharing ideas within a sales office is a powerful technique. By developing a friendly and sincere attitude within an office, an individual sales associate has access to the brainpower and experience of all of the other sales associates within that office. But outside of one's own office there may be a reluctance to share ideas, especially among local competitors. With this resistance in mind, it is suggested that sales associates look to out-of-town seminars and conferences where the participants may be more willing to share ideas. The atmosphere may be more relaxed and the participants are not constrained to cooperate with out-of-town non-competitors. The quality of one's program for self-development is critical to that sales associate's success. It cannot be given anything less than high priority in one's career.

On the lighter side, a very successful Florida real estate broker always seemed to include the following statement in his training program lecture series. "If you were arrested for impersonating a real estate salesperson, would the case be thrown out of court for lack of evidence!" Think about it!

Personal Goals

Here are some of the reasons why women and men choose to enter the field of residential real estate sales. (It will be noted that reference has been made to women and men. The reason for that particular order is that almost 70% of all licensed residential real estate salespeople are women. They also comprise about 60% of all brokers/owners and sales managers).

1. *Earnings* are proportional to effort expended. In most real estate brokerage firms, the higher one's production, the higher the commission rate. Combined with Item 4 below puts one on the road to financial security.

2. *Independence* gives one choices comparable to running one's own business.

3. *Flexibility* permits the salesperson to schedule one's own work day to fit an individual's personal schedule. It is said jokingly, "We only work half-days in real estate . . . and we get to pick which 12 hours". Salespeople have almost complete command of their time.

4. *Investment opportunities* are brought to salespeople's attention because they are in the market daily and therefore are in a position to be among the first to learn about such opportunities.

5. *Job satisfaction* in that salespeople are dealing with home ownership, the great American dream that is currently at 65% of all households in the United States. Salespeople are helping their clients select a home where these clients can enjoy living and provide the setting for molding the character of their children. To paraphrase Norman Vincent Peale once again, "Find people with problems . . . real estate problems and help them solve those problems." That certainly has a professional tone to it.

In setting a performance goal for the year ahead, the sales associate is making a commitment to perform at a stated level. This goal, of course, is the end result for the year and therefore one needs to have a game plan for the 12 months ahead to get there. One approach is illustrated by the great basketball star, Michael Jordan. When asked how he was able to maintain a 32 point average per game throughout most of his career he replies, "I simplified it a few years ago. 32 points per game is really just 8 points per quarter. I figure I can get that in some kind of way during the course of a game." From a management point of view, what he was doing was taking a goal and dividing into doable parts.

The importance of listings comes into play at this point. Can increased listings increase a sales associate's earning power? Look at it this way. If a sales associate deals with buying prospects only, there appears to be an identifiable upper limit . . . related to the number of hours in a day that limit the number of buying prospects that one can possibly service. By balancing selling efforts with listing efforts, the sales associate can have other sales associates and other brokers (co-brokers) help the listing agent earn additional commissions. There is no doubt that new listings mean new ads, new prospect calls, new open houses, new exciting news for buyers and obviously, more sales for everyone concerned.

Setting listing goals can be a very logical process based on personal, company and MLS information. However, a total goal is not enough in itself. The end goals must be broken down into do-able parts in order to set daily, weekly, monthly and ongoing targets. The following chart sets the series of procedures necessary to plan a successful listing year.

CHART 11 – 1
GOAL SETTING – STEPS TO INCREASED LISTING EARNINGS

Average Earnings

A.	Average Listing Price (Associate's Experience)	$90,000
B.	Percent of Listed Price Received (MLS)	93%
C.	Average Sales Price (A x B)	83,700
D.	Net Commission Paid to Associate by Broker	1.5%
E.	Average Commission Share Per Listing Sold (C X D)	1,256

Goal Breakdown – Listings and Effort

F.	Annual Earnings Goal from Listings	$20,000
G.	Average Commission per Listing Sold (Line E, above)	1,256
H.	Sold Listings Needed (rounded)	16
I.	Sales Rate of Listings Sold (Associate's Experience)	60%
J.	Total Number of Listings Needed (rounded)	27
K.	Presentations Made to Obtain One Listing (3:1 ratio)	3
L.	Total Annual Presentations Needed	81

Goal for 50 Weeks (two weeks vacation)

M.	Weekly Presentations Needed	1.6
N.	Contacts Needed for Each Listing Presentation Appointment	10
O.	Weekly Contacts Needed (M X N)	16

Goal for One Week (Five Working Day Listing Program)

P.	Daily Contacts Needed (Line 0 ÷ 5)	3.2
Q.	Average Time per Contact (Associate's Experience)	15 minutes
R.	Contact Minutes per Day (P x Q)	48 minutes

Goal per Day (Re: Making Listing Appointments)

S.	Hours per Day Making Contacts for Listing Appointments	.8 hours

Average Listing Inventory

T.	Average Listed Price (Associate's Experience)	$90,000
U.	Total Listings Needed (Line J above)	27
V.	Total Annual Listing Volume (T X U)	$2,430,000
W.	Turnover Rate (360 days ÷ 90 day average)	4
X.	Continuing Listing Inventory Needed	$607,500
Y.	Minimum Number of Listings Needed in Inventory (X ÷ T)	6.75
Z.	Minimum Number of Listings Needed in Inventory (Y rounded)	7

Based on the sales associate's average listing price and MLS experience on percent of asking price received by the seller combined with the firm's commission policy, the average commission earned in this illustration is $1,256. With an annual earnings goals of $20,000 on listings and an experience ratio of one out of three listing presentations resulting in an actual listing, a total of 81 presentations must be scheduled in order to meet the annual goal. The listing presentation time as well as the contact time needed to schedule presentations are translated into weekly and daily time amounts. Finally, the average number of listings in inventory throughout the year is calculated as an ongoing reminder of consistent effort needed to achieve the annual goal. One midwestern sales manager believes that a sales associate should have at least 60% of his/her listings sold but not more than 80%, otherwise that sales associate is not reaching his/her potential as a listing agent.

A well defined listing plan gives the sales associate the direction needed to achieve an established goal.

A similar system can be set up for a selling goal. The components would be average selling price, sales commissions, number of showings, ratio of showings to an accepted offer, number of contacts needed for a showing, time involved and fallout ratio of accepted offers that fail to close.

Setting goals is much the same as treating one's individual career like a business. It is an accepted fact in management circles that people who write down their goals on paper are much more likely to achieve them. Others go a step farther in making a commitment toward achieving a goal. Besides going on record, they share their goal with their spouses, with close friends, mentors and ask those confidants to remind them about their progress towards such goals at the start of each month.

One of the greatest deterrents to success in the real estate field is the fear of failure. The fear to make a phone call, the fear to make a commitment, the fear of rejection, the fear to face up to a problem and the fear of looking bad (feeling foolish) are some examples. An old German philosopher summed up his own situation in these words, "I've worried about many things in my life, but oddly enough, some of the things that I worried about the most, never happened!" So it is with fear. In most cases, it is an imagined fear and constitutes a mental block in the way of one's ability to act. The usual byproduct of fear is excuse. Excuses are fabricated reasons for inaction. It seems as if some salespeople can find excuses why they can't sell real estate . . . and the excuses are without end.

January	–	people are paying their Christmas bills
February	–	people don't like to go out in the cold weather
March	–	people are too busy with Holy Week and Easter
April	–	people are broke from paying their income taxes
May	–	people are getting "spring fever" – want to be out-of-doors
June	–	people are busy with weddings and graduations
July	–	people are all out on vacation
August	–	people don't like to go out in very hot weather
September	–	people are busy getting their kids back to school
October	–	people are all wound up with the World Series
November	–	people are busy watching TV football games
December	–	people are too busy with the holiday season

It's amazing how hard they work at complaining and explaining why they can't sell. The same amount of energy could be harnessed in a positive way to change their selling style from mediocrity to a respectable level of success.

It should be remembered that clients will often reflect the sales associate's attitude . . . if he/she is dull or negative, the prospective buyers will most likely be negative . . . and find it easier to say, "No". But if the sales associate is positive and enthusiastic, he/she has a much higher probability of getting "Yes" answers. The public prefers to deal with winners and enjoy the process. The advice is to "get in the game!" Athletic coaches describe the psychological lift that a player experiences by "getting into the game".

Baseball   –   the first catch or the first time at bat
Football   –   the first clean block or the first tackle
Golf   –   getting off that first tee
Basketball –   making that first basket or getting that
                first rebound

And so it is in the field of real estate sales . . . right after you get an offer accepted. You feel great. You are full of enthusiasm. Everything is right. Everything is positive.

In a previous chapter, the "First 100 days Theory" was explained. It was another way of saying, "Your future is now!" It is believed that what a sales associate does in the first 100 days of each calendar year, highly influences what that sales associate is going to do for the rest of the year. It establishes a kind of personal momentum . . . it establishes one's pace of doing things.

Professional Designations

As one moves up the ladder of success, it may be easy to become complacent and start to lose some of that hunger for success that had been a motivating force on the way up. One dimension of that driving force is contained in the words of Calvin Coolidge, who wrote: "Nothing in the world can take the place of persistence. Talent will not; nothing is more common than unsuccessful men with talent. Genius will not; unrewarded genius is almost a proverb. Education will not; the world is full of educated derelicts. Persistence and determination alone are omnipotent." These seemingly harsh words reflect his colonial New England background and straight forward manner of speech. It also reflects strains of "Britannia" . . . whose citizens were known worldwide for their "tenacity of purpose". From all of this we can surmise that, among other qualifications, persistence is one of the most important ingredients of success. Of course, that does not rule out the role of talent and education. While not top-ranked, they are major contributing factors in the development of a successful career.

Relevant education focused on real estate subject matter and performance at a professional level are key factors that distinguish salespeople from their competitors. The National Association of Realtors® has developed a program offering professional designations to members that meet the training requirements in 17 real estate related fields.

Designation	Description	Sponsoring Group
ABR	Accredited Buyer Representative	Real Estate Buyer's Agent Council
ABRM	Accredited Buyer Representative Manager	Real Estate Buyer's Agent Council
ALC	Accredited Land Consultant	Realtors® Land Institute
AMO	Accredited Management Organization	Institute of Real Estate Management
ARM	Accredited Residential Manager	Institute of Real Estate Management
CCIM	Certified Commercial Investment Member	Commercial Investment Real Estate Institute
CIPS	Certified International Property Specialist	National Association of Realtors®
CPM®	Certified Property Manager®	Institute of Real Estate Management
CRB	Certified Real Estate Brokerage Manager	Real Estate Brokerage Managers Council – Realtors National Marketing Institute®
CRE®	Counselor of Real Estate®	The Counselors of Real Estate
CRS®	Certified Residential Specialist	Residential Sales Council Realtors National Marketing Institute®
GAA	General Accredited Appraiser	National Association of REALTORS® Business Specialties
GRI	Graduate, Realtor® Institute	National Association of Realtors®
LTG	Leadership Training Graduate	Women's Council of Realtors®
RAA	Residential Accredited Appraiser	National Association of REALTORS® Business Specialties
RCE	Realtor® Association Certified Executive	National Association of Realtors®
SIOR®	Society of Industrial and Office Realtors®	Society of Industrial and Office Realtors®

Information on the previous designations available to real estate professionals can be obtained from the National Association of Realtors®, 430 North Michigan Avenue, Chicago, Illinois 60611-4087.

Code of Ethics

As a general statement, ethics comprise a set of guidelines for conduct and level of behavior requirements based on relevant moral standards. As far back as the 18th century, B.C., the King of Babylon, Hammurabi, was given credit for introducing a code of laws in Mesopotamia. Historically, it is referred to as the "Code of Hammurabi" and encompassed the idea of justice and reason within the law. Prior to that time most collections of laws were patently arbitrary in the sense that they represented "the will of the gods". Justice under the new code was administered by judges at hearings that were governed by a "like kind" principle. For example, if one's home collapsed and killed the owner through a fault of the builder, that builder was put to death. In the event the owner's son was killed as a result of the collapse, the builder's son was put to death. Another part of the code provided that if one charged another with a crime that called for the death penalty and the accuser failed to prove the case, that accuser was subject to the same death penalty. While these penalties were harsh, the code did demonstrate an awareness of the natural moral side of justice that previously had not been considered.

A somewhat similar approach is found in the Old Testament of the bible as part of the Hebrew culture of that time. In the Book of Exodus, Chapter 21, verses 23-25, it states, " . . . you shall give life for life, eye for eye, tooth for tooth, hand for hand, foot for foot, burn for burn, wound for wound, stripe for stripe". This stern approach is also revealed in the Ten Commandments with the dominance of "thou shall not" commands. This is in sharp contrast to the positive tone of the New Testament with its emphasis on "love thy neighbor" and "forgiveness".

In today's business world, each profession develops its own code of behavior based on the experiences that relate to that profession. Those members who fail to follow such codes are liable to be reprimanded or ousted from that organization. A common complaint of code violation results when an association member takes "poetic license" or employs excessive "puffing" in promoting one's service in public advertising. There is a tendency on the part of critics to magnify ethical issues especially when the critic loses out on a transaction, contract, or assignment. It seems as if when one is on the losing side for the moment, the loser is right and the rest of the world is wrong. Displaying very human traits, the loser is usually reluctant to accept any of the blame for the loss. As one philosopher stated, ". . . learning to live ethically is learning to live with oneself".

A noticeable number of codes of ethics have a common content in the form of key words and phrases such as respect for others, honesty, trustworthy, fair, loyal, accountable, truthful, law abiding and confidentiality. The purpose of the code is to guide the conduct of the organization's members and to give the public the assurance that the services of its members will be delivered in a professional manner.

The Code of Ethics of the National Association of Realtors® consists of a Preamble and 17 Articles. It should be noted that the Standards of Practice are not an integral part of the Code but rather serve to clarify the ethical obligations imposed by the various Articles.

Code of Ethics and Standards of Practice
of the NATIONAL ASSOCIATION OF REALTORS®
Effective January 1, 1998

Where the word REALTORS® is used in this Code and Preamble, it shall be deemed to include REALTOR-ASSOCIATE®s.

While the Code of Ethics establishes obligations that may be higher than those mandated by law, in any instance where the Code of Ethics and the law conflict, the obligations of the law must take precedence.

Preamble...

Under all is the land. Upon its wise utilization and widely allocated ownership depend the survival and growth of free institutions and of our civilization. REALTORS® should recognize that the interests of the nation and its citizens require the highest and best use of the land and the widest distribution of land ownership. They require the creation of adequate housing, the building of functioning cities, the development of productive industries and farms, and the preservation of a healthful environment.

Such interests impose obligations beyond those of ordinary commerce. They impose grave social responsibility and a patriotic duty to which REALTORS® should dedicate themselves, and for which they should be diligent in preparing themselves. REALTORS®, therefore, are zealous to maintain and improve the standards of their calling and share with their fellow REALTORS® a common responsibility for its integrity and honor.

In recognition and appreciation of their obligations to clients, customers, the public, and each other, REALTORS® continuously strive to become and remain informed on issues affecting real estate and, as knowledgeable professionals, they willingly share the fruit of their experience and study with others. They identify and take steps, through enforcement of this Code of Ethics and by assisting appropriate regulatory bodies, to eliminate practices which may damage the public or which might discredit or bring dishonor to the real estate profession.

Realizing that cooperation with other real estate professionals promotes the best interests of those who utilize their services, REALTORS® urge exclusive representation of clients; do not attempt to gain any unfair advantage over their competitors; and they refrain from making unsolicited comments about other practitioners. In instances where their opinion is sought, or where REALTORS® believe that comment is necessary, their opinion is offered in an objective, professional manner, uninfluenced by any personal motivation or potential advantage or gain.

The term REALTOR® has come to connote competency, fairness, and high integrity resulting from adherence to a lofty ideal of moral conduct in business relations. No inducement of profit and no instruction from clients ever can justify departure from this ideal.

In the interpretation of this obligation, REALTORS® can take no safer guide than that which has been handed down through the centuries, embodied in the Golden Rule, "Whatsoever ye would that others should do to you, do ye even so to them."

Accepting this standard as their own, REALTORS® pledge to observe its spirit in all of their activities and to conduct their business in accordance with the tenets set forth below.

Duties to Clients and Customers

Article 1

When representing a buyer, seller, landlord, tenant, or other client as an agent, REALTORS® pledge themselves to protect and promote the interests of their client. This obligation of absolute fidelity to the client's interests is primary, but it does not relieve REALTORS® of their obligation to treat all parties honestly. When serving a buyer, seller, landlord, tenant or other party in a non-agency capacity, REALTORS® remain obligated to treat all parties honestly. *(Amended 1/93)*

- **Standard of Practice 1-1**
  REALTORS®, when acting as principals in a real estate transaction, remain obligated by the duties imposed by the Code of Ethics. *(Amended 1/93)*

- **Standard of Practice 1-2**
  The duties the Code of Ethics imposes are applicable whether REALTORS® are acting as agents or in legally recognized non-agency capacities except that any duty imposed exclusively on agents by law or regulation shall not be imposed by this Code of Ethics on REALTORS® acting in non-agency capacities.

  As used in this Code of Ethics, "client" means the person(s) or entity(ies) with whom a REALTOR® or a REALTOR®'s firm has an agency or legally recognized non-agency relationship; "customer" means a party to a real estate transaction who receives information, services, or benefits but has no contractual relationship with the REALTOR® or the REALTOR®'s firm; and "agent" means a real estate licensee acting in an agency relationship as defined by state law or regulation. *(Adopted 1/95, Amended 1/98)*

- **Standard of Practice 1-3**
  REALTORS®, in attempting to secure a listing, shall not deliberately mislead the owner as to market value.

- **Standard of Practice 1-4**
  REALTORS®, when seeking to become a buyer/tenant representative, shall not mislead buyers or tenants as to savings or other benefits that might be realized through use of the REALTOR®'s services. *(Amended 1/93)*

- **Standard of Practice 1-5**
  REALTORS® may represent the seller/landlord and buyer/tenant in the same transaction only after full disclosure to and with informed consent of both parties. *(Adopted 1/93)*

- **Standard of Practice 1-6**
  REALTORS® shall submit offers and counter-offers objectively and as quickly as possible. *(Adopted 1/93, Amended 1/95)*

- **Standard of Practice 1-7**
  When acting as listing brokers, REALTORS® shall continue to submit to the seller/landlord all offers and counter-offers until closing or execution of a lease unless the seller/landlord has waived this obligation in writing. REALTORS® shall not be obligated to continue to market the property after an offer has been accepted by the seller/landlord. REALTORS® shall recommend that sellers/landlords obtain the advice of legal counsel prior to acceptance of a subsequent offer except where the acceptance is contingent on the termination of the pre-existing purchase contract or lease. *(Amended 1/93)*

- **Standard of Practice 1-8**
  REALTORS® acting as agents of buyers/tenants shall submit to buyers/tenants all offers and counter-offers until acceptance but have no obligation to continue to show properties to their clients after an offer has been accepted unless otherwise agreed in writing. REALTORS® acting as agents of buyers/tenants shall recommend that buyers/tenants obtain the advice of legal counsel if there is a question as to whether a pre-existing contract has been terminated. *(Adopted 1/93)*

- **Standard of Practice 1-9**
  The obligation of REALTORS® to preserve confidential information provided by their clients continues after the termination of the agency relationship. REALTORS® shall not knowingly, during or following the termination of a professional relationship with their client:
  1) reveal confidential information of the client; or
  2) use confidential information of the client to the disadvantage of the client; or
  3) use confidential information of the client for the REALTOR®'s advantage or the advantage of a third party unless:
     a) the client consents after full disclosure; or
     b) the REALTOR® is required by court order; or

c) it is the intention of the client to commit a crime and the information is necesary to prevent the crime; or
d) it is necessary to defend the REALTOR® or the REALTOR®'s employees or associates against an accusation of wrongful conduct. *(Adopted 1/93, Amended 1/97)*

- **Standard of Practice 1-10**
  REALTORS® shall, consistent with the terms and conditions of their property management agreement, competently manage the property of clients with due regard for the rights, responsibilities, benefits, safety and health of tenants and others lawfully on the premises. *(Adopted 1/95)*

- **Standard of Practice 1-11**
  REALTORS® who are employed to maintain or manage a client's property shall exercise due diligence and make reasonable efforts to protect it against reasonably foreseeable contingencies and losses. *(Adopted 1/95)*

- **Standard of Practice 1-12**
  When entering into listing contracts, REALTORS® must advise sellers/landlords of:
  1) the REALTOR®'s general company policies regarding cooperation with subagents, buyer/tenant agents, or both;
  2) the fact that buyer/tenant agents, even if compensated by the listing broker, or by the seller/landlord will represent the interests of buyers/tenants; and
  3) any potential for the listing broker to act as a disclosed dual agent, e.g. buyer/tenant agent. *(Adopted 1/93, Renumbered 1/98)*

- **Standard of Practice 1-13**
  When entering into contracts to represent buyers/tenants, REALTORS® must advise potential clients of:
  1) the REALTOR®'s general company policies regarding cooperation with other firms; and
  2) any potential for the buyer/tenant representative to act as a disclosed dual agent, e.g. listing broker, subagent, landlord's agent, etc. *(Adopted 1/93, Renumbered 1/98)*

Article 2

REALTORS® shall avoid exaggeration, misrepresentation, or concealment of pertinent facts relating to the property or the transaction. REALTORS® shall not, however, be obligated to discover latent defects in the property, to advise on matters outside the scope of their real estate license, or to disclose facts which are confidential under the scope of agency duties owed to their clients. *(Amended 1/93)*

- **Standard of Practice 2-1**
  REALTORS® shall only be obligated to discover and disclose adverse factors reasonably apparent to someone with expertise in those areas required by their real estate licensing authority. Article 2 does not impose upon the

REALTOR® the obligation of expertise in other professional or technical disciplines. *(Amended 1/96)*

- **Standard of Practice 2-2**
  (Renumbered as Standard of Practice 1-12 1/98)

- **Standard of Practice 2-3**
  (Renumbered as Standard of Practice 1-13 1/98)

- **Standard of Practice 2-4**
  REALTORS® shall not be parties to the naming of a false consideration in any document, unless it be the naming of an obviously nominal consideration.

- **Standard of Practice 2-5**
  Factors defined as "non-material" by law or regulation or which are expressly referenced in law or regulation as not being subject to disclosure are considered not "pertinent" for purposes of Article 2. *(Adopted 1/93)*

Article 3

REALTORS® shall cooperate with other brokers except when cooperation is not in the client's best interest. The obligation to cooperate does not include the obligation to share commissions, fees, or to otherwise compensate another broker. *(Amended 1/95)*

- **Standard of Practice 3-1**
  REALTORS®, acting as exclusive agents of sellers/landlords, establish the terms and conditions of offers to cooperate. Unless expressly indicated in offers to cooperate, cooperating brokers may not assume that the offer of cooperation includes an offer of compensation. Terms of compensation, if any, shall be ascertained by cooperating brokers before beginning efforts to accept the offer of cooperation. *(Amended 1/94)*

- **Standard of Practice 3-2**
  REALTORS® shall, with respect to offers of compensation to another REALTOR®, timely communicate any change of compensation for cooperative services to the other REALTOR® prior to the time such REALTOR® produces an offer to purchase/lease the property. *(Amended 1/94)*

- **Standard of Practice 3-3**
  Standard of Practice 3-2 does not preclude the listing broker and cooperating broker from entering into an agreement to change cooperative compensation. *(Adopted 1/94)*

- **Standard of Practice 3-4**
  REALTORS®, acting as listing brokers, have an affirmative obligation to disclose the existence of dual or variable rate commission arrangements (i.e., listings where one amount of commission is payable if the listing broker's firm is the procuring cause of sale/lease and a different amount of commission is payable if the sale/lease results through the efforts of the seller/landlord or a cooperating broker). The listing broker shall, as soon as practical, disclose the existence of such arrangements to potential cooperating brokers and shall, in response to inquiries from cooperating brokers, disclose the differential that would result in a cooperative transaction or in a sale/lease that results through the efforts of the seller/landlord. If the cooperating broker is a buyer/tenant representative, the buyer/tenant representative must disclose such information to their client. *(Amended 1/94)*

- **Standard of Practice 3-5**
  It is the obligation of subagents to promptly disclose all pertinent facts to the principal's agent prior to as well as after a purchase or lease agreement is executed. *(Amended 1/93)*

- **Standard of Practice 3-6**
  REALTORS® shall disclose the existence of an accepted offer to any broker seeking cooperation. *(Adopted 5/86)*

- **Standard of Practice 3-7**
  When seeking information from another REALTOR® concerning property under a management or listing agreement, REALTORS® shall disclose their REALTOR® status and whether their interest is personal or on behalf of a client and, if on behalf of a client, their representational status. *(Amended 1/95)*

- **Standard of Practice 3-8**
  REALTORS® shall not misrepresent the availability of access to show or inspect a listed property. *(Amended 11/87)*

Article 4

REALTORS® shall not acquire an interest in or buy or present offers from themselves, any member of their immediate families, their firms or any member thereof, or any entities in which they have any ownership interest, any real property without making their true position known to the owner or the owner's agent. In selling property they own, or in which they have any interest, REALTORS® shall reveal their ownership or interest in writing to the purchaser or the purchaser's representative. *(Amended 1/91)*

- **Standard of Practice 4-1**
  For the protection of all parties, the disclosures required by Article 4 shall be in writing and provided by REALTORS® prior to the signing of any contract. *(Adopted 2/86)*

Article 5

REALTORS® shall not undertake to provide professional services concerning a property or its value where they have a present or contemplated interest unless such interest is specifically disclosed to all affected parties.

Article 6

When acting as agents, REALTORS® shall not accept any commission, rebate, or profit on expenditures made for their principal, without the principal's knowledge and consent. *(Amended 1/92)*

- **Standard of Practice 6-1**

  REALTORS® shall not recommend or suggest to a client or a customer the use of services of another organization or business entity in which they have a direct interest without disclosing such interest at the time of the recommendation or suggestion. *(Amended 5/88)*

- **Standard of Practice 6-2**

  When acting as agents or subagents, REALTORS® shall disclose to a client or customer if there is any financial benefit or fee the REALTOR® or the REALTOR®'s firm may receive as a direct result of having recommended real estate products or services (e.g., homeowner's insurance, warranty programs, mortgage financing, title insurance, etc.) other than real estate referral fees. *(Adopted 5/88)*

Article 7

In a transaction, REALTORS® shall not accept compensation from more than one party, even if permitted by law, without disclosure to all parties and the informed consent of the REALTOR®'s client or clients. *(Amended 1/93)*

Article 8

REALTORS® shall keep in a special account in an appropriate financial institution, separated from their own funds, monies coming into their possession in trust for other persons, such as escrows, trust funds, clients' monies, and other like items.

Article 9

REALTORS®, for the protection of all parties, shall assure whenever possible that agreements shall be in writing, and shall be in clear and understandable language expressing the specific terms, conditions, obligations and commitments of the parties. A copy of each agreement shall be furnished to each party upon their signing or initialing. *(Amended 1/95)*

- **Standard of Practice 9-1**

  For the protection of all parties, REALTORS® shall use reasonable care to ensure that documents pertaining to the purchase, sale, or lease of real estate are kept current through the use of written extensions or amendments. *(Amended 1/93)*

Duties to the Public

Article 10

REALTORS® shall not deny equal professional services to any person for reasons of race, color, religion, sex, handicap, familial status, or national origin. REALTORS® shall not be parties to any plan or agreement to discriminate against a person or persons on the basis of race, color, religion, sex, handicap, familial status, or national origin. *(Amended 1/90)*

- **Standard of Practice 10-1**

  REALTORS® shall not volunteer information regarding the racial, religious or ethnic composition of any neighborhood and shall not engage in any activity which may result in panic selling. REALTORS® shall not print, display or circulate any statement or advertisement with respect to the selling or renting of a property that indicates any preference, limitations or discrimination based on race, color, religion, sex, handicap, familial status or national origin. *(Adopted 1/94)*

Article 11

The services which REALTORS® provide to their clients and customers shall conform to the standards of practice and competence which are reasonably expected in the specific real estate disciplines in which they engage; specifically, residential real estate brokerage, real property management, commercial and industrial real estate brokerage, real estate appraisal, real estate counseling, real estate syndication, real estate auction, and international real estate.

REALTORS® shall not undertake to provide specialized professional services concerning a type of property or service that is outside their field of competence unless they engage the assistance of one who is competent on such types of property or service, or unless the facts are fully disclosed to the client. Any persons engaged to provide such assistance shall be so identified to the client and their contribution to the assignment should be set forth. *(Amended 1/95)*

- **Standard of Practice 11-1**

  The obligations of the Code of Ethics shall be supplemented by and construed in a manner consistent with the Uniform Standards of Professional Appraisal Practice (USPAP) promulgated by the Appraisal Standards Board of the Appraisal Foundation.

  The obligations of the Code of Ethics shall not be supplemented by the USPAP where an opinion or recommendation of price or pricing is provided in pursuit of a listing, to assist a potential purchaser in formulating a purchase offer, or to provide a broker's price opinion, whether for a fee or not. *(Amended 1/96)*

- **Standard of Practice 11-2**

  The obligations of the Code of Ethics in respect of real estate disciplines other than appraisal shall be interpreted and applied in accordance with the standards of competence and practice which clients and the public reasonably require to protect their rights and interests considering the complexity of the transaction, the availability of expert assistance, and, where the REALTOR® is an agent or subagent, the obligations of a fiduciary. *(Adopted 1/95)*

- **Standard of Practice 11-3**

  When REALTORS® provide consultive services to clients which involve advice or counsel for a fee (not a commission), such advice shall be rendered in an objective manner and the fee shall not be contingent on the substance of the advice or counsel given. If brokerage or transaction services are to be provided in addition to consultive services, a separate compensation may be paid with prior agreement between the client and REALTOR®. *(Adopted 1/96)*

Article 12

REALTORS® shall be careful at all times to present a true picture in their advertising and representations to the public. REALTORS® shall also ensure that their professional status (e.g., broker, appraiser, property manager, etc.) or status as REALTORS® is clearly identifiable in any such advertising. *(Amended 1/93)*

- **Standard of Practice 12-1**

  REALTORS® may use the term "free" and similar terms in their advertising and in other representations provided that all terms governing availability of the offered product or service are clearly disclosed at the same time. *(Amended 1/97)*

- **Standard of Practice 12-2**

  REALTORS® may represent their services as "free" or without cost even if they expect to receive compensation from a source other than their client provided that the potential for the REALTOR® to obtain a benefit from a third party is clearly disclosed at the same time. *(Amended 1/97)*

- **Standard of Practice 12-3**

  The offering of premiums, prizes, merchandise discounts or other inducements to list, sell, purchase, or lease is not, in itself, unethical even if receipt of the benefit is contingent on listing, selling, purchasing, or leasing through the REALTOR® making the offer. However, REALTORS® must exercise care and candor in any such advertising or other public or private representations so that any party interested in receiving or otherwise benefiting from the REALTOR®'s offer will have clear, thorough, advance understanding of all the terms and conditions of the offer. The offering of any inducements to do business is subject to the limitations and restrictions of state law and the ethical obligations established by any applicable Standard of Practice. *(Amended 1/95)*

- **Standard of Practice 12-4**

  REALTORS® shall not offer for sale/lease or advertise property without authority. When acting as listing brokers or as subagents, REALTORS® shall not quote a price different from that agreed upon with the seller/landlord. *(Amended 1/93)*

- **Standard of Practice 12-5**

  REALTORS® shall not advertise nor permit any person employed by or affiliated with them to advertise listed property without disclosing the name of the firm. *(Adopted 11/86)*

- **Standard of Practice 12-6**

  REALTORS®, when advertising unlisted real property for sale/lease in which they have an ownership interest, shall disclose their status as both owners/landlords and as REALTORS® or real estate licensees. *(Amended 1/93)*

- **Standard of Practice 12-7**

  Only REALTORS® who participated in the transaction as the listing broker or cooperating broker (selling broker) may claim to have "sold" the property. Prior to closing, a cooperating broker may post a "sold" sign only with the consent of the listing broker. *(Amended 1/96)*

Article 13

REALTORS® shall not engage in activities that constitute the unauthorized practice of law and shall recommend that legal counsel be obtained when the interest of any party to the transaction requires it.

Article 14

If charged with unethical practice or asked to present evidence or to cooperate in any other way, in any disciplinary proceeding or investigation, REALTORS® shall place all pertinent facts before the proper tribunals of the Member Board or affiliated institute, society, or council in which membership is held and shall take no action to disrupt or obstruct such processes. *(Amended 1/90)*

- **Standard of Practice 14-1**

  REALTORS® shall not be subject to disciplinary proceedings in more than one Board of REALTORS® or affiliated institute, society or council in which they hold membership with respect to alleged violations of the Code of Ethics relating to the same transaction or event. *(Amended 1/95)*

- **Standard of Practice 14-2**

  REALTORS® shall not make any unauthorized disclosure or dissemination of the allegations, findings, or decision developed in connection with an ethics hearing or appeal or in connection with an arbitration hearing or procedural review. *(Amended 1/92)*

- **Standard of Practice 14-3**

  REALTORS® shall not obstruct the Board's investigative or disciplinary proceedings by instituting or threatening to institute actions for libel, slander or defamation against any party to a professional standards proceeding or their witnesses. *(Adopted 11/87)*

- **Standard of Practice 14-4**

  REALTORS® shall not intentionally impede the Board's investigative or disciplinary proceedings by filing multiple ethics complaints based on the same event or transaction. *(Adopted 11/88)*

Duties to REALTORS®

Article 15

REALTORS® shall not knowingly or recklessly make false or misleading statements about competitors, their businesses, or their business practices. *(Amended 1/92)*

Article 16

REALTORS® shall not engage in any practice or take any action inconsistent with the agency or other exclusive relationship recognized by law that other REALTORS® have with clients. *(Amended 1/98)*

- **Standard of Practice 16-1**

  Article 16 is not intended to prohibit aggressive or innovative business practices which are otherwise ethical and does not prohibit disagreements with other REALTORS® involving commission, fees, compensation or other forms of payment or expenses. *(Adopted 1/93, Amended 1/95)*

- **Standard of Practice 16-2**

  Article 16 does not preclude REALTORS® from making general announcements to prospective clients describing their services and the terms of their availability even though some recipients may have entered into agency agreements or other exclusive relationships with another REALTOR®. A general telephone canvass, general mailing or distribution addressed to all prospective clients in a given geographical area or in a given profession, business, club, or organization, or other classification or group is deemed "general" for purposes of this standard. *(Amended 1/98)*

  Article 16 is intended to recognize as unethical two basic types of solicitations:

  First, telephone or personal solicitations of property owners who have been identified by a real estate sign, multiple listing compilation, or other information service as having exclusively listed their property with another REALTOR®; and

  Second, mail or other forms of written solicitations of prospective clients whose properties are exclusively listed with another REALTOR® when such solicitations are not part of a general mailing but are directed specifically to property owners identified through compilations of current listings, "for sale" or "for rent" signs, or other sources of information required by Article 3 and Multiple Listing Service rules to be made available to other REALTORS®

under offers of subagency or cooperation. *(Amended 1/93)*

- **Standard of Practice 16-3**

  Article 16 does not preclude REALTORS® from contacting the client of another broker for the purpose of offering to provide, or entering into a contract to provide, a different type of real estate service unrelated to the type of service currently being provided (e.g., property management as opposed to brokerage). However, information received through a Multiple Listing Service or any other offer of cooperation may not be used to target clients of other REALTORS® to whom such offers to provide services may be made. *(Amended 1/93)*

- **Standard of Practice 16-4**

  REALTORS® shall not solicit a listing which is currently listed exclusively with another broker. However, if the listing broker, when asked by the REALTOR®, refuses to disclose the expiration date and nature of such listing; i.e., an exclusive right to sell, an exclusive agency, open listing, or other form of contractual agreement between the listing broker and the client, the REALTOR® may contact the owner to secure such information and may discuss the terms upon which the REALTOR® might take a future listing or, alternatively, may take a listing to become effective upon expiration of any existing exclusive listing. *(Amended 1/94)*

- **Standard of Practice 16-5**

  REALTORS® shall not solicit buyer/tenant agreements from buyers/tenants who are subject to exclusive buyer/tenant agreements. However, if asked by a REALTOR®, the broker refuses to disclose the expiration date of the exclusive buyer/tenant agreement, the REALTOR® may contact the buyer/tenant to secure such information and may discuss the terms upon which the REALTOR® might enter into a future buyer/tenant agreement or, alternatively, may enter into a buyer/tenant agreement to become effective upon the expiration of any existing exclusive buyer/tenant agreement. *(Adopted 1/94, Amended 1/98)*

- **Standard of Practice 16-6**

  When REALTORS® are contacted by the client of another REALTOR® regarding the creation of an exclusive relationship to provide the same type of service, and REALTORS® have not directly or indirectly initiated such discussions, they may discuss the terms upon which they might enter into a future agreement or, alternatively, may enter into an agreement which becomes effective upon expiration of any existing exclusive agreement. *(Amended 1/98)*

- **Standard of Practice 16-7**

  The fact that a client has retained a REALTOR® as an agent or in another exclusive relationship in one or more past transactions does not preclude other REALTORS® from seeking such former client's future business. *(Amended 1/98)*

- **Standard of Practice 16-8**
The fact that an exclusive agreement has been entered into with a REALTOR® shall not preclude or inhibit any other REALTOR® from entering into a similar agreement after the expiration of the prior agreement. *(Amended 1/98)*

- **Standard of Practice 16-9**
REALTORS®, prior to entering into an agency agreement or other exclusive relationship, have an affirmative obligation to make reasonable efforts to determine whether the client is subject to a current, valid exclusive agreement to provide the same type of real estate service. *(Amended 1/98)*

- **Standard of Practice 16-10**
REALTORS®, acting as agents of, or in another relationship with, buyers or tenants, shall disclose that relationship to the seller/landlord's agent or broker at first contact and shall provide written confirmation of that disclosure to the seller/landlord's agent or broker not later than execution of a purchase agreement or lease. *(Amended 1/98)*

- **Standard of Practice 16-11**
On unlisted property, REALTORS® acting as buyer/tenant agents or brokers shall disclose that relationship to the seller/landlord at first contact for that client and shall provide written confirmation of such disclosure to the seller/landlord not later than execution of any purchase or lease agreement.

REALTORS® shall make any request for anticipated compensation from the seller/landlord at first contact. *(Amended 1/98)*

- **Standard of Practice 16-12**
REALTORS®, acting as agents or brokers of sellers/landlords or as subagents of listing brokers, shall disclose that relationship to buyers/tenants as soon as practicable and shall provide written confirmation of such disclosure to buyers/tenants not later than execution of any purchase or lease agreement. *(Amended 1/98)*

- **Standard of Practice 16-13**
All dealings concerning property exclusively listed, or with buyer/tenants who are subject to an exclusive agreement shall be carried on with the client's agent or broker, and not with the client, except with the consent of the client's agent or broker or except where such dealings are initiated by the client. *(Adopted 1/93, Amended 1/98)*

- **Standard of Practice 16-14**
REALTORS® are free to enter into contractual relationships or to negotiate with sellers/landlords, buyers/tenants or others who are not subject to an exclusive agreement but shall not knowingly obligate them to pay more than one commission except with their informed consent. *(Amended 1/98)*

- **Standard of Practice 16-15**
In cooperative transactions REALTORS® shall compensate cooperating REALTORS® (principal brokers) and shall not compensate nor offer to compensate, directly or indirectly, any of the sales licensees employed by or affiliated with other REALTORS® without the prior express knowledge and consent of the cooperating broker.

- **Standard of Practice 16-16**
REALTORS®, acting as subagents or buyer/tenant agents or brokers, shall not use the terms of an offer to purchase/lease to attempt to modify the listing broker's offer of compensation to subagents or buyer's agents or brokers nor make the submission of an executed offer to purchase/lease contingent on the listing broker's agreement to modify the offer of compensation. *(Amended 1/98)*

- **Standard of Practice 16-17**
REALTORS® acting as subagents or as buyer/tenant agents or brokers, shall not attempt to extend a listing broker's offer of cooperation and/or compensation to other brokers without the consent of the listing broker. *(Amended 1/98)*

- **Standard of Practice 16-18**
REALTORS® shall not use information obtained by them from the listing broker, through offers to cooperate received through Multiple Listing Services or other sources authorized by the listing broker, for the purpose of creating a referral prospect to a third broker, or for creating a buyer/tenant prospect unless such use is authorized by the listing broker. *(Amended 1/93)*

- **Standard of Practice 16-19**
Signs giving notice of property for sale, rent, lease, or exchange shall not be placed on property without consent of the seller/landlord. *(Amended 1/93)*

- **Standard of Practice 16-20**
REALTORS®, prior to or after terminating their relationship with their current firm, shall not induce clients of their current firm to cancel exclusive contractual agreements between the client and that firm. This does not preclude REALTORS® (principals) from establishing agreements with their associated licensees governing assignability of exclusive agreements. *(Adopted 1/98)*

Article 17

In the event of contractual disputes or specific non-contractual disputes as defined in Standard of Practice 17-4 between REALTORS® associated with different firms, arising out of their relationship as REALTORS®, the REALTORS® shall submit the dispute to arbitration in accordance with the regulations of their Board or Boards rather than litigate the matter.

In the event clients of REALTORS® wish to arbitrate contractual disputes arising out of real estate transactions, REALTORS® shall arbitrate those disputes in accordance with the regulations of their Board, provided the clients agree to be bound by the decision. *(Amended 1/97)*

- **Standard of Practice 17-1**

  The filing of litigation and refusal to withdraw from it by REALTORS® in an arbitrable matter constitutes a refusal to arbitrate. *(Adopted 2/86)*

- **Standard of Practice 17-2**

  Article 17 does not require REALTORS® to arbitrate in those circumstances when all parties to the dispute advise the Board in writing that they choose not to arbitrate before the Board. *(Amended 1/93)*

- **Standard of Practice 17-3**

  REALTORS®, when acting solely as principals in a real estate transaction, are not obligated to arbitrate disputes with other REALTORS® absent a specific written agreement to the contrary. *(Adopted 1/96)*

- **Standard of Practice 17-4**

  Specific non-contractual disputes that are subject to arbitration pursuant to Article 17 are:

  1) Where a listing broker has compensated a cooperating broker and another cooperating broker subsequently claims to be the procuring cause of the sale or lease. In such cases the complainant may name the first cooperating broker as respondent and arbitration may proceed without the listing broker being named as a respondent. Alternatively, if the complaint is brought against the listing broker, the listing broker may name the first cooperating broker as a third-party respondent. In either instance the decision of the hearing panel as to procuring cause shall be conclusive with respect to all current or subsequent claims of the parties for compensation arising out of the underlying cooperative transaction. *(Adopted 1/97)*

  2) Where a buyer or tenant representative is compensated by the seller or landlord, and not by the listing broker, and the listing broker, as a result, reduces the commission owed by the seller or landlord and, subsequent to such actions, another cooperating broker claims to be the procuring cause of sale or lease. In such cases the complainant may name the first cooperating broker as respondent and arbitration may proceed without the listing broker being named as a respondent. Alternatively, if the complaint is brought against the listing broker, the listing broker may name the first cooperating broker as a third-party respondent. In either instance the decision of the hearing panel as to procuring cause shall be conclusive with respect to all current or subsequent claims of the parties for compensation arising out of the underlying cooperative transaction. *(Adopted 1/97)*

  3) Where a buyer or tenant representative is compensated by the buyer or tenant and, as a result, the listing broker reduces the commission owed by the seller or landlord and, subsequent to such actions, another cooperating broker claims to be the procuring cause of sale or lease. In such cases the complainant may name the first cooperating broker as respondent and arbitration may proceed without the listing broker being named as a respondent. Alternatively, if the complaint is brought against the listing broker, the listing broker may name the first cooperating broker as a third-party respondent. In either instance the decision of the hearing panel as to procuring cause shall be conclusive with respect to all current or subsequent claims of the parties for compensation arising out of the underlying cooperative transaction. *(Adopted 1/97)*

  4) Where two or more listing brokers claim entitlement to compensation pursuant to open listings with a seller or landlord who agrees to participate in arbitration (or who requests arbitration) and who agrees to be bound by the decision. In cases where one of the listing brokers has been compensated by the seller or landlord, the other listing broker, as complainant, may name the first listing broker as respondent and arbitration may proceed between the brokers. *(Adopted 1/97)*

The Code of Ethics was adopted in 1913. Amended at the Annual Convention in 1924, 1928, 1950, 1951, 1952, 1955, 1956, 1961, 1962, 1974, 1982, 1986, 1987, 1989, 1990, 1991, 1992, 1993, 1994, 1995, 1996 and 1997.

Explanatory Notes

The reader should be aware of the following policies which have been approved by the Board of Directors of the National Association:

In filing a charge of an alleged violation of the Code of Ethics by a REALTOR®, the charge must read as an alleged violation of one or more Articles of the Code. Standards of Practice may be cited in support of the charge.

The Standards of Practice serve to clarify the ethical obligations imposed by the various Articles and supplement, and do not substitute for, the Case Interpretations in *Interpretations of the Code of Ethics.*

Modifications to existing Standards of Practice and additional new Standards of Practice are approved from time to time. Readers are cautioned to ensure that the most recent publications are utilized.

Experience has proven, that over the long run, the most successful real estate individuals and firms are those who give higher priority to their client's outcome in a transaction rather than their own. While they may experience a few setbacks along the way, they eventually rise above those competitors who may place higher priority on their own personal gain. There can be no respectable position that is *sometimes* ethical, or putting it more bluntly, one can't be half ethical. In the business world one is continually faced with making a moral choice, and in electing to choose the proper path, there is the precious reward of integrity . . . one of life's greatest rewards.

Organize Your Professional Career

Whether you are an owner/broker or an individual sales associate, it is very advisable to have a road map in order to stay on the road to success. There are seven key words that highlight that trip. They are:

1. Plan
2. Commit
3. Budget
4. Develop
5. Protect
6. Invest
7. Secure

A few of these have been touched on previously but are worthy of some degree of repetition. The others may have been addressed directly or indirectly, but only to a limited extent.

1. *Plan* – a good plan gives one direction and guidance toward a goal that should be reasonable and achievable. Annual goals should be divided into monthly and weekly goals with regard to contacts for appointments and showings. Projected annual earnings can be redefined in terms of "sides" . . . both listing and selling sides. Along with the satisfaction of increased earnings is that additional satisfaction of a psychological uplift

to know that one has achieved a level of success. This concept of fulfillment is applicable to all forms of work. For example, one community had a problem with garbage collection. The workers seemed to lack interest and motivation. They looked at their work as drudgery and exhibited no pride in their work. They also were targets of criticism and complaints. Things began to change when their supervisor developed a plan to address these problems. Under the supervisor's proposal the level of pay was kept the same for an eight hour day. However, the workers were invited to take on the challenge to perform the same volume of collections in less than eight hours. The reward was to be paid for the full eight hours even if they accomplished the collections in six or seven hours, permitting them to have off for the balance of the day. It was amazing to see how attitudes changed. They exhibited team-like spirit and actually enjoyed the challenge. Not only was their workday reduced to an average of six hours, but they took pride in their accomplishment. They became the subject of conversation by homeowners now pleased with their new and positive work habits. It is no longer a problem to find willing workers for these jobs. In fact, there is a waiting list of job applicants. The change in attitudes was attributable to the personal satisfaction of meeting a challenge. Goals are challenges and reward achievers with self-esteem.

2. *Commit* – success does not come to those who merely wish for it. While wishing may be the starting point, there needs to be a personal commitment to follow the plan toward the goal. This calls for a daily work habit to do a list of things contained in the plan. Consistent performance turns into good habits and part of one's work routine. One relatively new sales associate was heard to say, ". . . you know, it seems that the harder I work, the luckier I get!" That person may have mis-

taken the word harder for smarter. Which is it? High pay for smart work or low pay for mediocre work?

3. *Budget* – there is a tendency on the part of real estate salespeople to become so engrossed in the process of listing and selling that they unknowingly overlook the variations in their cash flow of earnings during the various seasons of the year. As long as their commission checks keep coming in, everything is fine. But when there are no more accepted offers in the closing process, they face the stark reality of coming to grips with a dry spell . . . no more commission checks. This may cause a mild panic and a serious disruption of what was once a positive attitude. A well capitalized firm can step in and provide cash advances to tide them over this cash crisis. The firm might also refer the sales associate to a neighborhood bank for a short-term loan. Regardless, it represents an interruption in personal production until the individual's concern is taken care of. Rather than spend each commission check entirely, the better procedure would be to have the sales associate build up a reserve fund in the form of a savings account. A portion of each commission check should be put aside in this account in order that the accumulated reserve fund is available to take care of such problems. Here again, this should not be a verbal commitment but rather stated in writing as part of the salesperson's plan.

4. *Develop* – in order to make progress in the real estate field, the salesperson needs to grow as an individual. It is recommended that a salesperson also make a plan to learn. Listen to an audio tape on real estate or related subjects for 10 or 15 minutes a day. An easy way to do this would be to have a cassette player in your car if one is not already built in. Attend an out-of-town real estate convention or conference once a year. Watch at

least one business video each quarter of the year. Or as one sales manager suggested, "on occasion, buy a book instead of a lunch . . . it will broaden your mind but not your waistline!" Exchange ideas by networking with other sales associates. Know what's going on in your field. As the old saying goes, "All work and no play makes Jack/Jackie a dull person". But one of the real damages is that a salesperson may become a workaholic . . . so wrapped up in one's work that he/she has little time for anything else except work. For the short term, this may not necessarily be harmful but over the long-term it may lead to occupational "burn-out". In this case a wise sales manager will advise, "Take time to sharpen your ax". That sales manager is alluding to the story of the north woods lumberjack who realized that as the blade of his ax grew dull, it required more effort to do the same amount of work in chopping down a tree. Experience taught him to sharpen his ax regularly in order to work effectively and conserve energy. The same lesson applies to the sales associate who puts in long hours day after day without realizing that he/she is gradually losing effectiveness. It is advisable to plan at least two week-long vacations a year . . . to get away form it all . . . to relax and "recharge your batteries". A weekend off every now and then will also prove to be helpful. Such a program will rekindle a positive attitude and elevate one's level of confidence. The same kind of advice would apply to a salesperson who has been experiencing success for an extended period of time because there is the risk of becoming complacent and losing the drive that got that salesperson there in the first place.

5. *Protect* – in this litigious society in which we all live, on occasion one can expect to be faced with a lawsuit resulting from a real estate transaction. There may not even be any actual evidence of one's negligence or mis-

representation. It may be that the seller who is at the center of this action has moved out of state, leaving the broker and sales associates as likely targets of this legal action. If the firm does not carry Errors and Omissions Insurance that covers the sales associates, it is very important that the sales associate obtain such coverage on his/her own. A large settlement, not covered by E & O insurance, could be a career ending blow to a seemingly innocent sales associate. A similar type risk applies to uninsured medical and/or hospitalization expenses whether they apply to the sales associate or his/her own family. The seriousness of this risk is evidenced by the fact that nearly nine out of ten real estate salespeople have some form of insurance coverage. Not to be overlooked in this category of risks is income protection insurance which becomes significant in the event of a disability that affects one's ability to perform. This would be especially vital if the salesperson was the breadwinner in the family. The same type of reasoning applies to life insurance coverage.

6. *Invest* – it seems natural for salespeople to invest in a business area that they know best . . . real estate. Not only do they have the background to analyze and confidence to decide, they are in the midst of that market on a continuing basis. They can be among the first to know of a real estate investment opportunity, giving them a distinct time advantage compared to other investments that require them to rely on information from third parties. They are able to get pertinent information firsthand. Good real estate investments at sound locations are bound to benefit from appreciation over the years. It is preferable to acquire those kind of real estate investments that require minimum amount of direct management, or that at least have the opportunity to place the management with capable parties in order to relieve the sales associate from that kind of

stress and time demands. Professional career growth and real estate investment growth should grow side by side. Not to be overlooked, is another form of investment in programs and equipment that will enhance one's personal production. It might be a television or radio program, a periodic newsletter, a lap top computer, a car telephone, or a fax machine. These sales assists will tend to improve one's professional image as well as increase one's service efficiency.

7. *Secure* – look to the future when the "golden years" will come about sooner than one would think. No matter how successful one's career has been, the inevitable aging process will bring the matter of retirement on the scene. By way of a general estimate, at this point in time it is said that social security payments may amount to about 20% of one's annual earnings, assuming that person's earnings were at about $50,000 a year on average. While such payments would be above the poverty level, they hardly provide a standard of living anywhere near what one would have been experiencing on a $50,000 a year income. It stands to reason that expected social security payments must be supplemented by other savings plans for retirement. Aside from the real estate investment portfolio that one has accumulated, there are other investment opportunities popularly used by salespeople in the real estate field. They are:

IRA	–	individual retirement account
SEP-IRA	–	simplified employee pension plan using IRA
KEOGH	–	profit sharing plan (401-k)

Most financial planners estimate that one will need about 70% – 75% of one's current income in order to maintain a reasonably comparable standard of living at the time of retirement. The appealing dimension of some of the above plans is that contributions to the plans may not count as income in the year of contribution. The income tax liability is assessed at the time of withdrawal. It is a deferment of income tax. There are limits, of course. If one is under 70½ years of age, one can put up to $2,000 of yearly earnings in an IRA. That participant's spouse may also contribute up to $2,000 a year whether or not that spouse is working. In the case of a SEP-IRA, one can contribute as much as 15 percent of pre-tax earnings up to $150,000 of income, with maximum contributions set at $22,500. Under the Keogh plan, one is able to contribute up to 15% of one's annual income subject to a limit of $9,500 a year. An important feature of the new tax law is that it allows penalty-free withdrawal from IRAs and 401(K) plans for first time home buyers, up to $10,000. Withdrawals can be made from current IRAs, beginning 1-1-98.

A first time home buyer is an individual (and his/her spouse) who has had no ownership interest in a home during the previous two years.

These are merely some highlights of the various plans. There are many other provisions of these plans that need to be examined in order to best fit a salesperson's particular situation. The advice is quite similar to that a sales associate might give to a for sale by owner prospective seller. Don't be a "do-it-yourselfer". Hire a professional for advice outside of one's area of expertise . . . in the field of insurance, investment and retirement programs.

CHAPTER 12 — YOUR CAREER: THE FUTURE OF THE PROFESSIONAL

"Put yourself in the right direction . . . on the path to
your goal." *Estelle Stone*

Historically, change has always been present in our society, but now the intensity of change is occurring at an increasing rate. What was once considered gradual change has now escalated to a high speed pace.

Over the past few centuries, our western civilization has seen major changes in the form of the agricultural revolution, the industrial revolution and the transportation revolution. Now our society is in the midst of an information revolution that is more dynamic than the previous major changes. The present information explosion impacts the real estate market and the manner in which business is transacted.

If one turns back the pages of history for fifty years or so . . . to review the real estate brokerage industry since the end of World War II . . . there are some noticeable changes that have taken place. By the middle 1940s, not all states in the U.S. had basic license laws and even fewer had real estate trust account regulations. The standard authorized blank forms were comparatively brief in size and in content. The illustration in Chart 12 – 1 shows a residential exclusive listing contract form whose actual size was five inches by eight and one-quarter inches with space on the rear side for property information. A separate carbon sheet was used in order to make a duplicate copy. There were no copy machines and the cost of multiple carbon forms put them out of reach. The offer to purchase blank form was equally as brief. Local newspapers were the dominant vehicle for real estate advertising. Television was not introduced until the late 1940s. For the most part, *caveat emptor* (Let the buyer beware!), seemed to be the tolerated standard of practice in the real estate marketplace.

RESIDENTIAL EXCLUSIVE LISTING CONTRACT

LISTING DATE.., 19...... EXPIRATION DATE.., 19...... LISTING No...........................

TO ....
BROKER:

In consideration of your agreement to list and to use your efforts to find a purchaser for the property hereinafter described, the undersigned hereby gives you the sole and exclusive right to sell the property known as

No. ....

in the.................... of.., County of.., Wisconsin, for the

sum of..Dollars, ($........................),

subject to adjustment for accrued interest, prepaid insurance, rents and current taxes as of time of closing, on the

following terms: Cash: ....

Balance: ....

STRIKE OUT THOSE NOT INCLUDED

Included in the purchase price are such of the following items as may now be on the premises, which will be delivered free and clear of encumbrance: all shrubs and trees; screen doors and windows; storm doors and windows; awnings; electric lighting fixtures, but not bulbs; window shades, curtain rods and venetian blinds; bathroom accessory fixtures; stokers; oil burners; gas heating units; hot water heaters; linoleum cemented to floors; carpeting in living room, dining room,

hallways and stairs; also ....

If a sale or exchange is made or a purchaser procured therefor by you, by the undersigned, or by any other, at the price and upon the terms specified herein, or at any other terms and price accepted by the undersigned, during the life of this contract, or if sold or exchanged within six (6) months after the termination hereof to anyone with whom you negotiated during the life of this contract and whose name you have filed with me in writing prior to the termination of this

contract, the undersigned agrees to pay you a commission of........................ per cent (..........%) of the sale price.

The undersigned agrees to furnish his choice of either a full and complete abstract of title by a responsible abstract company, extended to date, showing marketable title to the seller, at the time of sale, or an owner's title guaranty policy, and will convey title in fee simple by warranty deed, free and clear of legal liens and encumbrances except

....

All deposits made shall be retained by you in a trust account. If forefeited by the buyer, said monies shall first pay for cash advancements made by you; one-half the balance, but not in excess of the commission agreed upon, shall belong to you. The balance shall belong to the undersigned.
(SEE REVERSE SIDE FOR BALANCE OF CONTRACT)

THE OWNER WARRANTS THAT THE FOLLOWING INFORMATION IS CORRECT:

Legal Description: ....

....

.... Size of Lot.................................... Age................

Building .... (Stone) (Frame) (Brick) (Stucco) Roof........................

1st Floor .... Bath........................

2nd Floor .... Bath........................

3rd Floor .... Bath........................

Basement.................................... Foundation.................................... Garage........................

Refrigeration.................... Insulation.................... Heating.................... (Coal) (Oil) (Gas) (Stoker)

Insurance .... Taxes 19........, $........................

Assessed Valuation— Land $.................... Imp. $.................... Total $.................... Keys at........................

Mortgage ....

Leases .... Rents........................

When can Occupancy be given?.................................... Sign?........................

General Information: ....

....

This contract shall remain in force until ...., 19........   ....(SEAL)
Owner

The above contract is hereby accepted...................., 19........   ....(SEAL)
Owner

....   Address ....
Broker

By ....   Telephone ....
(EXECUTED IN DUPLICATE)

FORM 1702 REVISED 7-1-50 WISCONSIN LEGAL BLANK CO., MILWAUKEE 21771

CHART 12 – 1

This brings to mind the actual story of a young real estate professor in the mid-1950s. He was all enthused about the new computer facility installed at the local university. It was housed in a separate temperature controlled room somewhat larger than an average size classroom. It consisted of a large mainframe loaded with electronics and wheel spinning/searching tapes. Decks of eighty column punch cards were the form of input that was processed through programs that were also in decks of sequenced key punched cards. There was an aura of mystique and excitement over the printouts. The processing and analyzing of large quantities of data at that point in time were almost mind boggling. Carried away with the excitement of the situation, the energetic professor unilaterally changed the topic of his address before a luncheon meeting of local real estate brokers. Rather than talk about the market forecast for the coming year, he decided to talk about the future of the real estate industry in the years to come. He told of the technological breakthrough of the computer and its capabilities of processing information. He then explored the idea of collecting real estate market related information in a central place and making it a part of the public record. Sellers and buyers, being reasonably well informed, could then bargain with each other and arrive at a mutually agreeable transaction price. The transaction could then be closed at the office of a lender or title company. This short-cutting of the marketing process would materially reduce the role of the real estate broker, which of course displeased the members of the audience to no end. It was suggested that he take his "long-haired" ideas back to the campus because he was out of touch with the real world in which business was transacted.

In summary, there was some substance to his prediction but he overlooked the all important fact that the real estate broker had reasonably good control of the market transaction information. Back then, what he didn't realize was that transaction information was not a "free good" in the marketplace. While title companies had direct access to a good deal of this information, the price to reassemble it was not very cost-effective. On the other hand, the most efficient and lowest cost assemblers of real estate market information were the Multiple Listing Services that generated this information as a byproduct of their primary service: providing a market of listings for sale and subsequent related transactions with attendant sale data. Thus, over the years, possession of current market data added another valuable dimension to the real estate brokers' services. But in recent years things have started to change. The technology of the 1990s permits access to real estate related data, and interpretation and transmission thereof, to any and all points in and outside of the real estate field. In short, organized real estate no longer enjoys the special privilege of a "quasi-monopoly" on real estate transaction information. That advantage is gradually eroding away.

Incidently, most current personal computers have greater speed and capacity than all of the "magic" contained in those huge mainframes of yesteryear. But it also should be noted that other changes have taken place. For example, the National Association of Real Estate Boards (now the National Association of Realtors®) has grown from 45,000 members in the early 1950s to over 700,000 in the mid 1990s.

The Eighties and the Nineties

As the real estate industry approaches the twenty-first century, here is a partial list of the more important "tools" that a successful broker needs to be competitive:
- a Personal Computer with modem, color printer and software programs
- access to source information systems - including M.L.S.
- a Fax Machine
- Voice Mail (or at least a telephone pager)
- a Copy Machine
- a Cellular Phone

Depending on the quality of the equipment purchased, the capital expenditure involved to acquire these items could be about $5,000. It should not be overlooked that this is the initial expenditure. Along with it are installation fees and monthly service charges as well as rental fees for those items available for lease only. What is equally important is the rate of functional obsolescence of most of the above items. It is not unusual to see technological advance so rapid that replacement may be in order within five years' time. In short, this type of equipment will most likely become outmoded before it becomes worn out.

Concerns of Real Estate Practitioners in the 1990s

The major concerns of real estate brokers in the 1990s seem to fall into four general categories:

1. Legal
2. Consumer
3. Competition
4. Environment

1. *Legal* – At the top of the list is the interpretation of the legal concept of "dual agency". Traditionally, the real estate broker has been considered the agent of his or her principal, the seller. It is the seller who pays the commission in nearly all cases. In turn, the broker owes the seller loyalty, disclosure, diligence and skill among other duties. But many buyers mistakenly assume that the same broker is their agent due to their direct contact with him or her. The trend is to have a clear-cut understanding of the agency status involved by using written disclosure to the seller at the time of the listing and to the buyer at the time of the first showing. From this has emerged an increasing role of the "buyer's broker" as sole and exclusive agent of the buyer only.

2. *Consumer* – There are an ever increasing number of sources to which a dissatisfied buyer or seller may turn to in order to register a complaint with the expectation of having a real estate problem resolved. These services include the State License Board, local and state Trade Associations, the local Better Business Bureau, other state bureaus assigned such responsibility by statute, and investigative media reporters. In our litigious society, the wave of law suits has permeated

all levels of service activity. It was first noticeable in the medical profession, then it appeared in the practice of law, certified public accounting, real estate brokerage and now real estate appraisal. There is no doubt that the offended consumer is entitled to just relief; but, in a noticeable number of instances, it seems to be more expedient to settle out of court rather than to go to trial and have the case judged on its merits. It can be described as a kind of "sue and settle" approach. Not all problems are economic in nature. Various types of discrimination can be the subject of consumer complaints. This list has expanded over the years to include such subjects as race, color, creed, national origin, handicap, marital status, source of income, sex and sexual orientation and children.

3. *Competition* – The deregulation movement on the part of the federal government in many business and commerce areas has affected the general intensity of competition in those and related areas. Newer forms of competition have been gaining stature in the real estate market since the mid-1980s. They are:

- Franchising real estate brokerage firms by well-organized, well capitalized, large national organizations
- The acquisition and merging of existing brokerage firms into larger regional and national entities
- Vertical integration of the full range of real estate services — brokerage, title service, mortgage lending, insurance and relocation into a single, large company (one-stop shopping)
- Real estate market information made available to the public (individuals and firms) on a fee basis by non-real estate related data companies

The concept of protection does not seem to be very high on the scale of values as far as competition in a free market economy is concerned. Soliciting other brokers' listings before they have expired is one example. Fifty years ago estimates indicated that perhaps only one-third of all residential listings were sole and exclusive. The balance were so-called "open listings" wherein a seller would pay a commission to the broker who brought in an offer that was accepted by the seller. While this certainly encouraged competition, some homes had two or three different for sale signs on their front lawns.

In line with anti-trust regulations, brokers cannot conspire to fix commission rates on properties for sale. Regulators expect that each commission fee will be arrived at as an independent negotiation between seller and broker.

4. *Environment* – The increasing concern of the general public toward the state of the environment has focused attention on these factors in connection with real estate transactions. Among the list of related environmental and contamination factors are: asbestos, contaminated water, radon gas, underground storage tanks, urea formaldehyde insulation, petroleum spills, lead based paint and many others. While the real estate broker is not expected to be an expert in each of these areas, the broker is bound to disclose knowledge of the presence of these possible problems on or near the property which is being offered for sale. It is considered reasonable for the broker to arrange for current technical reports to be prepared on these subjects by a competent, independent professional possessing expertise in the appropriate area.

The Closing Years of the 20th Century

In the last dozen years or so of the twentieth century there appeared to be parallels between what has happened in professional sports and what has happened in real estate brokerage. In the fields of baseball, football and basketball, club owners competed with one another and continually raised the salaries of their better players in an effort to hold what they believed to be the necessary player talent to keep their clubs in championship and play-off contention. Player compensation escalated faster than revenue from gate receipts. As a result, profit margins became thinner and thinner. Accordingly, club owners looked for more revenue from other sources such as radio and television rights, inside-the-park billboards, colorful sportswear and apparel bearing the team's logo, luxury boxes for affluent sports fans and larger stadiums subsidized, in part, by local and state governments.

Similar events happened in the field of real estate brokerage. Sales associates, especially the better producers, were paid a higher and higher share of the gross commission. This caused the broker's profit margin to become smaller and smaller. As a result, the owner/broker had to look to other sources of revenue to offset the increasing share of commission paid to sales associates. These additional sources of revenue came from sources such as computerized mortgage loan initiations, title policy applications, home warranty policy applications, cooperative advertising, joint purchasing of signs and supplies and other forms of innovative savings. However, it should be carefully noted that many of these attractive sources of additional revenue are strictly regulated by the federal government's Real Estate Settlement Procedures Act (RESPA). Here again, one of the most important requirements of the act is disclosure to the consumer.

Aside from the necessary pursuit of other sources of revenue, this commission trend impacts the real estate brokerage firm in several other ways related to efficiency and economies of scale, such as:

1. Size, number and design of offices
2. Role of the top, middle and marginal producers
3. Management of incoming leads

These three categories of change and concern are discussed in the following pages.

1. *Size, Number and Design of Offices* – In order to achieve further economies of scale, the trend will most likely be toward fewer, but larger, offices. Out of ne-

cessity, every square foot of an office must be functional with little or no room for luxury features. This follows the corporate trend of "down-sizing" that is merely corporate jargon for increased efficiency, less waste and a "leaner" organization. The new look will emphasize more conference rooms for client service that double as video training centers for small groups based on the different levels of experience and specific needs. Outmoded desks will be replaced by work stations equipped with wireless telephone headsets that can access any number of systems. Touch tone telephones will be replaced by portable telephone key pads. Another alternative will be the use of cellular phones both inside and outside of the office.

2. *Role of Top, Middle and Marginal Producers* – The number of top producers is bound to continue to increase. The 80-20 principle of Pareto's Law may very well become 90-10 by the year 2000. Top producers, with their 100 percent commitment to achievement and their attendant financial capability to afford the latest electronic equipment, will increase their dominance in the real estate market. While the number of these top producers increases, the total number of sales associates in the overall market will most likely decrease. This will be due, in part, to higher productivity per sales associate. Middle level producers will not spend as much time in the office as top producers and will not be willing to invest as much for capital equipment. Middle level producers may prefer to work more at home due to household and/or family responsibilities. These producers will be able to function at home with minimal equipment such as a telephone, fax machine and copy machine. Regular visits to the office will still be necessary in order to use the MLS system, other equipment and to seek the advice and guidance of the broker/ manager. Marginal producers may not want to

buy the necessary equipment and therefore may find it necessary to be in the office more frequently than middle level producers to use the firm's equipment. From management's point-of-view, each licensee should be viewed as a profit center. Logically, not all licensees will be given the same level of physical equipment, support and direct personal attention. Consistently low producers who are not making progress in sales but are good at detail and follow-up will become capable assistants for the top producers. Low producers should become effective service agents for top producers rather than remain marginal independent sales associates. Low producers who do not have the required qualifications to serve as assistants to top producers will go the way of the corner grocery store and the two pump gas stations that were left behind in the wave of economic change.

3. *Management of Incoming Leads* – One of the more inefficient functions of many real estate brokerage firms is the handling of incoming inquiries. The fact that sales associates are independent contractors gives them a lot of leeway with very little control over their work procedures. Are your customers satisfied with the service you provide? Are the sales associates at times too busy to adequately service all leads? What happens to the leads generated through your company when a sales associate decides to leave the organization? Who actually owns the leads? As in any other phase of the real estate brokerage business, incoming leads can be more efficiently managed if the broker is willing to invest the capital. One such investment is the "UP DESK" designed by The Enterprise Ltd. of Milwaukee, Wisconsin, innovators of new marketing, electronic processing and communication systems for the residential real estate market. This company is headed by Mr. Roger Scommegna, a forward thinking CEO.

The "UP DESK" System

The main purpose of the "Up Desk" is to facilitate professional handling of incoming property prospect calls.

The "Up Desk" is a user friendly interactive computer system with the following components:

- CPU – a Pentium Windows operating system, 16 megabytes of RAM
- PRINTER – Epson Stylus, color ink jet, uses copy paper
- MONITOR – 14" color screen
- MODEM – 28.8
- KEYBOARD – standard

The entire MLS database is downloaded into the "Up Desk" before the start of each business day. *Property searches* can be made by street name or number, MLS number, broker's property code number, municipality, price range and/or property features. A *comparable search* can be made by number of bedrooms, number of baths, and municipality within 10 percent of a target price. The *mortgage calculator* uses a specific down payment or percent of price to calculate the monthly mortgage payment.

Printouts include a complete property description, a color picture and information about the responding agent with his/her picture in color as well.

Property information can also be faxed directly from the "Up Desk" computer.

Training time for a sales associate is usually fifteen to thirty minutes. Information requests require no more than entering a few letters or numbers on the keyboard and/or directing the cursor arrow by moving the mouse. With regular use, the sales associates' understanding broadens and their confidence increases. Typical sales associates learn and adapt rather quickly when they realize that property information, comparables and monthly mortgage payments are at their fingertips. The ability to immediately print out a color flyer or send a fax transmission during the course of a single incoming telephone call adds tremendous efficiency that must be respected.

A less technical but perhaps more invasive avenue into the area of independent contractor domain of the sales associate is what some call "Prospect Management," "Lead Management", or "Manager Directed Sales". The system works like this:

The broker/owner hires a special clerk/secretary to handle all incoming telephone calls. This specialist assures that callers receive the information they want within a matter of minutes (or longer, if the situation dictates a longer time delay). A few brokers are installing telephone identification systems to supplement this procedure. Some brokers maximize "on-hold" by using recorded information about mortgage loans, current interest rates, new listings, or home warranty programs. Names and phone numbers of callers are given to agents on a list of sales associates that sign up in advance to take such calls. Sales associates sign up for designated time periods and therefore should be available in the office at those designated times. Only those sales associates who sign up in advance are eligible to take turns at receiving incoming prospect calls. In the event the sales associate next in line is not available to take the call, it is passed on to the following person on the list. In this system, the sales manager has a detailed record of assigned prospects and is in a better position to follow up on the sales associates' progress with these leads. The system affords improved efficiency in handling and tracking incoming prospect calls. It also provides a work program for a newcomer to service prospects that provide the age-old bothersome complaint so often heard by the sales manger, ". . . but they never called back."

Looking Ahead into the 21st Century

Not too long ago, this author had the opportunity to read a fascinating book that focused on the future . . . the future of progressive business leaders in the decade ahead. These predictions can be found in a book written by Daniel Burrus with Roger Gittines entitled *Technotrends* published by Harper Business, a Division of Harper Collins Publishers. This author has taken the liberty of expanding on some of Burrus' key points in order to focus on the real estate brokerage business.

1. PAST SUCCESS IS YOUR WORST ENEMY[1]

Past success can build up barriers to improvement in both personnel and internal systems. Paradigms provide the way we tend to look at things. The comfort of success may cause one's paradigms to become too deeply rooted and inflexible. Resistance to new ideas may develop. Management can easily interpret constructive criticism as threatening in nature. Pessimistic comments such as "We tried that years ago . . . it will never work!" and "Don't rock the boat!" are heard now and then. Other kinds of resistance take the form of commissioning a survey, or the age-old tactic of appointing a committee to study the matter. The real solution to the problem may be found in re-examining one's paradigms . . . meaningfully shifting with the changing times.

Total Quality Management (TQM) can provide a continuous process of quality improvement for the long term, but on a gradual day by day basis. Most members of a sales team will resist change if it is introduced too abruptly. Change is almost always more acceptable if team members are involved in

---

[1]Daniel Burrus with Roger Gittines, *"Technotrends – How to Use Technology to Go Beyond Your Competition,"* Harper Business, A Division of Harber Collins Publishers, 1994, Appendix E, *Thirty New Rules.*

formulating the components of change. Increasing annual sales volume alone is just part of the total improvement program. To not improve is equivalent to standing still . . . the competition will pass you by.

2. IF IT WORKS, IT'S OBSOLETE[2]

Change for change's sake alone is the equivalent of walking on a treadmill. While the exercise may be beneficial, you'll remain in the same place. Complacency is satisfaction and contentment with the status quo. Some may defend this situation on the grounds that "if it ain't broke, don't fix it." However, we live in a dynamic world in which the business community plays an integral part. Change is constant.

Consider the case of the personal computer over a past decade, 1985 through 1995. New models were introduced in the form of the 286 . . . 386 . . . 486 . . . and now they are all obsolete. The machines didn't wear out, they simply became obsolete as newer and better models were introduced with improved speed, greater capacity and simpler operating features. This rapid change was brought about by fierce competition among product developers and producers.

As part of one's TQM program, present systems, operating procedures and leadership techniques must be continually questioned. "How can this be improved?" "Is there a better way?" Suggestions and recommendations should come from any and all sources within the organization . . . not from management alone. Contributions should be recognized and rewarded in an appropriate manner.

3. BUILD CHANGE INTO THE PLAN OR PRODUCT[3]

In the middle of the 1930s, author Frederick M. Babcock, who trained appraisers for the Federal Housing Administration (FHA), was apparently the first to describe the "three components of value" as ". . .location. . .location. . .location." That statement has

---

[2]Ibid., p. 353.
[3]Ibid., p. 353.

been repeated thousands of times over the years. While physical location is a fixed point on the surface of the earth, it's intangible components are subjected to continual change. The relocation of highways, the construction of shopping malls and the expansion of an airport are examples of major changes that affect the quality of specific locations. Locational changes are interactive . . . a kind of multi-directional reaction of value forces.

Change can be seen in the form of *life cycles* in people, houses, neighborhoods and even cities. It is unusual to see a real estate brokerage office stay at the same location over several generations due to the changing urban scene. As the focus of a residential market shifts, the broker's marketing efforts should shift accordingly. The role of women in real estate marketing, the extension of life expectancy, the increasing speed of electronic communication and the growing importance of consumerism are some of the major changes that will certainly affect the manner in which business will be conducted in the real estate field in the 21st century. There is an old axiom in business: "If we always do things the way we always did them, we'll always get what we already have."

4. RE-BECOME AN EXPERT[4]

An expert is a person who is very skillful or highly trained and informed in some special field. Education is a continuous, lifelong process. True scholars readily admit that the more they learn, the more they realize how much more there is to know. Successful real estate brokers and sales associates relish the opportunity to read newly released publications from the various trade associations at the local, state and national levels. Some leaders in the field recommend that every month or so, one should buy a book instead of a lunch.... it's good for the mind as well as the waistline! Not all of the material may be new to the reader but it can serve to stimulate other ideas. For example, step back and reexamine the way you look at things. Which of the following symbols is most out of place?

---

[4]Ibid., p. 354.

$$\begin{array}{c|c} b & c \\ \hline d & q \end{array}$$

Are these lower case letters of the English alphabet? Are these abbreviated forms of musical notes and signs? Does the arrangement of the symbols in four quadrants have any significance? Depending on the paradigm that one employs, "c" is different because it lacks a stem. On the other hand, "c" can be superimposed more effectively on "d" and "q" than on "b". From another point of view, "b", "c" and "d" are in alphabetical order and "q" is the most out of place since "q" is not in that sequence. The point is not to jump hastily to what appears to be the obvious conclusion. Aside from these four letter-type symbols, did you consider the crossed line diagram that creates the four quadrants? Or didn't you even notice it? Perhaps its "+" shape is the symbol that is the most out of place. Look at alternatives, try to "see" things that others fail to "see".

Consider the case of a marginal business operating at a good location in an urban area. Day after day hundreds of people drive by but fail to recognize the real estate opportunity. The business operator has years on his lease that can't expire soon enough in view of his low profits. The investor/owner is not pleased with the rent that is locked in without escalation provisions. The creative real estate broker sees and understands the situation and brings in a strong buyer that appreciates the location's true retail potential. The present investor/owner likes the idea of liquidating his investment in order to get a new start and the tenant/operator likes the idea of getting out from under the lease. A sale takes place and all parties (seller, buyer and tenant) have improved their respective positions. It took the expertise of the real estate broker to "see" what others could not "see".

5. FOCUS ON YOUR CUSTOMER'S FUTURE NEEDS[5]

One of the broker's marketing strengths lies in his/her list of satisfied clients – an excellent source of referrals and repeat busi-

---

[5]Ibid., p. 354.

ness. As we learned in an earlier chapter, households experience change over time. Some occupants may become underhoused while others may become overhoused. The typical examples are younger married couples with a growing family in need of more space and older "empty nesters" who have much more living space than they need. These changing housing needs ripen into demand on both sides of the real estate transaction, with some in need to list for sale and others in need to buy. These needs can be anticipated by tracking two obvious sources. The first would be to store transaction information in a computer database and project it for review every several years or so. A second source would be local census data that would reveal population trends such as "baby boomers" changing status, growth of the senior citizens and the rate of household formations. While such statistics may describe the amount of changing demand and some of the characteristics of such demand, it is also important to anticipate the kind of service likely to be expected on the part of those future clients. Some insight into clients' future needs and expectations might be obtained through a brief survey as part of a biennial follow-up effort with satisfied clients.

6. BUILD A BETTER PATH TO THE CUSTOMER[6]

Don't wait for the customer to come to you, take the initiative and pursue the potential customer. It's the natural course of action in the competitive business world. This applies to past clients as well as "clients to be". The latter category is dominated by present renters. In a series of surveys, about seven out of ten renters stated that owning a home was a good investment and that they would like to own a home some day. Bear in mind that renters occupy about 35% of all housing units in this country. While not all of them will become home buyers, nearly one-half of them will buy in the years ahead. A broker can put his or her firm in a favorable position with this segment of the market by providing home buying information seminars for first-time home buyers. This group would most likely include young couples, immigrants and single

---

[6]Ibid., p. 353.

heads of households desiring to pursue the "great American dream" of home ownership. Topics covered in the seminars could include information on housing components, floor plans, mortgage financing, title evidence, maintenance, real estate taxes and insurance.

Both past clients and expected future clients should be kept informed with updated news on interest rates, price trends and tax law changes via mail or telephone contact. The broker's credibility is enhanced as prospective clients rely more and more on information provided to them over an extended period of time.

7. ENTER THE COMMUNICATION AGE[7]

To gain the confidence of customers and clients and to maintain a competitive position in the real estate industry, it is absolutely necessary to utilize new technology in your business. The fact that personal computers are now outselling television sets in nearly all major market areas across the country underscores the critical nature of the oncoming change. The computerized Multiple Listing Service opened the floodgates for the introduction of fax machines, car phones, voice mail and portable computers. Today nearly eight out of ten real estate firms are using some type of computer system in their business. The typewriter is being phased out gradually. It is just a matter of time before the majority of listing contracts and offers to purchase are computer generated. As more and more households acquire personal computers, some experts are starting to wonder about the need for the laptop computer as a real estate marketing tool. They ask, "If nearly all households have their own personal computers, how much need will there be for a portable laptop computer?"

It is quite apparent that consumers are demanding more real estate information. They want it quickly and they want it to be easily accessible. Real estate brokerage firms have no other choice but to tool up with the appropriate equipment for their market and to be flexible enough to keep up with changes in communications technology. The near future will generate more combinations of video, telephone and computer applications. Progressive brokers

---

[7]Ibid., p. 354.

and sales associates will ride this exciting wave of change, while others will be left behind.

8. TIME IS THE CURRENCY OF THE 90's[8]

Many households in today's society are headed by two full-time wage earners. This arrangement provides adequate income but subtracts from the time available for other activities. Aside from being busy with their respective careers, people have pressing demands from their children with school and extra-curricular activities, social responsibilities, church affiliations, recreation and relatives. Time is at a premium. While these couples may have the financial wherewithal to participate in these various activities, they are short of time in their very crowded calendars. These are the same households that are most likely to have a personal computer. When it comes to entering the real estate market, they tend to prefer to have a real estate firm handle the matter. This is the same approach they use back at the office . . . hire a consultant to handle the specialized tasks.

With increasing government regulations regarding environmental issues, disclosure, consumer protection, tax reports and property reports, the real estate transaction is becoming more complex and therefore requires more time and more careful effort. The increased volume of information involves more time to process and distribute. Efficient use of time is a critical component of management. The Latin motto, *"carpe diem"*, means "seize the day" . . . but in this case it would not be for fun and pleasure but rather for efficient and productive use of one's time. Time waits for no one . . . it passes you by . . . with no instant replays.

9. GIVE YOUR CUSTOMERS THE ABILITY (TO DO WHAT THEY CAN'T DO, BUT WOULD HAVE WANTED TO DO, IF ONLY THEY KNEW THEY COULD HAVE DONE IT).[9]

With regard to prospective home buyers, what would be more helpful in their home search?

---

[8]Ibid., p. 353.
[9]Ibid., p. 353.

a. If they only knew what they wanted (If they don't know, help them find out . . . if you don't know, you better find out!)
b. Easy access to information (Make it available but try to limit it to what is important to them . . . don't bury them in facts and figures!)
c. A good agent (Look at things through the buyers' eyes . . . from the buyers' point of view – give your opinion only when asked)
d. A more efficient way to shop (Let the buyers set the pace, ask the questions and make decisions in a private setting)

Another real estate marketing concept being developed and introduced in this country by the Enterprise organization is what is known as MARKET VALUE PRICING. The basic idea originated in Australia as a broker response to a declining real estate commission rate schedule. The purpose was to attempt to reduce the time/cost of the broker's role in the real estate transaction in view of a declining commission rate. Most brokers already quote price ranges to prospective sellers in the process of preparing a Comparative Market Analysis as part of the listing procedure. Now brokers introduce the concept of price range to buyers as well. This sets the stage for what might be termed, the "Fair Compromise".

In a majority of the cases, the seller wants the best price possible and the buyer doesn't want to pay more than he or she has to. Add to that, the notion that in today's society, there are a noticeable number of people that want to buy major items at a discounted price . . . in search of that elusive "bargain". This situation creates one of the inefficiencies of the real estate market as buyers and sellers "search" and "fish" for the transaction price. Unfortunately, there is no *exact price* for a specific residential property. Price does not necessarily equal value. Value is not found in printed tables but it is established by the interaction of willing sellers and qualified buyers in the marketplace. This can be a time consuming process especially when the parties involved are lacking experience and/or complete information.

How does the broker get the parties into the "comfort zone" wherein buyers are willing to make an offer and sellers are willing to negotiate? Market Value Pricing has many of the answers . . . the broker does not market the property with a single list price but rather with a price range.

This could result in —

- Getting buyers on the "negotiating track" sooner than usual because the value range is defined (. . . no guessing game)
- Encouraging sellers to negotiate more readily with sincere buyers
- Encouraging sellers to counteroffer, knowing buyers have seemingly accepted the value range
- Getting more offers . . . and sooner!
- Reducing the selling time (number of days on the market)

An adaptation of Market Value Pricing can be found in the automotive field. A 1996 newspaper article tells of General Motors Corp. expanding its "Value Pricing" program on the west coast of the United States. Under the plan GM sells cars and trucks equipped with popular options at special low prices that discourages haggling. The program was introduced in California in 1993 and helped the company to become the state's largest vehicle seller. In general, the end result of using Value Packaging in the automotive field approximates that of using the Market Value Pricing in the real estate field . . . less haggling and moves the transaction along faster.

In the United States there are some states wherein a price range in the real estate listing contract may not meet the statutory requirement of "expressing the price" at which real estate may be sold. In these cases it is suggested that both the specific price and the price range at which the property should be marketed appear in the listing agreement. The specific price would have to be agreed upon by the seller and the broker at the time of signing the listing contract.

When properly and tactfully employed, Market Value Pricing transforms the broker's role from that of an adversary to that of an ambassador/advocate. Further, it enables the real estate broker to play his or her role as an agent for the seller. At the same time, it also aids the buyer's broker/agent in assisting the buyer in making a price decision.

In summary, Market Value Pricing creates a win-win situation on all sides of the real estate transaction.

Threat or Opportunity?

There is an important message interwoven among Mr. Burrus' words. These words should cause one to start thinking above the level of fear . . . to elevate one's curiosity . . . to stimulate progressive thinking . . . to recognize challenges as opportunities . . . to dream, but in a reasonably constructive manner. Yet there seems to be a problem of trying to make a decision in an environment of overworked hyperbole about the Information Revolution. In due time this inflated peak of expectation will be followed by a downward drift toward reality generated by disillusionment. As the air is gradually cleared of hype, things will begin to settle down and common sense will prevail. This will establish an operating level at which the Information Revolution can be widely applied in a productive manner. A review of history reminds us that it took nearly two centuries for the Industrial Revolution to fully develop. Current innovation is on a much faster track. At the start of the 20th century, over 80 percent of all workers in this country were engaged in agricultural work. Now, as we near the end of this century, less than 5 percent are involved in agricultural work. Due to mechanization and biological innovations, the size of the agricultural work force has been drastically reduced while production has been significantly increased. Technological change has had its impact in a similar manner in the manufacturing field. At mid-century, over 70 percent of all U.S. employees were working in manufacturing jobs. As we near the close of this century, that percentage is now less than 15 percent. This drastic exodus has been in the direction of service industries. The information Revolution will take place in due time . . . but not overnight. Like with the introduction of most pioneering innovations, mistakes in judgment will be made. The "one size fits all" approach of some of the less successful social reform programs provides some insight on trying to apply a simple solution to a complex problem. These mistakes may manifest themselves in the form of buying total systems when only parts are actually needed. Or of trying to fit one's needs to a total system, rather than the other way around. It might be more advisable to select new equipment "cafeteria style", using only those components that suit one's needs. It is generally agreed that change will happen, but it may take a generation or two. What should you do in the meantime? It is important that you keep abreast of what is happening. Don't isolate yourself . . . don't be satisfied with the status quo. Attend seminars, conventions, talk to leaders in the field and read newsletters and bulletins to know what is going on. Being informed of change is critical to management because change can create obsolescence faster than any one of your competitors can. But there is a price to be paid. It should be recognized that constant change means constant management discomfort. That is part and parcel of welcoming and accepting change.

Some Challenging Questions

It may be advisable to reevaluate the probable future of your own market area. How might your local market change? Consider what the impact on your business might be if some of the following "What if" assumptions take place:

WHAT IF commission rates are competed downward?

WHAT IF more and more financial institutions decide to go into the real estate business?

WHAT IF large insurance companies acquire other insurance companies (casualty, title insurance, home warranty, etc.)?
WHAT IF super franchisors integrate vertically, offering complete one-stop shopping for real estate buyers?

Are you prepared to compete with large firms on *their* terms? Do you have a real estate specialty that could survive competitive challenge and establish itself as a high quality and unique service in a special niche of the market? Such a specialty would be an in-depth knowledge of one particular segment of the real estate market . . . that would make you an expert because you know more about it than anyone else. Such a specialty might be in the field of premium priced homes, vacant land, waterfront properties, smaller apartment buildings, condominiums, leased property, etc.

Where do you and/or your company want to be five years from now?
Where do you and/or your company want to be ten years from now?

Bear in mind that forecasting five or ten years into the future is very risky business. The word to the wise is to keep your options open. Leasing for the shorter term (five years or less) may provide some flexibility. Leasing, rather than owning the real estate office as well as leasing capital equipment, may shift some of the risk to other investors. Would you lease an automobile for a term of ten years even if it was proved to be more economical on paper? Perhaps not, because there may be other relevant factors involved besides economics.

Do you expect to have more "100%-percenters" on your sales staff in the future? Would such a change in sales personnel create space and remodeling problems? Do you expect increased competition from so-called "discounters"? Perhaps you should reconsider some of the analysis contained in Chapter 8 by seeking other sources of revenue.

Free advice . . . unwarranted assumptions . . . puffing of advertisements can lead to disappointed business decisions. New ideas always seem attractive and as a result some shortcomings are easily overlooked. Eventually we are able to adjust to marketing hype.

All through life we are faced with venturing into new areas . . . the so-called "unknown". In some ways you, in the real estate industry, are venturing into the unknown once again. But this should not be anything new to most of you. Remember your experience in grade school . . . your educational challenges were belittled by the warnings of older teenagers' . . . "that's nothing —

wait 'til you get in high school!" While in high school your academic efforts were again downgraded by older students cautioning you with the warning . . . "wait 'til you get into college!" On the college level your scholarly endeavors were minimized with the cautioning . . . "wait 'til you get into the real world!" Through your personal experience you have discovered that you can meet the challenges in the real world just as you have at all of the previous levels of educational challenges. One of the main differences is that in the real world, we not only have to make our own decisions but we have to live with the consequences - - - be they good or bad. Effective decision making is based on sound information, confidence, determination and the will to succeed. You may not come up with the right decision every time but it is important to have the courage to make decisions rather than putting them off.

Procrastination can fill one's life with a lengthy list of missed opportunities . . . a litany of "if only" lamentations.

IF ONLY I had taken that specialized training.
IF ONLY I had the courage to go into business for myself.
IF ONLY I had purchased that property ten years ago when the price was low.
IF ONLY I had purchased those shares of stock when they were initially offered.

While it may be too late to seize some missed opportunities, let this serve as a call for an abrupt turnaround in your thinking. Instead of dwelling on the negatives of the past, turn to positive thoughts about the future. New opportunities will present themselves. New opportunities are bound to turn up all around us. Filled with new enthusiasm and a positive attitude, you can and will reach higher heights in your field of endeavor.

Ace, 95
Affordability, 95,96
Andrews, Richard B., 11
Anti-trust laws, 236
Appraising, 100
Assessed value approach, 108
Association of Real Estate
   License Law Officials, 28

Babcock, Frederick M., 304
Break-even analysis, 241
Broker, 14
   functions, 16
   responsibility to Buyer, 116
   responsibility to Seller, 115
Broker pyramid, 12
Brokerage business, 14
Budgets, 251
   Expense, 252
   Revenue, 252
Building starts, 75
Burrus, Daniel, 303
Business organization, 203
   Capital, 204
   Control, 205
   Forms, 203
   Liability, 206
   Tax position, 206
Business plan, 239
Business value, 253
Buyer interest (creating), 165
Buyers, 140
   sources of, 158
Buyer's psychology, 160

Capital requirements, 204
Capitalization of net income, 183, 184
Career – organizing, 284
Cash flow, 195
Challenging questions, 313
Changes,
   last fifty years, 291
   80's and 90's, 294
Closing years of 20th century, 297
Code of Ethics, 274
Company name, 210
Comparative market analysis, 132
Competitive market problems, 135
Concerns of practitioners, 295
Cone of value, 181
Consumer behavior, 160
Contract for deed, 128

Convenience, 181
Conversions, 39
Cost of replacement, new, 109

Dampeners (market), 74
Days on market, 77
Debt service, mortgage, 151
Degree of control, 218, 261
Demographic factors, 74
   age distribution, 80, 81
   birth rate, 43
   households, 48
   migration, 79
   natural increase, 43
Demolition, 39
Depreciation, 178
Designations (professional), 272
Dis-investment, 196
Dorau, H.B., 23

Economies of scale, 236
Education, 265
Ely, Richard T., 23
Employment, 81
Enthusiasm, 228
Equity gap, 191
Exclusive agency, 127
Expenses of sale, 125
Expenses per desk, 241
Experience, 19

Favorable exposure, 213
Federal Housing Administration, 23, 161, 304
Federal National Mortgage Association, 146
Filtering, 42
Financing terms, 78
Fisher, Ernest M., 23
Focus on the future,
   nine statements re: future, 303-310
   twenty-first century, 303
For sale by owner, 137
Forecasts, 93
Forms of business organization, 203
   corporation, 204, 205, 206
   limited liability company, 209
   partnership, 204, 205
   sole proprietorship, 204, 205

Gaumnitz, Erwin A., 239
Goal setting, 267, 269
Goldberg, Charles, 140
Gross rent multiplier, 27

Index

Highest and best use, 34
Hilton, Walter, 197
Hinman, A.G., 23
Home building, 75
Home ownership, 143
Household cycle, 49
Households, 48
  demographic factors, 55
Housing, 48
  decisions, 53
  market model, 36
  turnover, 75
Hoyt, Homer, 23

Income statement, 176
Income tax aspects, 191
Independent contractor, 208
Indicators (market), 87, 88
Inflation, 82, 260
Interest rates, 151
  resistance to increases, 153
Internal rate of return, 196
Investment, 170
  leverage, 188
  models, 185
  pyramiding, 186
Investment analysis, 175
Investment theory of city growth, 21
Investor, 171
  benefits, 172
  kinds of investors, 173

Land contract, 128
Land development, 198
Leverage, 188
Liability, 206
License laws, 21
Lindemann, John A., 85
Liquidating the investment, 196
Listings,
  importance, 118
  open, 127
  probability of obtaining, 120
  types of contract, 126
Location, 181

Management control, 218, 261
Management principles, 214
Management talent, 234
Market (real estate), 32
  buyer's market, 47
  change –seasonal, 59

  cyclical, 63
  trend, 70
  irregular, 71
defined, 32
demand, 45
functions, 32
indicators, 74
patterns of change, 58
predictions, 89
seller's, 47
sub-markets, 37
supply, 45
Market imperfections, 34, 45, 262
Market price, 103
Market share, 247
Market value pricing, 310
Mission statement, 252
Monthly payment, 148
Mortgage recordings, 76
Motivating salespeople, 232, 233
Multiple listing, 127

National Association of Real Estate Boards, 24
National Association of Realtors®, 24, 283
Net cash flow, 178

Offer to purchase, 166
Office location, 212
Older home owners, 138
Operating functions, 198
Operating expenses, 240
Overpricing, 109, 136
Ownership turnover, 75
Owning vs. renting, 145

Paine, Charles L., 170
Pareto's law, 227
Personal goals, 267
Pockets of activity, 121
Policy manual, 217
Population change, 43, 79
Pre-qualifying buyers, 149
Price estimate, 108
Price range, 131
Pricing, 98
Profession, 262
  definition, 262
Property management, 201
Public records, 87
Public relations, 237

Ratcliff, Richard U., 23, 32
Rate of return, 183
Real estate, 12
  body of knowledge, 15
  courses, 18
  field of activity, 12
  functions, 13
Realtor®, 211, 273
Rental housing, 38
Residential market model, 36
Revenue pace, 248
Risk, financial, 190
Rules of thumb, 25

Sales manager, 231-236
  role, 231
  selection, 234
Sales quotas, 245-247
  company, 245
  sales staff, 246
Sales staff, 223
  size, 224
Salespeople, 223-227
  recruiting, 225
  training, 225
  why they leave, 221
Sellers, 111
  pricing rationale, 104
  reasons for selling, 113
Shapiro, Nathan, 111
Standing stock, 38

Starker type exchange, 193
Stimulators (market), 74
Stone, Estelle, 291
Straight capitalization, 27
Straight-line depreciation, 185
Success, 219
  commitment, 285
  defined, 219

Taxation, 206
Theory vs. practice, 22
Threat or opportunity, 312
Timing of sale, 129
Trading on equity, 141, 188
Tuccillo, John A., 260

UP-DESK, 301
Urban renewal, 39

Vacancies, 76
Value, 180-182
  components, 180
  cone of, 181
Veterans Administration, 140, 161
von Schledorn, Ernie, 124

Wehrwein, George S., 23
Weimer, Arthur, 23

Young, Charles, 219, 229
Younger market, 142